Shakespeare Criticism

Anne Bradby

ATLANTIC
PUBLISHERS & DISTRIBUTORS (P) LTD

Published by
ATLANTIC
PUBLISHERS & DISTRIBUTORS (P) LTD
7/22, Ansari Road, Darya Ganj, New Delhi-110002
Phones : +91-11-40775252, 40775214, 23273880, 23275880
Fax: +91-11-23285873
Web: www.atlanticbooks.com
E-mail: orders@atlanticbooks.com

Printed & bound in India by Atlantic Print Services

Contents

Introduction

'Assuredly that criticism of Shakespeare will alone be genial which is reverential', Coleridge said in a lecture. And George Darley wrote to Allan Cunningham in 1835:

'How it would unglorify Shakespeare, and soil imagination, if he were brought down to the kennel in which real existence runs'!

Those opinions will serve to define something of the attitude towards Shakespeare which was held in the period at which the previous collection of criticism in this series ended, and to stress the contrast with the present. The development from Coleridge's style into the sentimental dithyramb of less brilliant men, in a time when the amount of Shakespearian criticism hugely increased, and in which there was change in standards of scholarship but little in those of criticism, is not traced in this book, which is a collection made from writers since the War.

The picture of an extremely self-occupied Shakespeare, boldly rebuking his characters for faults which he thereby corrects in himself, and checking his own over-rapid growth, which is found in Dowden's criticism, is a little ridiculous to us. Alien, also, is Pater's moral approach, holding that poetry is to help us to make 'finer appreciations'; and so is the practice of character-extraction, brilliantly though it has been done in this century by A.C. Bradley. For one of the chief critical maxims of the day is that nothing must be extracted from its proper context, least of all in the case of Shakespeare. Darley was perhaps saying that very thing in the passage quoted above, but we disagree as to the nature of the context. Poetry is not to be treated as religion, nor a poet as a philosopher: Coleridge's reverence for Shakespeare's 'philosophical mind' has been countered by Mr. Shaw's ribald remarks on the conventional morality of that mind, such as his comment on Orlando's 'If ever been where bells have knolled to church': 'How perfectly the atmosphere of the rented pew is caught in this incredible line'!

Shakespeare's context as it is now seen is the theatre, and England under Elizabeth. This would seem to imply a Crocean aesthetic which considers the medium in which the artist works as the essential shape of his thought, through which alone it has existence; as opposed to the aesthetic which Carlyle expressed — '*Disjecta membra* are all that we find of any Poet', where the medium is only an imperfect vessel for the thought. A passage from Mr. Eliot's *The Use of Poetry* . . . may illustrate this: '*If* poetry is a form of "communication", yet that which is to be communicated is the poem itself, and only incidentally the experience and the thought which have gone into it'. And it is always true, he writes elsewhere, to say that form and content are the same, and always true to say that they are different. Perhaps the case in which they are not the same for the reader is when a clumsy or obscure expression leaves him to find a content which may be different from what the words are really saying, or to add something to what they say. But at any rate the two are inevitably separated for the purpose of criticism, and the stress on context mentioned above has led to an increased study of the way a poet wrote, so often before neglected for what he wrote about.

The scholarship which is allied to this is the particular emphasis of this age. It existed before: for instance Johnson, writing of the supernatural in *Macbeth*, said 'In order to make a true estimate of the abilities and merit of a writer, it is always necessary to examine the genius of his age and the opinions of his contemporaries'. But Johnson acknowledged that he excelled in pointing out what he ought to have done and in explaining why he had not done it. And most often the functions of the scholar and the critic were divided in activity, even when they existed in one mind. They have now come nearer to each other, even though exploration is so highly specialized, though Shakespeare's images are card-indexed and his texts purged.

Where knowledge is ordered and centralized, each writer of any worth may use it as a foundation; it is a State socialism rather than a monarchy. But it has not abolished hobbyhorses; it has produced many fantastic theses, which would argue Shakespeare into being the 'ally of the ministers of Elizabeth and James', make *The Tempest* an allegory of the old rites of initiation, and the Scottish succession the concern of *Hemlet.*

The change in attitude was defined by Sir Walter Raleigh in *Shakespeare*, published in 1909. 'Our sin', he said, 'is not indifference, but superstition. . . . His poetry has been used like wedding-cake, not to eat but to dream upon . . . Let us make an end of this, and do justice to Shakespeare the craftsman'.

Certainly Shakespeare the craftsman has been recognized, as is shown here: his craft of the theatre by the criticism of Mr. Granville-Barker, with the discoveries of Mr. W.J. Lawrence and Sir Edmund Chambers as its scholastic roots; his poetic craft in various ways by various investigators. Scientific study of texts, sources, and customs it is impossible to represent by extracts, least of all in a volume of mainly critical essays. But the necessary combination of science and inspiration in scholarship is relevant, as set out in Mr. W.W. Greg's *Principles of Emendation*. . . .

The more general criticism here needs no comment; it is in the tradition of English literature, which has not agreed with Warton that 'general criticism is on all subjects useless and unentertaining'. For if criticism tends, like philosophy, to reconcile us with our nature by increasing self-knowledge, and by the actual process to give pleasure, this is best accomplished in those flashes which make the principles of things known, as when Johnson shows the whole scope of one of the Unities: 'Time is, of all modes of existence, most obsequious to the imagination'. This gets its effect by the imperiousness of language, especially in the power of the unexpected word *obsequious*. And it can be objected that this is the right of poetry and emotion stirring prose, not of criticism. But what moves us is not necessarily an inexact statement of fact; it simply enforces itself by appealing to the senses as well as to the mind, as do the great axioms of St. Thomas Aquinas.

In such infrequent sayings as Johnson's, *attitude* and critical classification count for nothing in particular. It is, in any case, by the application to criticism of a mind where, in Coleridge's phrase, 'truth has become domesticated into power', rather than by the unchangeable truth of the conclusions reached, that our understanding is enlarged. Most steadily, also, it is by general truths rather than by particular interpretations: Bradley's general analysis of Shakespearian tragedy will not vary its value according as critical standards vary, where his analysis of the plays often will.

In criticism, while the histories and generalizations record revolutionary changes of attitude, the phrases of the great critics remain to refute them. Johnson's remarks on emendatory criticism are in accord with the modern essay here reprinted; refuting those who called it a dull, undistinguished activity, he said it demanded more than humanity possessed, and the first requisite was 'that intuition by which the poet's intention is immediately discovered'. Again, he foreshadows in a narrower and verbal sense Mr. Eliot's theory of the behaviour in a crisis of Shakespeare's heroes: 'His persons, however distressed, have a conceit left them in their misery, a miserable conceit'. He was concerned with the same problem of wasted energy in criticism, deploring the discovery of trivial likenesses to other writers in Shakespeare, as used to prove what he did or did not read; and disposing of a type of commentator which we still have — 'Upton, who did not easily miss what he desired to find'. Coleridge had stated that ideal identity of form and content spoken of above: 'the infallible test of a blameless style; namely, its untranslatableness in words of the same language without injury to the meaning'. And Coleridge at his most enthusiastic did not exceed Dryden's just praise: 'Shakespeare, who has many times written better than any poet in any language'.

It may seem that a volume of modern Shakespeare criticism ought to begin at least with Raleigh, even if Bradley were excluded. But because of difficulties with copyright this was not possible. The book, accordingly, keeps to the time since the War, even though a writer such as Robertson may have done work before it. There are obvious omissions, but only with good reason: Professor Dover Wilson, for instance, is not represented, but this is because there was no suitable essay of his available. It was not possible to represent American criticism in a volume of this scope, but Professor Stoll's work has a necessary place in a survey of English criticism.

But at best the survey is partial; one cannot know absolutely what is important in the criticism of one's own age, any more than in its poetry. And it is hard to give even a glance at an activity which swings the whole way between art and science. At least, however, this makes it possible to read good essays otherwise difficult or expensive to come by.

Acknowledgements for permission to include copyright material are due to Messrs. George Allen & Unwin for a chapter from *The Problem of Hamlet* by J. M. Robertson; to Mr. Edmund Blunden and Messrs. Jonathan Cape for *Shakespeare's Significances*; to the Cambridge University Press for two chapters from E. E. Stoll's *Art and Artifice in Shakespeare*; to Professor H. B. Charlton for 'Romanticism in Shakespearian Comedy', reprinted from *the Bulletin of the John Rylands Library*; to Mr. T. S. Eliot and Messrs. Faber and Faber for *Shakespeare and the Stoicism of Seneca*; to Mr. H. Granville-Barker who has revised and rewritten the essay on 'King Lear' which appeared in *Prefaces to Shakespeare* (Ist ser.) published by Messrs. Sidgwick & Jackson; to Mr. W. W. Greg and the President of the British Academy for *Principles of Emendation in Shakespeare*; to Dr. G. B. Harrison and the Editor of *The Times Literary Supplement* for 'Shakespeare's Topical Significances'; to Professor L. L. Schücking and Messrs. G. Harrap for the extract from *Character Problems in Shakespeare's Plays*; to Mr. J. Isaacs for 'Shakespeare as Man of the Theatre' from *Shakespeare and the Theater* published by the Shakespeare Association; to Mr. G. Wilson Knight for 'The Othello Music' from *The Wheel of Fire*, and to Mr. J. Middleton Murry for 'Metaphor' from *Countries of the Mind*, ii, both published by the Oxford University Press; to Mr. G. Rylands, the Hogarth Press, and Messrs Harcourt Brace & Co. for two chapters from *Words and Poetry*; to Dr. Caroline Spurgeon for *Leading Motives in the Imagery of Shakespeare's Tragedies*; to Mr. Charles Williams and the Delegates of the Clarendon Press for *Henry V* and the extract from *The English Poetic Mind*.

Anne Bradby, 1936

1
Shakespeare's Work of Transmutation[1]
J.M. Robertson

1. Old Action: New Psychosis

It remains to note how Shakespeare's handling has turned a Hamlet who was very little of a mystery into a Hamlet who is very much one. The first step in counter-sense, certainly, was taken by Kyd, when he combined the revelation by the Ghost with the mock madness of the old story given him in Belleforest. In that, no Ghost is needed, the murder being known to all, though the traitorous brother (Fengon) persuades the people that he killed Hamblet's father (Horvendile) only in defence of Geruth, Hamblet's mother, who is secretly Fengon's paramour. Hamblet's madness, accordingly, is assumed in the manner of the old myth of Brutus and David, to save his life, he feeling sure that otherwise Fengon will slay him. It is not primarily a matter of wild talk but of demented action, though Hamblet proceeds to make 'sub till answers' which arouse Fengon's suspicion, leading him to seek to entrap the youth by means of a 'fair and beautiful woman' and 'certain courtiers'. Here we have the germs of Ophelia and Rosencrantz and Guildenstern; and in the foster-brother who puts Hamblet on his guard we have a hint of Horatio. Another attempt is made by Fengon to entrap Hamblet in a talk with his mother, with a counsellor concealed behind the hangings,[2] and the counsellor is killed by Hamblet in the manner

1. *The Problem of Hamlet* (1919).
2. Under straw in Saxo Grammaticus; under a quilt in Belleforest. The hangings appear in the English translation, of which only a copy dated 1608 exists.

of the play, which here also follows the story. Before the slaying scene, however, Kyd had previously composed the play-within-the-play, which gratuitously reveals to the King Hamlet's ghost-given knowledge of the murder — a fresh confusion of the old plot. In that, the killing of the courtier is followed by Hamblet's dispatch to England; his counterfeiting of the letters, so as to doom the messengers, as in the play; and his manifold English adventures, which the play ignores.

Whereas, then, the barbaric Hamblet shams madness to save his life, Kyd's Hamlet, who shams madness after supernaturally learning of a wholly secret murder, thereby begins at once to endanger his. Apprised by the Ghost, he had no occasion to alter his behaviour: it was his business to behave as before, the King having thus far no designs on him. And the play-within-the-play is another supererogation. Kyd loved to complicate his motives thus. In *Arden* he introduces items of sacrilege and avarice which are dramatically needless, being motived only by the academic principle that he who suffers must have sinned; and he invents two wronged men, one of whom appears merely to curse, doing nothing further in the action. By thus confusing the original Hamlet-plot through his favourite Ghost-motive, Kyd, led to retain the mock-madness by his success with the semi-madness of Jeronymo, prepared the divagation which Shakespeare so wonderfully develops. The Ghost-warned Hamlet who shams madness to no purpose grows naturally into the Hamlet who unintelligibly swerves from revenge.

That Kyd's inconsistencies of construction thus inhere in Shakespeare's play is a fact which criticism must sooner or later face. Lowell, rightly arguing that 'if you deprive Hamlet of reason there is no truly tragic motive left', confuses his position by accepting the absurd pronouncement of early Victorian 'experts' that Hamlet really exhibits in perfection the symptoms of madness, and explains that 'if such a man assumed madness, he would play his part perfectly'. Then he remembers that the assumed madness is 'one of the few points in which Shakespeare keeps close to the old story', and accordingly declares him to have done so with 'unerring judgment'. Hamlet, that is to say, shams madness merely because he does not know what else to do:

'the scheme of simulated insanity is precisely the one he would have been likely to hit upon, because it enabled him to follow his own bent, and to drift with an apparent purpose', and so forth. Then we are to believe that Shakespeare saw in the expedient of the barbarian of the story, a man of action absolutely, 'precisely' what would be done by a man of exactly opposite structure. To such shifts does idolatry conduct us.

We shall ultimately do much more for Shakespeare's credit by honestly acknowledging that his Hamlet pretends madness because Kyd's Hamlet did so before; and that in Kyd's Hamlet the device is put out of joint, first by Kyd's own further device of the Ghost's revelation, which cancels the prudential motive of the saga Hamblet, making Hamlet on the contrary at once arouse the King's suspicion; and secondly by the device of the play-within-the-play, which is anything but a madman's plan, though Jeronymo gave the precedent. In a word, Hamlet's mock-madness is now ill-motived. Lowell, in his best 'high priori' manner, writes that 'Voltaire complains that he [Hamlet] goes mad without any sufficient object or result. Perfectly true, and precisely what was most natural for him to do, and, accordingly, precisely what Shakespeare meant that he should do'. What Voltaire really said[3] was that 'pour ne pas donner d'ombrages à Gertrude, il contrefait le fou pendant toute la pièce' — a jest which incidentally suggests a better motive for Hamlet's mock madness than any given by the idolaters. As criticism, Voltaire's fling is perfectly just; and, like some of his other flings, it is to be met, not by brazening things out, but by granting that Shakespeare did at times make himself answerable for other men's artistic sins.[4] He did so when, essaying his immortal task of transmuting the crude play of Kyd into a dramatic marvel, he retained all the archaic machinery while transfiguring all the characters. A marvel his *tour de force* remains; but no jugglery can do away with the fact that the construction is incoherent, and the hero perforce an enigma, the snare of idolatrous criticism.

3. *Lettre à messieurs de l'académie fraçaise,* 15 auguste, 1776.
4. E.g. the scene between Henry and Catherine in *Henry V,* which Voltaire condemned. Most of his attacks on Shakespeare turn on real blemished, and they are bracketed with very high praise. The sin of his criticism is its want of final balance.

It is of no avail to plead, as Mr. Widgery so eloquently does after Werder, that Hamlet in the play has an insuperably difficult task, seeing that he cannot prove the King's guilt by citing the testimony of a ghost. Why did he not at the outset tell both Horatio and Marcellus what the Ghost had told him? They would have believed, and been believed, readily enough. Given a Ghost who is credited by the *audience*, why should he not be credited by the characters? When, again, the King rushes away in confusion from the play it is surely idle to argue, as does Mr. Widgery, that Hamlet has failed in his object because the King does not *speak*. Is not his confusion a sufficient proof of his guilt? To say that the courtiers do not so recognize it is to argue in a circle. Shakespeare would never have *planned* a play on such lines and with such a thesis, any more than he would have invented the prayer-scene and the motive that there withholds Hamlet.

All these devices, once more, are but the machinery of Kyd, adapting a barbaric story in which the barbarian *must* delay his revenge because he is only one against a powerful chief whom the people heartily support, believing him to have saved the youth's mother from her husband's violence. It all goes back, possibly, to a sun myth; but the barbaric tale is fairly coherent. Kyd needed a tale of delayed vengeance, and for him, though he makes Hamlet indirectly accuse himself in the closet-scene with the Ghost,[5] there was no more mystery in Hamlet's delay than there was in Jeronymo's, or in the halting and hindered movement of the action in *Arden,* with the baffled attempts, and the two reconciliations of the doomed man with his enemy. Kyd's tragedy-method was not psychological or didactic, with all his devotion to Seneca: it is one of protracted and long-baffled action; and he of necessity ekes out the time with incidents and expedients, especially where, as in *Hamlet*, he has a plot full of delays given to his hand.

In the closet-scene in the First Quarto the Ghost says nothing of an 'almost blunted purpose'; that is Shakespeare's modification. Kyd has no such conception. His Hamlet says:

---

5. In Q.l the dialogue is clearly in part Kyd's; and in the *Brudermord* we have the same deprecation of the supposed wrath of the Ghost at delay.

> Do you not come your tardy son to chide,
> That I thus long have let revenge slip by?

but the Ghost replies only:

> Hamlet, I once again appear to thee
> To put thee in remembrance of my death.
> Do not neglect, nor long time put it off,—

going on to urge him to comfort his mother. This is wholly in the spirit of the *Spanish Tragedy*, where the partly unavoidable and partly artificial delay of revenge is the great preoccupation of the distracted Jeronymo, who delays in order to obtain a grand finale of slaughter by means of his play-within-the-play. He begins plotting immediately after the murder:

> Meanwhile, good Isabella, cease thy plaints,
> Or at the least dissemble them awhile:
> So shall we sooner find the practice out.
>
> (II. v. 113.)

When he gets Bellimperia's letter he is suspicious:

> Hieronimo, beware, — thou art betrayed.
> And to entrap thy life this train is laid.
> Advise thee, therefore, be not credulous. . . .
> Dear was the life of my beloved son,
> And of his death behoves me be reveng'd:
> Then hazard not thine own, Hieronimo,
> But live t' effect thy resolution.
> I therefore will by circumstances try
> What I can gather to confirm this writ. . . .
>
> (III. ii. 37-49.)

He contemplates suicide and refrains:

> For if I hang or kill myself, let's know
> Who will revenge Horatio's murther then?

He thinks of appealing to the King, but decides to 'go by, go by'. He

> will revenge his [Horatio's] death,
> But how? not as the vulgar wits of men,
> With open but inevitable ills,
> As by a secret yet a certain mean,
> Which under friendship will be cloakèd best.
> Wise men will take their opportunity
> Closely and safely, fitting things to time;

But in extremes advantage hath no time;
And therefore all times fit not for revenge.
Thus therefore will I rest me in unrest,
Dissembling quiet in inquietness —

(III. xiii.)

and so on. Revenge, awaked from sleep by Andrea's ghost (an item which has been mistakenly ridiculed), replies:

Sufficeth thee that poor Hieronimo
Cannot forget his son Horatio,
Nor dies Revenge although he sleep awhile.

(III. xii.)

Bellimperia bitterly reproaches Hieronimo for his delay, but he reassures her and plots on; Isabella, committing suicide, denounces his negligence; but he is all the while at work. For Kyd, Hamlet was substantially in the same case; and in making the prince excuse himself to the Ghost he is not implying that Hamlet has been really remiss. That is Shakespeare's development of the situation. Professor Bradley subtly argues[6] that when the Ghost says 'Remember me' he is touching, not accidentally, on a faculty of forgetting known to him in Hamlet; but in all probability the touch came from Kyd. When Jeronymo says (III, vi. 103):

This makes me to *remember thee*, my son,

he does not mean that he had ever forgotten him.

2. The Infusion of Pessimism

The vital dramatic difference, however, between Jeronymo and Hamlet was that while the audience saw and followed Jeronymo's purpose, there was no very clear purpose in Kyd's Hamlet to follow. The question, put to this day by the unsophisticated, 'Why doesn't he kill his uncle and live happy ever afterwards with Ophelia'? was forestalled by Kyd only in so far as he offered the explanation given in the *Brudermord*, that the King is always surrounded by his guards. That explanation, given him in the old story, probably seemed to him sufficient. But he in effect partly qualified it when, multiplying his episodes after his manner, he staged the play-scene, which put the King

6. *Shakespearean Tragedy*, p. 126.

on his guard, and then the prayer-scene. If meantime, as we have surmised, there had been going on an action in connexion with Fortinbras, Elizabethan audiences would be apt to be impatient.

True, once more, there has been no great delay in all: indeed, save for the indefinite interval between Acts I and II there has been none at all! The play-scene is only a day after the arrival of the players; and on that night the action rushes on to the point of the decreeing of Hamlet's voyage to England. After being convinced by the King's behaviour, Hamlet has had but one chance to slay him; and to stress that one recoil as the critics do is to pay a remarkable tribute to the 'time-devouring' power of Shakespeare's dramatization. Hamlet, when all is said, is commonly condemned on the strength of a single recoil from assassination, and that under circumstances in which, religion apart, any high-minded man would have recoiled. To stab the King in the back while he knelt praying would have been truly a precious proof of 'resolution' and 'faculty for action'. But the fact remains that, as Shakespeare's added soliloquies imply, the audiences, disregarding under the dramatic spell all questions of real time, fidgeted, without the modern critics to help them. They would have scouted the suggestion that a ghost was not a good witness; after the convincing play-scene they would grow suspicious; and after the prayer-scene many must have been moved to sarcasm, though doubtless Kyd's edifying theology impressed some. The broad fact is that, time apart, Hamlet as it were willfully delays in our play, while Jeronymo is constantly planning his comprehensive vengeance and loses no clear opportunity, though he too is slow, to the extent of angering his wife and Bellimperia.

Now, Shakespeare's handling of the play is above all things a masterly effort to hint a psychological solution of the acted mystery, while actually heightening it by the self-accusing soliloquies. It is he who makes Hamlet keep the Ghost's tale secret : in the *Brudermord* it is at once revealed to Horatio; and in our play we learn at the play-scene that it *had* been revealed in the interim. It is he who stresses the Queen's guilt, here reverting to the original story as against the treatment indicated in the *Brudermord*, where the King makes no charge against his wife, though Hamlet speaks doubtfully of her at the close. In the First Quarto we have the Ghost's speech on the battlements from the text given in the Second; but in the closet-scene the Queen protests her absolute ignorance of the murder and pledges herself, in lines that are obviously Kyd's, to assist Hamlet against the King. Here Kyd follows the Belleforest story in which Geruth protests her innocence of the murder, saying nothing of other matters. In the Second Quarto these passages disappear, and though Hamlet does not accuse the Queen of complicity in the murder, his tone is that of one who has suffered tortures on the score of his mother's degradation.

This, if there be any, is the new ground-note of Shakespeare's Hamlet. The guilt of a mother is an almost intolerable motive for drama, but it had to be maintained and emphasized to supply a psychological solution, or rather a hint of one. The childlike subservience of poor Ophelia tells to the same effect.[7] Utter sickness of heart, revealing itself in pessimism, is again and again dramatically obtruded as if to set us feeling that for a heart so crushed revenge *is no remedy.*[8] And this implicit pessimism is Shakespeare's personal contribution: his verdict on the situation set out by the play.[9] But the fact remains that he has not merely

7. Professor Bradley's gallant and brilliant defence of the ill starred child does not alter her relation to the action.
8. Never that it is forbidden by religion.
9. Over thirty years ago I put the thesis of Hamlet's pessimism in an essay on *The Upshot of Hamlet* (1885). It has since been independently put by several German writers who, however, leave the issue at that. See Hermann Türck's *Hamlet ein Genie* (1888) and *Das psychologische Problem in der Hamlet-Tragödie* (1890); also his polemic with Kuno Fischer over their respective originalities: *Die Uebereinstimmung von Kuno Fischer's und Hermann Türck's Hamlet-Erklärung* (1894); and *Kuno Fischer's kritische Methode* (1894). Both writers, as it happened, were repeating a British thesis. But Türck has the phrase: 'Hamlet is the tragedy of idealism' (*Hamlet ein Genie,* p. 17), partly endorsed by Professor Bradley, p. 113. On the other hand, my proposition that Shakespeare imports a temporary pessimism of his own into Hamlet's situation was partly anticipated by Rumelin in his *Shakespearestudien* (1866), p. 96: 'So war auch in Shakespeare die Hamlet-Natur nur ein Theil seines Gemüthslebens'. But he again was anticipated a century earlier by a British critic who far out went his age in psychological penetration : 'For what is Falstaff, what Lear, what Hamlet or Othello, but different modifications of Shakespeare's thought?' — Maurice Morgann, *Essay on Falstaff* (1777), p. 16.

not been explicit — as he could not be — he has left standing matter which conflicts with the solution of pessimism; he has exhibited Hamlet as roused to determination by the spectacle of the march of Fortinbras and declaring that he knows not why he has refrained; and he has further exhibited him acting with abundant vigour in the sea episode, as he had previously done in planning the Court play. These displays of vigour, like the killing of Polonius, do not consist with a pessimism so laming as to preclude revenge. And the ultimate fact is that Shakespeare *could not* make a psychologically or otherwise consistent play out of a plot which retained a strictly barbaric action while the hero was transformed into a supersubtle Elizabethan.

3. The Upshot

If this be pronounced aspersive criticism, I have but to say that for me the play becomes only more wonderful when the manner of its evolution is realized. What Shakespeare could not do, no man could have done. What he did remains a miracle of dramatic imagination. In the place of one of the early and crude creations of Kyd, vigorous without verisimilitude,[10] outside of refined sympathy, he has projected a personality which from the first line sets all our sympathies in a quick vibration, and so holds our minds and hearts that even the hero's cruelties cannot alienate them. The triumph is achieved by sheer intensity of presentment, absolute lifelikeness of utterance, a thrilling and convincing rightness of phrase and of feeling where wrong feeling is not part of the irremovable material. He who will may argue that Shakespeare should not have accepted intractable material. Let him tell us whether he would rather have been without *Hamlet*, and whether he cannot see that the practical compulsion to handle or retain intractable material underlies half a dozen of the Shakespeare plays as well as *Hamlet — Timon*, *Pericles*, *Cymbeline*, *Henry V*, the *Winter's Tale*, *Measure for Measure*, *All's Well*, to say nothing of other comedies. Till that is seen Shakespeare is not revealed.

---

10. This, of course, does not apply to *Arden*, which is later and psychologically very much superior to the *Tragedy*, though little better in point of verse technique.

He was, as usual, adapting an old play for his company, in the way of business. Its main features he had to preserve, else the public would miss what they looked for. *Hamlet* must retain its Ghost and its mock-madness no less than the real madness of Ophelia. To satisfy the poet as well as his cultured patrons the Prince must be made truly princely; and every stroke to that end was an element of success. But the revenge of the refined Hamlet must be delayed as was that of the barbaric Hamblet, without the original reason; the old machinery must be retained, down to the prayer-scene; and so there emerged a puzzling and unexplained character in place of one analogous to the rudely and clearly outlined Jeronymo, never puzzling to anybody save the characters alongside him, who are not in his counsels as the audience are.

Evolving a Hamlet of the highest mental lucidity, Shakespeare himself at one point accepted the inference of an 'almost blunted purpose', a will that will not act when it should; and by a score of subtle strokes he tacitly suggests how a man may feel the barrenness of a revenge to which he is vowed. But this is only half of his composite Hamlet : the other is the presentment of a man who can act with lightning speed and force, and will 'make a ghost of him that lets me'. Of all the explanatory formulas that of Mackenzie, so little discussed, is the best.[11] He posits an excess of sensibility which yields uncertain and divergent action — a spirit which recoils as uncontrollably from straightforward killing as from another's villainy or unworthiness. With a difference, Professor Bradley pronounces that Hamlet 'tries to find reasons for his delay in pursuing a design which excites his aversion'.[12] Such a conception may as easily be read into Shakespeare as that of psychic shock, or pessimism arising out of personal disillusionment. But it also is inadequate to the data. Hamlet thrusts through the arras without hesitation, and shows no horror at his deed. He has no scruple about sending his schoolfellows to their death on the bare surmise that they knew the contents of the King's dispatch. A 'sensibility' which yields at once these results and an insuperable recoil from vengeance on

11. The essay on *Hamlet* is not included in the collected edition of Mackenzie's *Miscellaneous Works*, 3 vols. (1820).
12. *Shakespearean Tragedy*, p. 226.

a villain is not finally thinkable. In the words of Salvini, 'A man like Hamlet has never existed, nor could exist'.[13] This, as we must admit in the conclusion, is not really an ultimate indictment of Shakespeare : but it is a necessary estoppels of certain theorists who turn an aesthetic suggestion into a false historic theorem.

For it is idle to pretend that Shakespeare was deeply concerned to secure perfect artistic consistency. As an adaptor and reconstructor he worked wonders; but he had to let pass many incongruities in many plays. To those already noted we may add the retention of the Dumb Show in which, before the play, the murder is enacted even as it is after the speeches. As it is the action and not the speaking that upsets the King, he ought either to have been upset by the Dumb Show or to have collected himself for the repetition.[14] Shakespeare at this point merely let stand what he found, as he let stand the episodes which we have seen to be 'out of the frame'. Whether or not by reason of the play being originally in two parts, it is full of fortuitous retardations; and it is not surprising that in a recent revival the actor-manager dropped such matters as the advice to the players and Polonius' advice to Laertes; even as the Reynaldo scene had been dropped long before.

It is possible, indeed, to exaggerate the incongruities of the piece. Though Hamlet's age is certainly a conundrum Professor Bradley has perhaps made needless difficultly[15] as to Hamlet's proposed return to Wittenberg. 'Going *back* to school in Wittenberg' does not necessarily mean that he has just come thence; and his reception of Horatio and Marcellus does not imply, as Professor Bradley says, that he and Horatio are supposed to have left Wittenberg 'for Elsinore less than two months ago'. Hamlet may have left it years before; and his 'Horatio, or I do forget myself', suggests long severance. As Professor Trench remarks, 'the city' may very well be Copenhagen, where Hamlet may have spent time after leaving Wittenberg. But there is real incongruity in his telling Horatio (III. ii) how he has prized him

13. Art. 'Salvini on Shakespeare', by Helen Zimmern, *Gentleman's Magazine*, February 1884.
14. This was commented on a century ago.
15. In Note B on *Hamlet in Shakespearean Tragedy.*

'since my dear soul was mistress of her choice', after greeting him with 'Horatio, or I do forget myself'. Even Professor Trench, who assures us that Shakespeare is 'regular and orderly in his work with the regularity and order of a classical genius',[16] and warns us that when we fail to understand it may be our own fault,[17] also declares[18] that 'when we fail to understand him [Shakespeare], it certainly is often his own fault'.

It is most true, if we must say 'fault' in a case where the master is performing a miracle of transmutation, vitalizing, elevating, and irradiating a crude creation into a world's wonder, and finally missing artistic consistency simply because consistency was absolutely excluded by the material. He leaves it possible for some (including Professor Trench) to think Hamlet more or less really mad. He indicates no totally explanatory formula because he could not: the play will not now go into any. In paying ourselves with saving formulas of Hamlet's mystery we are but obscuring Shakespeare's mystery, which is here finally so legible and so vividly interesting. *Hamlet* is only the more wonderful for being rightly 'understood'. When Furnivall indignantly rejected[19] the thesis of the Clarendon Press editors that the First Quarto in its construction is mainly the work of the earlier playwright, he was but revealing the uncritical temper of the older Shakespeare-worship. Disregarding the real tests of diction and psychology, he was staking Shakespeare's greatness on such positions as the invention of the idea of a play-within-the-play and the creation of such dialogue as Hamlet's 'chaff' with Polonius — work within the capacity of lesser men than Kyd. The assailed editors had made a loyal induction from the documents; and Furnivall and Dowden, refusing to make it, were seeking for Shakespeare the wrong kind of credit. His real triumph was to turn a crude play into the masterpiece which he has left us. It is a perfectly magnificent *tour de force* and its ultimate æsthetic miscarriage is only the supreme illustration of the vulgar but ancient truth that an entirely satisfactory silken

---

16. *Shakepearse's* Hamlet (1913), p. 187.
17. p. 166.
18. p. 109.
19. *Academy*, August 7, 1880.

purse cannot be constructed, even by a Shakespeare, out of a sow's ear — if one can without indecency apply that figure to a barbaric saga which ultimately yielded us *Hamlet.*

Aesthetically, it is improper. For, when all is said, the 'pragmatic' test is practically final for such a thing as a drama. *Hemlet* has 'made good' : it has enormously over passed the simple end of the playwright, to entertain. The miraculous puppetry of the actor manager has kept millions at gaze for centuries now; and if Shakespeare could be recreated and asked why he managed here and there so oddly, he might with an unanswerable effect open eye of wonder and ask what should make us thus put his mechanism to the rack. 'Do you want an *absolute*', he might ask, 'as a stage entertainment?' And though we might make play with Hamlet's dictum about holding up a mirror to Nature, we should be met by the reminder that that, too, is part of the *play*; and we should know that Shakespeare had non-suited us.

And so he might silence us if we sought to debate with him on the character of Iago, which in Professor Bradley's fine dissection we almost feel to be drawn from life itself. 'Did you mean to make a study of moral insanity'? we might ask him : 'Is the formula of Iago simply that he is at bottom *the* criminal type, crafty in will-worship and stupid in craft — a reversion to the ape or savage?' 'Does that really matter?' He might reply. 'Has not the play sufficed to *occupy* intelligent people? What matters it whether Iago could or could not have really existed? Could Othello? Could Falstaff? For that matter, could *any* imagined person? What *is* fiction? . . . The play works. Would anything but Iago serve to drive a tragedy that hinges on a handkerchief? If you think so, try another'. And there an end.

But the critical intellect, too, has its rights: *its* concern is simply conceptual truth; and as against — *not* Shakespeare but — those who formulate Ptolemaic schemes of his works, its rights are absolute. The 'purpose of playing is' — well, not exactly what Hamlet-Shakespeare alleges! But the purpose of science is indisputably to know how things actually went; and it is time we had done with Ptolemaic methods, though the literary Ptolemaists have included some remarkably able men, recalling the distinguished prototype, who was a very able man indeed.

2
Leading Motives in the Imagery of Shakespeare's Tragedies[1]

Caroline F.E. Spurgeon

It has not, so far as I know, ever yet been noticed that recurrent images play a part in raising, developing, sustaining, and repeating emotion in the tragedies, which is somewhat analogous to the action of a recurrent theme or 'motif' in a musical fugue or sonata, or in one of Wagner's operas.

Perhaps, however, a more exact analogy to the function of Shakespeare's images in this respect is the unique work of another great artist, of the peculiar quality of which they constantly remind one, that is, Blake's illustrations to his prophetic books. These are not, for the most part, illustrations in the ordinary sense of the term, the translation by the artist of some incident in the narrative into a visual picture; they are rather a running accompaniment to the words in another medium, sometimes symbolically emphasizing or interpreting certain aspects of the thought, sometimes supplying frankly only decoration or atmosphere, sometimes grotesque and even repellent, vivid, strange, arresting, sometimes drawn with an almost unearthly beauty of form and colour. Thus, as the leaping tongues of flame which illuminate the pages of *The Marriage of Heaven and Hell* show the visual form which Blake's thought evoked in his mind, and symbolize for us the purity, the beauty, and the two-edged quality of life and danger in his words, so the recurrent images in *Macbeth* or *Hamlet* reveal the dominant picture or sensation —

1. Shakespeare Association Lecture (1930).

and for Shakespeare the two are identical — in terms of which he sees and feels the main problem or theme of the play, thus giving us an unerring clue to the way he looked at it, as well as a direct glimpse into the working of his mind and imagination.

These dominating images are a characteristic of Shakespeare's work throughout, but whereas in the earlier plays they are often rather obvious and of set design, taken over in some cases with the story itself from a hint in the original narrative; in the later plays, and especially in the great tragedies, they are born of the emotions of the theme, and are, as in *Macbeth*, subtle, complex, varied, but intensely vivid and revealing; or as in *Lear*, so constant and all-pervading as to be reiterated, not only in the word-pictures, but also in the single words themselves.

Any reader, of course, must be aware of certain recurrent symbolic imagery in Shakespeare, such as that of a tree and its branches, and of planting, lopping, or rooting up, which runs through the English historical plays; they are conscious of the imaginative effect of the animal imagery in *Lear*, or of the flash of explosives in *Romeo and Juliet*, but it was not until the last few years, when in the course of an intensive study of Shakespeare's imagery I had listed and classified and card-indexed and counted every image in every play thrice over, that the actual facts as to these dominating pictures stared me in the face.

I found that there is a certain range of images, and roughly a certain proportion of these, to be expected in every play, and that certain familiar categories, of nature, animals, and what one may call 'everyday' or 'domestic', easily come first. But in addition to this normal grouping, I have found, especially in the tragedies, certain groups of images which, as it were, stick out in each particular play and immediately attract attention because they are peculiar either in subject or quantity, or both.

These seem to form the floating image or images in Shakespeare's mind called forth by that particular play, and I propose now, as briefly as possible, just to look at the tragedies from the point of view of these groups of images only.

In *Romeo and Juliet* the beauty and ardour of young love is seen by Shakespeare as the irradiating glory of sunlight and starlight in a dark world. The dominating image is *light*, every form and manifestation of it; the sun, moon, stars, fire, lightning, the flash of gunpowder, and the reflected light of beauty and of love; while by contrast we have night, darkness, clouds, rain, mist, and smoke.

Each of the lovers thinks of the other as light; Romeo's overpowering impression when he first catches sight of Juliet on the fateful evening at the Capulets' ball is seen in his exclamation,

> O, she doth teach the torches to burn bright!

To Juliet, Romeo is 'day in night'; to Romeo, Juliet is the sun rising from the east, and when they soar to love's ecstasy, each alike pictures the other as stars in heaven, shedding such brightness as puts to shame the heavenly bodies themselves.

The intensity of feeling in both lovers purges even the most highly affected and euphuistic conceits of their artificiality, and transforms them into the exquisite and passionate expression of love's rhapsody.

Thus Romeo plays with the old conceit that two of the fairest stars in heaven, having some business on earth, have entreated Juliet's eyes to take their place till they return, and he conjectures,

> What if her eyes were there, they in her head?

If so,

> The brightness of her cheek would shame those stars,
> As day-light doth a lamp:

and then comes the rush of feeling, the overpowering realization and immortal expression of the transforming glory of love,

> her eyes in heaven
> Would through the airy region stream so bright
> That birds would sing and think it were not night.

And Juliet, in her invocation to night, using an even more extravagant conceit such as Cowley or Cleveland at his wildest never exceeded, transmutes it into the perfect and natural expression of a girl whose lover to her not only radiates light but is, indeed, very light itself:

> Give me my Romeo; and, when he shall die,
> Take him and cut him out in little stars,
> And he will make the face of heaven so fine,
> That all the world will be in love with night,

> And pay no worship to the garish sun.

Love is described by Romeo, before he knows what it really is, as

> a smoke raised with the fume of sighs;
> Being purged, a Fire sparkling in lovers' eyes;

and the messengers of love are seen by Juliet, when she is chafing under the nurse's delay, as one of the most exquisite effects in nature, especially on the English hills in spring, of the swift, magical, transforming power of light; 'love's heralds', she cries, 'should be thoughts,

> Which ten times faster glide than the sun's beams,
> Driving back shadows over louring hills'.

The irradiating quality of the beauty of love is noticed by both lovers; by Juliet in her first ecstasy, when she declares that lovers' 'own beauties' are sufficient light for them to see by, and at the end by Romeo, when, thinking her dead, he gazes on her and cries

> her beauty makes
> This vault a feasting presence full of light.

There can be no question, I think, that Shakespeare saw the story, in its swift and tragic beauty, as an almost blinding flash of light, suddenly ignited and as swiftly quenched. He quite deliberately compresses the action from over nine months to the almost incredibly short period of five days; so that the lovers meet on Sunday, are wedded on Monday, part at dawn on Tuesday, and are reunited in death on the night of Thursday. The sensation of swiftness and brilliance, accompanied by danger and destruction, is accentuated again and again; by Juliet when she avows their betrothal

> Is too rash, too unadvised, too sudden,
> Too like the lightning, which doth cease to be
> Ere one can say 'It lightens';

and by Romeo and the Friar, who instinctively make repeated use of the image of the quick destructive flash of gunpowder (III. iii. 103, 132; v. i. 63). Indeed the Friar, in his well-known answer to Romeo's prayer for instant marriage, succinctly, in the last nine words, sums up the whole movement of the play,

> These violent delights have violent ends,

And in their triumph die; like fire and powder
Which as they kiss consume?

Even old Capulet, whom one does not think of as a poetical person, though he uses many images — some of great beauty — carries on the idea of light to represent love and youth and beauty, and of the clouding of the sun for grief and sorrow. He promises Paris that on the evening of the ball he shall see at his house

Earth-treading stars that make dark heaven light,

and when he encounters Juliet weeping, as he thinks for her cousin Tybalt's death, he clothes his comment in similar nature-imagery of light quenched in darkness,

When the sun sets, the air doth drizzle dew;
But for the sunset of my brother's son
It rains downright.

In addition to this more definite symbolic imagery we find that radiant light, sunshine, starlight, moonbeams, sunrise and sunset, the sparkle of fire, a meteor, candles, torches, quick coming darkness, clouds, mist, rain, and night, form a pictorial background or running accompaniment to the play, which augments unconsciously in us this same sensation.

We meet it at once in the Prince's description of the attitude of the rival houses

That quench the fire of your pernicious rage
With purple fountains issuing from your veins;

and later, in the talk of Benvolio and Montagu about the rising sun, the dew, and clouds (I. i. 117-18, 130-36), followed by Romeo's definition of love (I. i. 189-90), Capulet's words just quoted, Benvolio's riming proverb about fire (I. ii. 46), the talk of Romeo and Mercutio about torches, candles, lights, and lamps (I. iv. 35-45), the flashing lights and torches of the ball, four times accentuated (I. v. 28, 45, 88, 126), Romeo's conception of Juliet as a 'bright angel', 'as glorious to this night'

As is a winged messenger of heaven;

the moonlight in the orchard, the sunrise Friar Lawrence watches from his cell, the sun clearing from heaven Romeo's sighs (II. iii. 73), the exquisite light and shadow swiftly chasing over Juliet's words in the orchard (II. v. 4-II), the 'black fate' of the day on which Mercutio was killed, the 'fire-eyed fury' which leads Romeo to challenge Tybalt, their fight, to which they go like lightning', the sunset which Juliet so ardently desires to be swift 'and bring in cloudy night immediately', the exquisite play of quivering light from darkness through dawn, till

> jocund day
> Stands tip-toe on the misty mountain tops,

which forms the theme of the lovers' parting song; and at the last, Romeo's anguished reply to Juliet, pointing the contrast between the coming day and their own great sorrow,

> More light and light: more dark and dark our woes!

And then at the end we see the darkness of the churchyard, lit by the glittering torch of Paris, quickly quenched; Romeo's arrival with his torch, the swift fight and death, the dark vault, which is not a grave but a lantern irradiated by Juliet's beauty, Romeo's grim jest on the 'lightning before death', followed immediately by the self-slaughter of the 'star-crossed' lovers, the gathering together of the stricken mourners as the day breaks, and the 'glooming' peace of the overcast morning when

> The sun for sorrow will not show his head.

Shakespeare's extraordinary susceptibility to suggestion and readiness to borrow is well exemplified in this running imagery. He took the idea from the last place we should expect, from the wooden doggerel of Arthur Brooke, and the germ of it is in the sing-song line in which Brooke describes the attitude of the lovers,

> For each of them to other is as to the world the sun.

Their mutual feeling and the feud of the families is constantly referred to by Brooke as 'fire' or 'flame'; in the beginning, he speaks of the feud as a 'mighty fire'; the families 'bathe in blood of smarting wounds', and the Prince hopes he may 'quench the sparks that burned within their breast'. These three images are combined and unified by Shakespeare in the two lines already quoted (I. i. 83-84).

Other suggestions also come from Brooke, such as the emphasis on the bright light of the torches at the ball; and Romeo's first sight of Juliet, which is a 'sudden kindled fire'; her first impression of him when he

> In her sight did seem to pass the rest as far

As Phœbus' shining beams do pass the brightness of a star; and his description in his first talk to her, of the

> quick sparks and glowing furious glead . . .

. . . from your beauty's pleasant eyne, Love causéd to proceed
Which have so set on fire each feeling part of mine
That lo, my mind doth melt away, my outward parts do pine,

which is transmuted to the delightful image of the stars which have changed places with her eyes (II. ii. 15-22).

But although Shakespeare took the idea from his original it scarcely needs saying that, in taking it, he has transformed a few conventional and obvious similes of little poetic worth into a continuous and consistent running image of exquisite beauty, building up a definite picture and atmosphere of brilliance swiftly quenched, which powerfully affects the imagination of the reader.

In *Hamlet*, naturally, we find ourselves in an entirely different atmosphere, and if we look closely we see this is partly due to the number of images of sickness, disease, or blemish of the body in the play, and we discover that the idea of an ulcer or tumour, as descriptive of the unwholesome condition of Denmark morally, is, on the whole, the dominating one.

Hamlet speaks of his mother's sin as a blister on the 'fair forehead of an innocent love', and as in *Lear*, the emotion is so strong and the picture so vivid, that the metaphor overflows into the verbs and adjectives; heaven's face, he tells her, is *thought-sick* at the act; her husband is a *mildew'd ear*, *blasting* his *wholesome* brother, and to have married him her sense must be not only *sickly* but *apoplex'd*, and at the end of that terrific scene (iii. 4) he implores her not to soothe herself with the belief that his father's apparition is due to her son's madness and not to her own guilt, for that

> Will but skin and film the ulcerous place,
> Whiles rank corruption, mining all within,
> Infects unseen.

So also, later, he compares the unnecessary fighting between Norway and Poland to a kind of tumour which grows out of too much prosperity. He sees the country and the people in it alike in terms of a sick body needing medicine or the surgeon's knife. When he surprises Claudius at his prayers, he exclaims

> This physic but prolongs thy sickly days,

and he describes the action of conscience in the unforgettable picture of the healthy, ruddy countenance turning pale with sickness (III. i. 84). A mote in the eye, a 'vicious mole', a galled chilblain, a probed wound and purgation, are also among Hamlet's images; and the mind of Claudius runs equally on the same theme.

When he hears of the murder of Polonius he declares that his weakness in not sooner having had Hamlet shut up was comparable to the cowardly action of a man with a 'foul disease' who

> To keep it from divulging, let it feed
> Even on the pith of life;

and later, when arranging to send Hamlet to England and to his death, he justifies it by the proverbial tag :

> Diseases desperate grown
> By desperate appliance are relieved,
> Or not at all;

and adjures the English king to carry out his behest, in the words of a fever patient seeking a sedative,

> For like the hectic in my blood he rages,
> And thou must cure me.

When working on Laertes so that he will easily all in with the design for the fencing match, his speech is full of the same underlying thought of a body sick or ill at ease,

> Goodness, growing to a pleurisy,
> Dies in his own too much,

and finally, he sums up the essence of the position and its urgency with lightning vividness in a short medical phrase,

> But, to the quick o' the ulcer:
> Hamlet comes back.

In marked contrast to *Lear*, though bodily disease is emphasized, bodily action and strain are little drawn upon; indeed, only in Hamlet's great speech is it brought before us at all (*to be shot at* with slings and arrows, *to take arms against* troubles and *oppose* them, *to suffer* shocks, *to bear* the lash of whips, and *endure* pangs, to *grunt* and *sweat* under burdens, and so on), and here, as in *Lear*, it serves to intensify the feeling of mental anguish. In *Hamlet*, however, anguish is not the dominating thought, but *rottenness*, disease, corruption, the result of *dirt*; the people are 'muddied', Thick and unwholesome in their thoughts and whispers, and this corruption is, in the words of Claudius, 'rank' and 'smells to heaven', so that the state of things in Denmark which shocks, paralyses, and finally overwhelms Hamlet, is as the foul tumour breaking inwardly and poisoning the whole body, while showing

> no cause without
> Why the man dies.

Thus, to Shakespeare's pictorial imagination, the problem in Hamlet is not predominantly that of will and reason, of a mind too philosophic or a nature temperamentally unfitted to act quickly; he sees it pictorially, *not as the problem of an individual at all*, but as something greater and even more mysterious, as a *condition* for which the individual himself is apparently not responsible, any more than the sick man is to blame for the cancer which strikes and devours him, but which, nevertheless, in its course and development impartially and relentlessly annihilates him and others, innocent and guilty alike. That is the tragedy of Hamlet, as it is, perhaps, the chief tragic mystery of life.

It is hardly necessary to point out, in a play so well known and of such rich imaginative quality, how the ugliness of the dominating image (disease, ulcer) is counteracted, and the whole lighted up by flashes of sheer beauty in the imagery; beauty of picture, of sound and association, more particularly in the classical group and in the personifications. Thus the tragic, murky atmosphere of Hamlet's interview with his mother, with its ever-repeated insistence on physical sickness and revolting disease, is illumined by the glow of his description of his father's portrait, the associations of beauty called up by Hyperion, Jove and Mars, or the exquisite picture evoked by the contemplation of the grace of his father's poise,

> like the herald Mercury
> New-lighted on a heaven-kissing hill.

These beauties are specially noticeable in the many personifications, as when, with Horatio, we see 'the morn in russet mantle clad', as she 'walks o'er the dew of yon high eastward hill', or with Hamlet watch Laertes leaping into Ophelia's grave and ask

> whose phrase of sorrow
> Conjures the wandering stars and makes them stand
> Like wonder-wounded hearers?

Peace, with her wheaten garland, Niobe all tears, Ophelia's garments 'heavy with their drink', who pull her from her 'melodious lay' to muddy death, or the magnificent picture of the two sides of the Queen's nature at war, as seen by the elder Hamlet,

> But look, amazement on thy mother sits:
> O, step between her and her fighting soul:

these, and many more, are the unforgettable and radiant touches of beauty in a play which has, as images, much that is somber and unpleasant.

Troilus and *Hamlet* are very closely connected in their imagery. Did we not know it for other reasons we could be sure from the similarity and continuity of symbolism in the two plays that they were written near together, and at a time when the author was suffering from a disillusionment, revulsion, and perturbation of nature, such as we feel nowhere else with the same intensity.

The same two groups of images run through and dominate both plays, disease and food; in *Hamlet* the first is predominant, and in *Troilus* the second.

The main emotional theme in *Troilus* — passionate, idealistic love followed by disillusion and despair — is pictured with overwhelming vividness through physical taste; the exquisite anticipation by a sensitive palate of delicious food and wine, and the sick revolt and disgust on finding on one's tongue only 'greasy relics' or rotting fruit.

The disgust at woman's wantonness seems to express itself instinctively to Shakespeare, especially in these two plays and in *Antony*, in terms of physical appetite and food. 'Heaven and earth!' cries Hamlet,

> she would hang on him,
> As if increase of appetite had grown
> By what it fed on: and yet, within a month—

Let me not think on't.

So lust, says the elder Hamlet, 'though to a radiant angel link'd', will 'prey on garbage'.

Cleopatra, like Cressid, is thought of as a tempting and delicious piece of food, 'a dish for the gods';

other women cloy
The appetites they feed, but she makes hungry
Where most she satisfies;

and in moments of revulsion both alike become a cold and greasy remnant: 'I found you', says Antony,

'as a morsel cold upon
Dead Caesar's trencher.'

In like manner, before Troilus has been undeceived he thinks of his sweet love as 'food for fortune's tooth', and when the revulsion of disgust follows her treachery, he cries bitterly,

The fractions of her faith, orts of her love,
The fragments, scraps, the bits and greasy relics
Of her o'er-eaten faith, are bound to Diomed.

In that amazing image of the anticipation of her love it is the sense of taste which comes naturally to Troilus's lips as the means of expressing it:

I am giddy, expectation whirls me round.
The imaginary relish is so sweet
That it enchants my sense : what will it be,
When that the watery palates taste indeed
Love's thrice repured nectar?

and it is an image drawn from the same sense, as applied to 'the poor creature, small beer', which Cressid uses when Pandarus urges her to moderate her emotion at the thought of parting from Troilus,

how can I moderate it?
If I could temporise with my affection,
Or brew it to a weak and colder palate,
The like allayment could I give my grief.

Troilus, in the vivid, passionate speeches, the metaphors of which throw so much light on his character (II. ii. 26-32, 37-50, 61-96), twice draws upon food to make his thought more clear. Thus, for instance, when he is fulminating against the prudent counsels of his brothers to let Helen go, based on reason, he uses a curious metaphor from a jugged or stuffed hare, which is clearly an associative one. He scorns their timidity, and in true Shakespearean fashion he expresses the quality by the concrete example of the most timid animal of the fields in England, turning it into an adjective; this, in turn, calls up the memory of the succulent dish still a favourite one with English country folk, and he applies the process of the larding and cooking of it (which he clearly knows well) to the dulling of men's minds and the sapping of their fiery manhood with overmuch reason and caution:

> Nay, if we talk of reason,
> Let's shut our gates and sleep: manhood and honour

Should have hare-hearts, would they but fat their thoughts With this cramm'd reason.

And a little later, when he is again urging them to stand firm by honour, though it may not be the easiest way or suit them at the moment, he takes an example from ordinary, thrifty household management to illustrate this:

> nor the remainder viands
> We do not throw in unrespective sieve,
> Because we now are full.

The force of this dominating symbol is so great that we find that fourteen of the characters make use of images of food, taste, or cooking, and that there are no less than forty-four such images in the play : seething, stewing, mincing, baking, larding, stuffing, broiling, basting, brewing, frying, kneading, boiling, and stirring the ingredients for a pudding, are among the various kinds of cooking described or referred to, sometimes at considerable length, as in the metaphor on grinding the wheat, bolting, leavening, kneading, making the cake, heating the oven, baking, and cooling, carried on with expert knowledge by Pandarus and complete understanding by Troilus in the opening of the play (I. i. 14-26).

A 'crusty batch' (of bread), cheese served for a digestive, or mouse-eaten and dry, an addled egg, mincemeat seasoned with spice and salt and baked in a pie, porridge after meat, a dish of fool (stewed fruit crushed with cream), a fusty nut, a hard sailor's biscuit, fair fruit rotting untasted in an unwholesome dish, and greasy remnants of food are, in addition, all pressed into service; as are also hunger, appetite, ravenous eating, digestion, fasting, feeding, tasting, drinking up the lees and dregs of wine, tossing off a toast, sauce, flavouring, salt, sweet and sour.

Indeed, images of cooking seem so constantly with the speakers that they cannot refrain from using them even in the most far-fetched way; as when Pandarus describes how, when Helen was playing with Troilus, Queen Hecuba laughed so that her eyes ran o'er, and Cassandra laughed, to which Cressida quickly retorts,

> But there was more temperate fire under the pot of
> her eyes: did her eyes run o'er too?

Or when Ulysses refers to Achilles as the proud lord

> That bastes his arrogance with his own seam [lard],

and declares that if, as had been suggested, Ajax went to him,

> That were to enlard his fat-already pride.

The imagery in *Macbeth* appears to me to be more rich and varied, more highly imaginative, more unapproachable by any other writer, than that of any other single play. It is particularly so, I think, in the continuous use made of the simplest, humblest, everyday things, drawn from the daily life in a cottage, as a vehicle for sublime poetry. But that is beside our point here.

The ideas in the imagery are in themselves more imaginative, more subtle and complex than in other plays, and there are a greater number of them, interwoven the one with the other, recurring and repeating. There are at least four of these main ideas and many subsidiary ones.

> One is the picture of Macbeth himself.

Few simple things — harmless in themselves — have such a curiously humiliating and degrading effect as the spectacle of a small, ignoble man enveloped in a coat far too big for him. Comic actors know this well — Charlie Chaplin, for instance — and it is by means of this homely picture that Shakespeare shows us his imaginative view of the hero, and expresses the fact that the honours for which the murders were committed are, after all, of very little worth to him.

The idea constantly recurs that Macbeth's new honours sit ill upon him, like a loose and badly fitting garment belonging to someone else. Macbeth himself first expresses it, quite early in the play, when, immediately following the first appearance of the witches and their prophecies, Ross arrives from the King and greets him as thane of Cawdor, to which Macbeth quickly replies,

> The thane of Cawdor lives: why do you dress me
> In borrow'd robes?

And a few minutes later, when he is rapt in ambitious thoughts suggested by the confirmation of two out of the three 'prophetic greetings', Banquo, watching him, murmurs,

> New honours come upon him,
> Like our strange garments, cleave not to their mould
> But with the aid of use.

When Duncan is safely in the castle, Macbeth's better nature for a moment asserts itself and, in debate with himself, he revolts from the contemplated deed for a threefold reason : because of its incalculable results, the treachery of such action from one who is both kinsman and host, and Duncan's own virtues and greatness as king. When his wife joins him his repugnance to the deed is as great, but it is significant that he gives three quite different reasons for not going ahead with it, reasons which he hopes may appeal to her, for he knows the others would not.

So he urges that he has been lately honoured by the king, people think well of him, and therefore he should reap the reward of these things at once, and not upset everything by this murder which they have planned.

There is irony in the fact that to express the position he uses the same metaphor of clothes:

> I have bought
> Golden opinions from all sorts of people,
> Which would be worn now in their newest gloss,
> Not cast aside so soon.

To which Lady Macbeth retorts contemptuously, and quite unmoved:

> Was the hope drunk
> Wherein you dress'd yourself?

After the murder, when Ross says he is going to Scone for Macbeth's coronation, Macduff uses the same simile:

> Well, may you see things well done there: adieu!
> Lest our old robes sit easier than our new!

And, at the end, when the tyrant is at bay at Dunsinane and the English troops are advancing, the Scottish lords still have this image in their minds. Caithness sees him as a man vainly trying to fasten a large garment on him with too small a belt:

> He cannot buckle his distemper'd cause
> Within the belt of rule;

while Angus, in a similar image, vividly sums up the essence of what they all have been thinking ever since Macbeth's accession to power,

> now does he feel his title
> Hang loose about him, like a giant's robe
> Upon a dwarfish thief.

This imaginative picture of a small, ignoble man encumbered and degraded by garments unsuited to him, should be put against the view emphasized by some critics (notably Coleridge and Bradley) of the likeness between Macbeth and Milton's Satan in grandeur and sublimity.

Undoubtedly Macbeth is built on great lines and in heroic proportions, with great possibilities — there could be no tragedy else. He is great, magnificently great, in courage, in passionate, indomitable ambition, in imagination and capacity to feel. But he could never be put besides, say Hamlet or Othello, in nobility of nature; and there *is* an aspect in which he is but a poor, vain, cruel, treacherous creature, snatching ruthlessly over the dead bodies of kinsman and friend at place and power he is utterly unfitted to possess. It is worth remembering that it is thus that Shakespeare, with his unshrinking clarity of vision, repeatedly *sees* him.

Another image or idea which runs through *Macbeth* is the reverberation of sound echoing over vast regions, even into the limitless spaces beyond the confines of the world. Echoing sound, as also reflected light, always interested Shakespeare; he is very quick to notice it, and in the earlier plays he records it often, quite simply and directly, as in the reverberating roll of drums in *King John*, the smack of Petruchio's kiss resounding through the church, Juliet's delicate picture of Echo with her airy tongue repeating 'Romeo', Viola's assertion that if she were Orsino she would make the

> babbling gossip of the air
> Cry out 'Olivia'!

or her more fanciful remark to the Duke that the tune he likes

> gives a very echo to the seat
> Where love is throned.

He specially loves and describes repeatedly (in the *Dream, Titus,* and the *Shrew)* the re-echoing sound of hounds and horn,

> the musical confusion
> Of hounds and echo in conjunction:

its doubling and mocking quality attracts him,

> the babbling echo mocks the hounds,
> Replying shrilly to the well-tuned horns,
> As if a double hunt were heard at once,

and it is this quality which Warwick applies most appositely, when having been roused in the small hours to soothe the sleepless and fretful king he finally loses patience with Henry's fears that the revolutionaries must be fifty thousand strong, and retorts, somewhat tartly,

> It cannot be, my lord;
> Rumour doth double, like the voice and echo,
> The numbers of the fear'd. Please it your grace
> To go to bed.

It is not until after 1600, and most noticeably in *Troilus*, that Shakespeare uses this same idea of reverberation and reflection to illustrate subtle and philosophic thought. Ulysses' mind is full of it, and he applies it constantly; Kent, in *Lear,* seizes on an analogous natural fact to point the truth that noise and protestation do not necessarily indicate deep feeling, while in *Macbeth* the peculiar quality of echoing and re-echoing sound is used to emphasize in the most highly imaginative and impressive way a thought constantly present with Shakespeare in his middle years, the incalculable and boundless effects of evil in the nature of one man.

Macbeth himself, like Hamlet, is fully conscious of how impossible it is to 'trammel up the consequence' of his deed, and by his magnificent images of angels pleading trumpet-tongued, pity, like a naked new-born babe striding the blast,

> or heaven's cherubin horsed
> Upon the sightless couriers of the air,

who

> Shall blow the horrid deed in every eye,
> That tears shall drown the wind,

he fills our imagination with the picture of its being broadcast through great spaces with reverberating sound.

This is taken up again by Macduff, when he cries,

> each new morn
> New widows howl, new orphans cry, new sorrows
> Strike heaven on the face, that it resounds
> As if it felt with Scotland and yell'd out
> Like syllable of dolour,

and again by Ross, when he is trying to break the terrible news of Macbeth's latest murders to Macduff — the destruction of his own wife and children —

> I have words
> That would be howl'd out in the desert air,
> Where hearing should not latch them.

One can scarcely conceive a more vivid picture of the vastnesses of space than this, and of the overwhelming and unending nature of the consequences or reverberations of the evil deed.

Another constant idea in the play arises out of the symbolism that light stands for life, virtue, goodness; and darkness for evil and death. 'Angels are bright', the witches are 'secret, black and mid-night hags', and, as Dowden says, the movement of the whole play might be summed up in the words, 'good things of day begin to droop and drowse'.

This is, of course, very obvious, but out of it develops the further thought which is assumed throughout, that the evil which is being done is so horrible that it would blast the sight to look on it, so darkness or partial blinding is necessary to carry it out.

Like so much in the play it is ironic that it should be Duncan who first starts this simile, the idea of which turns into a leading motive in the tragedy. When he is conferring the new honour on his son, he is careful to say that others, kinsmen and thanes, will also be rewarded:

> *Signs of nobleness like stars, shall shine*
> On all deservers.

No sooner has the king spoken than Macbeth realizes that Malcolm, now a Prince of the realm, is an added obstacle in his path, and suddenly, shrinking from the blazing horror of the murderous thought which follows, he cries to himself,

> Stars, hide your fires;
> Let not light see my black and deep desires.

And from now on, the idea that only in darkness can such evil deeds be done is ever present with both Macbeth and his wife, as is seen in their two different and most characteristic invocations to darkness; her blood-curdling cry

> Come thick night,
> And pall thee in the dunnest smoke of hell,

which takes added force when we hear later the poignant words, 'She has light by her continually'; and his more gentle appeal in the language of falconry,

> Come, seeling night,
> Scarf up the tender eye of pitiful day.

And when Banquo, sleepless, uneasy, with heart heavy as lead, crosses the courtyard on the fateful night, with Fleance holding the flaring torch before him, and, looking up to the dark sky, mutters,

> There's husbandry in heaven,
> Their candles are all out,

we know the scene is set for treachery and murder.

So it is fitting that on the day following 'dark night strangles the travelling lamp', and

> darkness does the face of earth entomb
> When living light should kiss it.

The idea of deeds which are too terrible for human eyes to look on is also constant; Lady Macbeth scoffs it, 'the sleeping and the dead', she argues, 'are but as pictures':

> 'tis the eye of childhood
> That fears a painted devil;

but Macduff, having seen the slain king, rushes out, and cries to Lennox,

> Approach the chamber, and destroy your sight
> With a new Gorgon.

Macbeth boldly asserts he dare look on that 'which might appal the devil', and the horror and fear he feels on seeing one 'too like the spirit of Banquo' in the procession of kings is expressed in his agonized cry,

> Thy crown does sear mine eye-balls;

while in his bitter and beautiful words at the close, the dominant thoughts and images are the quenching of light and the empty reverberation of sound and fury, 'signifying nothing'.

The fourth of the chief symbolic ideas in the play is one which is very constant with Shakespeare and is to be found all through his work, that sin is a disease — Scotland is sick.

So Macbeth, while repudiating physic for himself, turns to the doctor and says if he could by analysis find Scotland's disease

> And purge it to a sound and pristine health,
> I would applaud thee to the very echo,
> That should applaud again . . .
> What rhubarb, senna, or what purgative drug,
> Would scour these English hence?

Malcolm speaks of his country as weeping, bleeding, and wounded, and later urges Macduff to

> make us medicines of our great revenge,
> To cure this deadly grief,

while Caithness calls Malcolm himself the 'medicine of the sickly weal', 'the country's purge'.

It is worth noting that all Macbeth's images of sickness are remedial or soothing in character; balm for a sore, sleep after fever, a purge, physic for pain, a 'sweet oblivious antidote', thus intensifying to the reader or audience his passionate and constant longing for well-being, rest, and, above all, peace of mind.

Other subsidiary motives in the imagery, which work in and out through the play, insensibly but deeply affect the reader's imagination.

One of these is the idea of the *unnaturalness* of Macbeth's crime, that it is a convulsion of nature. This is brought out repeatedly and emphasized by imagery, as are also the terrible results of going against nature.

Macbeth himself says that Duncan's wounds 'look'd like a breach in nature'

> For ruin's wasteful entrance,

and compares his murder to the sacrilege of breaking open the Lord's anointed temple.

The events which accompany and follow it are terrible because unnatural; an owl kills a falcon, horses eat each other, the earth was feverous and did shake, day becomes night; all this, says the old man, is unnatural,

> Even like the deed that's done.

Macbeth's greatest trouble is the unnatural one that he has 'murdered sleep', and the whole feeling of dislocation is increased by such images as 'let this frame of things disjoint', or by Macbeth's conjuration to the witches with the terrible list of the convulsions of nature which may result from their answering him. Indeed, if from one angle the movement of the play may be summed up in Macbeth's words,

> Good things of day begin to droop and drowse,

from another it is completely described by the doctor in his diagnosis of the doomed Queen's malady as 'a great perturbation of nature'.

In addition to these running images symbolizing or expressing an idea, there are groups of others which might be called atmospheric in their effect, that is, they raise or increase certain feelings and emotions.

Such is the action of rapid riding which contributes and emphasizes a certain sense of rushing, relentless, and goaded motion, of which we are very conscious in the play. This is symbolized externally by the rapid ride of the messenger to Lady Macbeth arriving 'almost dead for breath', ahead of Macbeth, who himself has out ridden Duncan, who remarks in unconscious irony,

> he rides well,
> And his great love, sharp as his spur, hath holp him
> To his home before us.

It is noticeable what a large part riding plays in the images which crowd on Macbeth's heated brain when he is weighing the *pros* and *cons* of his plan; the new-born babe 'striding the blast', heaven's cherubin horsed

> Upon the sightless couriers of the air,

and finally, the vision of his 'intent', his aim, as a horse lacking sufficient spur to action, which melts into the picture of himself as a rider vaulting into the saddle with such energy that it 'o'er-leaps itself', and he falls on the farther side.

The feeling of fear, horror, and pain is increased by the constant and recurring images of blood; these are very marked and have been noticed by others, especially by Bradley, the most terrible being Macbeth's description of himself wading in a river of blood, while the most stirring to the imagination, perhaps in the whole of Shakespeare, is the picture of him gazing, rigid with horror, at his own bloodstained hand and watching it dye the whole green ocean red.

The images of animals also, nearly all predatory, unpleasant, or fierce, add to this same feeling; such are a nest of scorpions, a venomous serpent and a snake, a 'hell-kite' eating chickens, a devouring vulture, a swarm of insects, a tiger, rhinoceros, and bear, the tiny wren fighting the owl for the life of her young, small birds with the fear of the net, lime, pitfall, or gin, used with such bitter ironic effect by Lady Macduff and her boy just before they are murdered, the shrieking owl, and the bear tied to a stake fighting savagely to the end.

Enough has been said, I think, to indicate how complex and varied is the symbolism in the imagery of *Macbeth*, and to make it clear that an appreciable part of the emotions we feel throughout of pity, fear, and horror are due to the subtle but definite and repeated action of this imagery upon our minds, of which, in our preoccupation with the main theme, we remain often largely unconscious.

The main image in *Othello* is that of animals in action, preying upon one another, mischievous, lascivious, cruel, or suffering, and through these, the general sense of pain and unpleasantness is much increased and kept constantly before us.

More than half the animal images in the play are Iago's, and all these are contemptuous or repellent, a plague of flies, a quarrelsome dog, the recurrent image of bird-snaring, leading asses by the nose, a spider catching a fly, beating an offenceless dog, wild cats, wolves, goats, and monkeys.

To this Othello adds his pictures of foul toads breeding in a cistern, summer flies in the shambles, the ill-boding raven over the infected house, a toad in a dungeon, the monster 'too hideous to be shown', bird-snaring again, aspics' tongues, crocodiles' tears, and his reiteration of 'goats and monkeys'. In addition Ludovico very suitably calls Iago 'that viper', and the green-eyed monster 'begot upon itself, born on itself', is described or referred to by Iago, Emilia, and Desdemona.

It is interesting to compare the animal imagery in *Othello* with that in *Lear*. The plays have certain likenesses; they were written near together (*Othello* probably in 1604, *King Lear* about 1605), they are the most painful of the great tragedies, and they are both studies of torture.

But the torture in *Lear* is on so vast and so inhuman a scale, the cruelty of child to parent in the doubly repeated plot is so relentless and ferocious, that the jealous and petty malignity of Iago shrinks beside it.

This difference in scale is expressed in the animal imagery. In *Othello* we see a low type of life, insects and reptiles swarming and preying on each other, not out of special ferocity but just in accordance with their natural instincts, mischievous and irresponsible wild cats, goats, and monkeys, or the harmless, innocent animal trapped or beaten. This reflects and repeats the spectacle of the wanton torture of one human being by another which we witness in the tragedy, the human spider and his fly; whereas in *Lear* our imagination is filled with the accumulated pictures of active ferocity, of wolf, tiger, wild boar, vulture, serpent, and sea-monster, all animals of a certain dignity and grandeur, though seen here only when

> their desires
> Are wolfish, bloody, starved and ravenous.

This represents the terrific scale of the suffering in *Lear*, which makes us feel — as we never do in *Othello* — that the vileness of humanity is so great, so unchecked and universal, that if the gods do not intervene, the end of such horrors must come and

> Humanity must perforce prey on itself,
> Like monsters of the deep.

But the gods, who 'keep this dreadful pother', do not intervene, and the most terrible lines in Shakespeare are those breathed by Gloucester in his agony, when he attributes to the gods themselves in their dealings with men, not only indifference and callousness, but the sheer wanton delight in torture, which in *Othello* we see exercised only by one human being on another.

If animals in action symbolize the main motive in *Othello*, there is another recurrent image which gives atmosphere and background. As is fitting, with a setting of two famous seaports, the sea, its images and language, play an important part throughout.

Iago, who possibly may have been seaman before he was soldier, uses it easily and very early; when complaining that Othello had passed him over for Cassio, he describes himself as 'be-lee'd and calm'd', he knows the state has not another of Othello's 'fathom', he says he must 'show out a flag and sign of love', that Brabantio will take action against Othello to whatever extent the law 'will give him cable'; later he coarsely describes his general's marriage in the terms of a pirate taking a prize galleon, he declares to Roderigo he is knit to his deserving 'with cables of perdurable toughness', and when he sees his plots shaping well, he murmurs with satisfaction,

> My boat sails freely, both with wind and stream.

The opening of Act II, when those in Cyprus are anxiously awaiting the arrival of Desdemona and of Othello, is full of sea-pictures and personifications, the ruffian wind upon the sea, the 'chidden billow' and the 'wind-shaked surge', so that it is well in keeping with the setting and atmosphere when Cassio, in high rhetorical terms, pictures the seas and rocks as traitors concealed to waylay the ship, who, on catching sight of the beauty of Desdemona, 'do omit their mortal natures' and let her go safely by.

Othello's use of sea-images is noteworthy; they come to him naturally, for on each occasion it marks a moment of intense emotion. The first, at the height of his happiness when he rejoins Desdemona, is an exclamation which to us, who know what lies before them, is in its opening one of the most poignant and moving in the play:

> O my soul's joy!
> If after every tempest come such calms,
> May the winds blow till they have waken'd death!

The next is at the height of his torture when, having been shown the handkerchief, suspicion becomes certainty and he vows vengeance. To clinch this Iago urges patience, and suggests that perhaps his mind may change; to which Othello instantly reacts as his torturer intends and affirms the unalterable quality of his resolve by comparing it to the 'icy current and compulsive course' of the ebbless Pontic Sea.

And at the end, when he has carried out his resolve and has suffered and realized all, again it is in sea-language that he expresses his equally set determination to follow Desdemona :

> Here is my journey's end, here is my butt
> And very sea-mark of my utmost sail.

The intensity of feeling and emotion in *Lear*, and the sharpness of its focus is revealed by the fact that in Shakespeare's imagination there runs throughout only one overpowering and dominating continuous image. So compelling is this that even well-marked different and subsidiary images are pressed into its service and used to augment and emphasize it.

In the play we are conscious all through of the atmosphere of buffeting, strain and strife, and, at moments, of bodily tension to the point of agony. So naturally does this flow from the circumstances of the drama and the mental sufferings of Lear, that we scarcely realize how greatly this sensation in us is increased by the general 'floating' image, kept constantly before us, chiefly by means of the verbs used but also in metaphor, of a human body in anguished movement, tugged, wrenched, beaten, pierced, stung, scourged, dislocated, flayed, gashed, scalded, tortured, and finally broken on the rack.

One can scarcely open a page of the play without being struck by these images and verbs, for every kind of bodily movement, generally involving pain, is used to express mental and abstract as well as physical facts. To name only a few of them. Lear, in his agonized remorse, pictures himself as a man *wrenched* and tortured by an 'engine', beating at the gate (his head) that let his folly in. Goneril has power to *shake* his manhood; he complains that she has *struck* him with her tongue; the hot tears *break* from him; his heart, he says, *will break into a hundred thousand flaws.* Albany wonders how far Goneril's eyes may *pierce*, Gloucester's *flaw'd heart*' is cracked, and finally it '*burst* smilingly'. Kent longs *to tread* Oswald into mortar, and in his heated description of the steward's character he evokes images of rats *biting* cords, weathercocks *turning*, dogs *following*, and geese being *driven. 'Tis worse than murder*, cries Lear, this *violent outrage* of putting Kent in the stocks, and his emotion on witnessing it *swells* and *climbs*, while the fool adds the picture of a man being dragged along by *holding on* when a great wheel *runs downhill,* and *letting go* only in time to save his *neck being broken.*

So also in scenes not directly concerned with Lear, such as Gloucester's conversations with Edmund, we find the same characteristic.

When Edmund, having roused his father's anger against the unwitting Edgar, desires to restrain him from immediate action until he has furnished further proof of his wickedness, he words his argument thus : If you will suspend your indignation until you have 'better testimony of his intent, you should *run a certain course*; where, if you *violently proceed against* him, mistaking his purpose, it would *make a great gap* in your own honour and *shake in pieces the heart* of his obedience'. And a little later, Gloucester being indeed shaken to the heart by Edmund's revelations, in the course of ten lines uses these verbs and nouns, *scourged, cools, falls off, divide, cracked, falls from bias, follow disquietly, mutinies, discord, machinations, hollowness, ruinous disorders.*

This use of verbs and images of bodily and generally anguished motion is almost continuous, and it is reinforced by similar words used in direct description, as in the treatment of

Gloucester; he is *bound* to a chair, *plucked* by the beard, his hairs are *ravished* from his chin, he is *tied to a stake*, like a bear to *stand the course*, and with his eyes blinded and bleeding, he is *thrust out* of the gates to *smell his way* to Dover.

All through the play the simplest abstract things, such as Cornwall's well-known obstinacy, are described in similar terms; the duke's disposition, says Gloucester, will not be *rubb'd* nor *stopp'd* even in a scene, pleasant in itself, such as the gentleman's ornate but delightful description of Cordelia's reception of his news (IV. iii), this sense of bodily movement and strain is constant. The letters *pierced* her to a demonstration of grief, her passion

> most rebel-like
> Sought to be king o'er her;

it *moved* her, patience and sorrow *strove*, she *heavea* the name of 'father' *pantingly forth* as if it *press'd her heart*; she *shook* the tears from her eyes, and away she *started*

> To deal with grief alone.

Look at the six lines which follow, in which Kent, having declared that Lear will not *yield* to see his daughter, describes his master's mental and emotional suffering in a series of pictures of physical buffeting, pain, and opposition, which, in addition to the two images of brutal dogs and poisonous serpents, have a cumulative and almost overwhelming effect on the mind:

> A sovereign shame so *elbows him*: his own unkindness

stripped Cordelia from his benediction, *turn'd* her to foreign casualties,

> these things *sting*
> *His mind so venomously*, that *burning* shame
> *Detains him* from Cordelia.

The idea of unnatural horrors, of human beings *preying on themselves* 'like monsters of the deep', or like wolves and tigers tearing one another's flesh, is also constantly before us. Lear is sure that Regan, when she hears how he has been mistreated, with 'her nails' will *flay* Goneril's *wolfish visage*; filial ingratitude is as if *the mouth should tear the hand*

> For lifting food to't.

Gloucester boldly avows to Regan he has sent Lear to Dover because

> I would not see *thy cruel nails*
> *Pluck out* his *poor old eyes,* nor thy *fierce sister*
> *In his anointed flesh stick boorish fangs;*

and Albany, crying to Goneril that she and Regan are 'tigers', not daughters, declares if he followed his inclination he would *dislocate* and *rear her flesh and bones.*

The large number of animal images, and their effect in the play, has often been noticed (notably by Bradley, *Shakespearean Tragedy*, pp. 266 and following). I would only point out here that in addition to the feeling they give us that 'humanity' is 'reeling back into the beast', they also, because portrayed chiefly in angry or anguished action, very distinctly augment the sensation of horror and bodily pain. In addition to savage wolves, tigers, and other animals there are *darting* serpents, the *sharp-toothed* vulture and *detested* kite, *stinging* adders and insects, *gnawing* rats, the *baited* bear, as well as *whipped, whining, barking, mad*, and *biting* dogs. All this helps to create and increase an unparalleled atmosphere of rapine, cruelty, and bodily pain.

To this is added as an overtone running through the crisis of the tragedy, the fury of the elements, described, be it remarked, wholly in terms of the human body. They are *wild, fretful unquiet*; the wind and rain are *to and fro conflicting;* with these, the old king, with his *heart-struck injuries is contending, tearing* his white hair

> Which the *impetuous* blasts, with *eyeless rage*,
> *Catch* in their *fury*;

and bidding the winds to blow and *crack their cheeks*, until at the height of his half-demented passion he commands the *all-shaking* thunder to '*smite flat* the thick rotundity o' the world'. This last amazing image is one of several in Shakespeare, notably in *Antony and Cleopatra*, which evoke the spectacle of devastating bodily action on so stupendous a scale that the emotions which give rise to it are lifted to a similar terrific and vast intensity. So the picture which follows here of the great gods, through the bursts of thunder and groans of roaring wind and rain, remorselessly seeking and finding out their enemies, while 'close *pent-up* guilts' *rive* their concealing continents, and *cry*

These dreadful summoners grace,

seems natural and only in keeping with the feeling aroused in the imagination of a Being or a Force mighty enough to remould the shape of the globe with one resounding blow.

The sense of bodily torture continues to the end. Gloucester catches the recurrent theme of the tragedy and crystallizes it forever in the terrible picture of men being torn limb from limb by the gods in sport, to whom they are but 'as flies to wanton boys'. Lear tells Cordelia he is bound

Upon a wheel of fire, that mine own tears
Do scald like molten lead;

Edgar sees the gods making instruments of torture with which to plague men; and, at the close, when Kent, who loved him, breathes the only valediction possible over his dead master's body, it is still the same metaphor which rises to his lips,

O, let him pass! he hates him
That would upon the rack of this tough world
Stretch him out longer.

The difference in imagery in the three Roman plays is arresting and very indicative of the difference in mood and temper in which they were written. All three owe much to North's *Plutarch*, but the difference in the way the material is handled well repays close study.

Julius Caesar is straightforward, slow moving, restrained, almost bare in style; it has relatively few images (less than half those in *Coriolanus*, and less than one third those in *Antony*), and a characteristic of these is that they are clear, definite, and worked out in a full and leisurely way.

Antony's comparison of Lepidus to the ass turned out to graze is a good example of the peculiar amplification and slow movement of these similes:

And though we lay these honours on this man,
To ease ourselves of divers slanderous loads,
He shall but bear them as the ass bears gold,
To groan and sweat under the business,
Either led or driven, as we point the way;

> And having brought our treasure where we will,
> Then take we down his load and turn him off,
> Like to the empty ass, to shake his ears
> And graze in commons.

Others of like nature are the ladder of ambition (II. i. 21), the state and kingdom of man (II. i. 66), the bonfire (I. iii. 107), the likeness of 'hollow men' and prancing mettlesome horses (IV. ii. 22), the stricken deer (III. i. 204), the setting sun (V. iii. 60), the turn in the tide (IV. iii. 216), and the northern star (III. i. 60).

There is no leading or floating image in the play; one feels it was not written under the particular stress of emotion or excitement which gives rise to a dominating image.

There is, however, a certain persistence in the comparison of the characters to animals; Caesar is a wolf, a lion, a falcon, a serpent's egg, an adder, a stricken deer; the Romans are sheep and hinds and bees; the conspirators are apes and hounds, Brutus is a lamb, Lepidus is an ass, a horse; Metellus and Casca are curs, Cassius is a showy, mettlesome steed which fails at the moment of trial, and Octavius and Antony are bears tied to the stake.

But this animal-imagery is not nearly so marked as in either *Lear* or *Othello*, and entirely lacks consistency of character, so it fails to produce the cumulative effect so strongly felt in both those plays.

Coriolanus, however, has a central symbol and a very definite one, but it is significant that this has not been born out of the creator's feeling of the tragedy, but has just been taken over by him wholesale, with much else, from North's *Plutarch*.

It is the old tale, with which the play opens, expounded by Menenius, of the rebellion of the various members of the body — the citizens — against the belly — the senate — which they accuse of being idle while they do all the work, and the belly's answer, somewhat developed by Shakespeare, that, on the contrary, it is the 'storehouse and the shop of the whole body', sending out, through rivers of blood, sustenance to all.

The images arising out of this central theme from the body and sickness are many, nearly one-fifth of the whole; and by means of them this idea is played upon throughout, though in a somewhat languid and artificial way.

The king, statesman, soldier, horse, and trumpeter are compared to the head, eye and heart, arm, leg, and tongue, and Menenius laughingly taunts one of the basest of the citizens with being the great toe of the rebellion. The people are the hands, the tribunes are the 'tongue o' the common mouth', or they are the mouths themselves, as when Coriolanus, turning on them, asks

> You being their mouths, why rule you not their teeth?

This conception is constantly with Coriolanus, as when he speaks of the 'navel' of the state, or asks

> How shall this bosom multiplied digest
> The senate's courtesy?

and goes on to tell the tribunes they are risking giving a dangerous drug to a body 'that's sure of death without it', recommending them at once to pluck out

> The multitudinous tongue; let them not lick
> The sweet which is their poison.

His action towards Rome is described by his mother as 'tearing his country's bowels out', and a similar image of hurt to the vitals of a body is used by Aufidius, when, after welcoming Coriolanus, he pictures them

> pouring war
> Into the bowels of ungrateful Rome.

Coriolanus refers to the people as 'measles'

> Which we disdain should tetter us, yet sought
> The very way to catch them,

and their discontent is as self-made sores on the body, brought about by 'rubbing the poor itch' of their opinion and so making themselves scabs.

Coriolanus himself is represented by the tribunes as a 'violent' disease which spreads infection and must be cut away, whereas Menenius argues that he is a A limb 'that has but a disease'

> Mortal, to cut it off; to cure it, easy;

and to Brutus's remark that when Coriolanus loved his country it honoured him, he answers drily,

The service of the foot
Being once gangrened, is not then respected
For what before it was.

The condition of the time is a 'violent fit' that craves physic, a sore which needs a physician, for it cannot be cured by self-probing, and so on; it is wearisome to pursue it further for it is very obvious, and a rather laboured and overworked metaphor at best.

It obtrudes itself throughout the play; any one on a first reading will notice and remember it, whereas it might be possible to know *Lear* or *Macbeth* very well without consciously realizing the dominating symbolic 'motives' in these plays. That is because in them the symbols are the outcome of the imagination at white heat, and thus become one with the movement and characters and could be no other than they are.

So one feels, for example, that Coriolanus is called a diseased limb or a gangrened foot because it fits in with a preconceived design, but Kent, in his agonized grief, sees the death of Lear as the release of a tortured body from the rack, not because bodily struggle and torture has been the dominating symbol throughout, but because, after the experience of burning through

the fierce dispute
Betwixt damnation and impassioned clay,

there was no other way possible to see it.

In *Antony and Cleopatra* we find ourselves emotionally in a different world, in an entirely different atmosphere from the other two Roman plays.

The difference in poetic fire between *Coriolanus* and *Antony* is as if, in the one case, the poet's imagination had caught alight three or four times only, and in burning had scattered sparks in the neighbourhood, while, in the other, it is a pure flame driving throughout, fanned by emotion, whose heat purifies, fuses, and transmutes into gold all kinds of material, and it is this fierce atmospheric heat which creates the pictures, dominating and directing them.

The group of images in *Antony* which, on analysis, immediately attracts attention as peculiar to this play, are images of the world, the firmament, the ocean, and vastness generally.

That is the dominating note in the play, magnificence and grandeur, expressed in many ways and pictured by continually stimulating our imaginations to see the colossal figure of Antony, 'demi-Atlas of this earth', 'triple pillar of the world', built on so vast a scale that the whole habitable globe is but a toy to him, as it were a ball or apple which he quarters with his sword, playing with 'half the bulk of it' as he pleases, 'making and marring fortunes'.

Antony himself touches this note at once in his royal love-making, when he tells Cleopatra that if she would put a bourne to the measure of his love, she must 'needs find out new heaven, new earth'.

Indeed, nothing short of the whole universe suffices for comparison with Antony, and in Cleopatra's lyrical elegies, wherein is concentrated all the passion and poetry of the most passionate and poetical of the plays, she likens him to one whose face was as the heavens,

> and therein stuck
> A sun and moon, which kept their course and lighted
> The little O, the earth.

In these soaring love-laments she sees him and makes us see him as a stupendous super-being, the 'crown o' the earth', whose 'legs bestrid the ocean', whose 'rear'd arm crested the world', and whose qualities can be compared only to the vast elemental forces of nature; his voice, to friends,

> was propertied
> As all the tuned spheres, . . .
> But when he meant to quail and shake the orb
> He was as rattling thunder.

Even the verbs used of his aspect are such as are applicable to the sun and planets; when he smiles, he would *shine* on those

> That make their looks by his,

and Alexas, lately come from him, is *gilded* with his *tinct*.

The perennial seasons themselves, with their wealth of association, become as mere adjectives to express the magnificence and scale of his bounty,

There was no winter in't; an autumn 'twas
That grew the more by reaping.

When, mortally wounded, he is borne aloft to her, Cleopatra calls on the sun to burn up the sphere in which it is fixed and so plunge the earth in darkness, and, when he dies, she knows there is

nothing left remarkable
Beneath the visiting moon.

Not only Cleopatra thinks of him thus; by a natural instinct all who know him compare him to great natural phenomena : he is a 'mine of bounty', says Enobarbus; in temper, reports Alexas,

Like to the time o' the year between the extremes
Of hot and cold, he was nor sad nor merry;

his faults in him, cries Lepidus,

seem as the spots of heaven,
More fiery by night's blackness;

and his messenger, Euphronius, is so conscious of his inferiority to his master, that he avows he was

of late as petty to his ends
As is the morn-dew on the myrtle-leaf
To his grand sea.

When the battle goes against him, Scarus remarks 'the greater cantle of the world is lost',

we have kissed away
Kingdoms and provinces;

and when he dies, so great a convulsion of nature is it that Caesar declares

the round world
Should have shook lions into civil streets,
And citizens to their dens. The death of Antony
Is not a single doom; in the name lay
A moiety of the world.

This vastness of scale is kept constantly before us by the use of the word 'world',[2] which occurs forty-two times, nearly double or more than double as often as in most other plays, and

2. In *Julius Caesar* 'world' occurs 17 times; in *Lear*, 18; in *Coriolanus*, 19; in *Othello*, 23; in *Hamlet*, 29.

it is continually employed in a way which increases the sense of grandeur, power, and space, which fills the imagination with the conception of beings so great that physical size is annihilated and the whole habitable globe shrinks in comparison with them. Caesar, lamenting his differences with Antony, cries,

> if I knew
> What hoop should hold us staunch, from edge to edge
> O' the world I would pursue it;

and Octavia declares that wars between these two mighty ones, her husband and her brother, would be

> As if the world should cleave, and that slain men
> Should solder up the rift.

The emotional effect of such a simile as this is incalculable, with its amazing picture of the gigantic gaping fissures in the round globe packed tight with the bodies of the dead. Were the feeling in it not so intense it would verge on the grotesque, as do some others among these vast world-images. Such, for instance, is the kind of huge gargoyle depicted by the saturnine Enobarbus when he hears that Caesar has deposed Lepidus, thus leaving only Antony and himself in power. He imagines them as the two mighty jaws in the world's face, grinding and destroying everything that comes between them, and exclaims,

> Then, world, thou hast a pair of chaps, no more;
> And throw between them all the food thou hast,
> They'll grind the one the other.

Antony's imagination moves on this same vast plane, and the pictures that he draws stimulate our vision and keep us ever conscious of the puny size of even the greatest of worldly princes, powers, and spaces compared to his stupendous force. Especially is this so when power is slipping from him, when the old lion is dying, and the tragedy is thus increased by contrast. With what a sublime sweep of simple words he sums up his earlier activities,

> . . . I, that with my sword
> Quarter'd the world, and o'er green Neptune's back
> With ships made cities;

and how vivid is the picture of the kings of the earth starting forth at his call, like small boys in a scramble, crying out to know what is his will. When he is angry, the insolent magnificence of his images surpasses all others in Shakespeare. Thus, after his defeat at sea, when, furious with Caesar's messenger, he has him soundly whipped and bids him get back to his master, he gives a characteristic picture in style and scale of the reason why it is particularly easy just then to anger him, for his 'good stars' that were his 'former guides'

> Have empty left their orbs and shot their fires
> Into the abysm of hell;

and when earlier, Cleopatra mischievously suggests that Caesar has sent for him, the thunder of his reply in majestic sweep and cadence still comes echoing down the centuries:

> Let Rome in Tiber melt, and the wide arch
> Of the ranged empire fall! Here is my space.

It has only been possible to sketch the merest outline of this particular point in the imagery of the tragedies, but this is perhaps sufficient to show how definite and how potent are these images within images.

No other writer, so far as I know, certainly no other dramatist, makes such continual use of the running and recurrent symbol as does Shakespeare.

Shelley, in his *Prometheus Unbound*, perhaps comes nearest to it when he brings out and emphasizes by means of his nature-imagery, certain philosophical and ethical thoughts; but the *Prometheus*, though nominally a drama, is really a lyrical poem in a single mood, which lends itself far more readily to such continuity of symbolism than do Shakespeare's varied and tremendous dramas.

This method of working by way of suggestion, springing from a succession of vivid pictures and concrete details, is, of course, of the very essence of 'romantic' art; and, in the case of Shakespeare, the poet's mind, unlike the dyer's hand, subdues to itself what it works in, and colours with its dominating emotion all the varied material which comes his way, colours it so subtly and so delicately that for the most part we are unconscious of what is happening, and know only the total result of the effect on our imaginative sensibility.

Hence, it seems to me that a study of his imagery from the angle from which we have just been looking at it helps us to realize a little more fully and accurately one of the many ways by which he so magically stirs our emotions and excites our imagination, and I believe it not only does this, but that it sometimes even throws a fresh ray of light on the significance of the play concerned, and — most important of all — on the way Shakespeare himself saw it.

3

From 'Art and Artifice in Shakespeare'[1]

E.E. Stoll

1. Comedy

Ever since the early days of Romanticism, critics have found a warrant for Shakespeare, as against the claims of classicism, legitimate or illegitimate, in the final words of the *Symposium*: 'The chief thing which he [Aristodemus] remembered was Socrates insisting to the other two [Aristophanes and Agathon] that the genius of comedy was the same as that of tragedy, and that the writer of tragedy ought to be a writer of comedy also'. But of this truth Shakespeare and the other great Elizabethans are not the only examples, whether within the single play or separately. Tirso, Lope, and Calderón have each left us both tragedies and comedies and also tragedies containing comic elements; and not only Corneille and Racine, but even (as in some few cases we happen to know) the Greek tragic poets wooed now and then the comic muse. And how much the two genres (like their counterparts in reality) have in common appears, on the one hand, from the fact that by masters like Shakespeare and Beaumont and the great Spaniards they are often made to blend felicitously; and, on the other, from the fact that by the serious-minded Romantic critics and actors the manifestly comic intentions of the author, whether Shakespeare or Molière, have, through mere shifting of the emphasis, been thwarted. *Behind* comedy there is always tragedy (indeed, since

1. *Art and Artifice in Shakespeare: a study in dramatic illusion and contrast* (1934).

the days of Romantic irony, behind tragedy there is comedy); and sometimes by the author himself its shadow is permitted to fall upon the scene. I have elsewhere spoken of the violence done to Molière and the comic Shakespeare by putting in the foreground what with them is in the background — and that thing, quite literally, the actors have done on the stage with Malvolio, when teased in the dark room.[2] Congreve, too, has been misinterpreted, his Lady Wishfort being made half tragic or pathetic in her affectation : the old or ugly we no longer have the heart to see mocked or flouted. Yet there are moments in his comedies when Mellefont and Cynthia, Valentine and Angelica sink back out of the merry mood, not into tragedy to be sure, but into seriousness or wistfulness, and the laughter dwindles into a sigh. 'Never let us know one another better', murmurs Angelica, 'for the pleasure of a masquerade is done when we come to show our faces'. And within the limits of comedy and tragedy both there is, of course, a still wider range of emotion and variety of tone in Shakespeare.

Nowadays, save by the mood and tone prevailing and the happy or unhappy ending, the two genres are scarcely to be distinguished. In 'drama' they are meant to coalesce. But in the Renaissance, as in ancient times, tragedy was more tragical, comedy more comical; and there was a difference also in the rank of the characters and the elevation of the style — distinctions which were, for the most part, observed by Shakespeare, though with greater latitude and (necessarily) greater skill. Yet with him, as at the Renaissance and in ancient times again, the central situation and the development of it were, in both genres, essentially the same. In both there was a duplicity, or doubleness, of effect. As with the ancients, it was the result of human intrigue or supernatural disposition; and while at the Renaissance the plotter or mischief-maker of classical comedy often appeared in tragedy also, no fundamental change took place in the structure of either. The villain was simply a more enterprising and aggressive Fate. He deceived and inveigled,

2. By E.H. Sothern; cf. G.P. Baker, *Shakespeare as a Dramatist* (1907), p. 242. The Steward is meant to be heard, not seen. For the critical misinterpretation see *Shakespeare Studies*, chapters on Shylock and Falstaff, especially pp. 305-6, 308-9.

instead of foreordaining and foretelling; and he actually trod the stage. As with the ancients, in comedy as in tragedy, there was, for a complication, the same sort of misunderstanding that we have been considering; whether it arose from deception, slander, or playing a part, or from misapprehension, mistaken identity, or disguise. And then the effect was comic irony, instead of the tragic. The comedies of Plautus and Terence, of Shakespeare and Molière, are alike examples. Of disguise or mistaken identity, in the open or in the darkness of a rendezvous, and of hoaxes or practical jokes there are instances in almost every comedy that Shakespeare penned. Of calumny credited there are, as we have already noticed, instances in *Much Ado, Cymbeline*, and *The Winter's Tale*; though these have, for the most part, effects not comic at all. The difference from those in tragedy lies only in the fact that they are not made so serious and are not so prolonged, the slander being but an episode. So far, however, the device serves the same constructive purpose. As in tragedy itself, this, like the others, produces compression and contrast.

Of such a structure as in *Othello*, however, Shakespeare has left us no comic parallel or counterpart. For that we must turn to Chapman, Marston, and Jonson, above all to *Volpone* and *The Alchemist*, with their equivalent to the ancient intriguing slave. In Shakespeare's comedies, as we have observed, positive and deliberate deception is often treated seriously; and although merrily enough in such as *Love's Labour's Lost, Midsummer Night's Dream*, and *The Merry Wives*, it involves no continuous intrigue by a single person. The situation is not central. Of disguise and feigning, misunderstanding and mistaken identity, there is more; but, except in the borrowed and adapted *Comedy of Errors*, it too is rather episodic. And his comedies being medleys, both light and serious in tone, there is for these devices not so much need, or opportunity either, to provide a special effect of illusion.

They are more definitely external and recognizably traditional than verbal deception; and besides, there was in comedy then, and there is still, less of realistic rigour. Fantasy, exaggeration, and even distortion, are part of the comic programme. In so far as Shakespeare does endeavour to make these expedients plausible, it is mainly by shifting the scene, as from Athens by day to the Forest by night in the *Midsummer Night's Dream*; or from England to Padua in *The Taming of the Shrew*; or to the Forest of Arden in *As You Like It*. There the thing might happen, we are readier to believe. Yet here is something of the same care as in the tragedies to keep the convention intact. Rosalind's disguise is impenetrable, not only to Orlando but to her father. And there is no reproach of stupidity attaching to these persons or to anyone else who fails to recognize the other disguised ladies in Romantic comedy, or the Duke in *Measure for Measure*, or Falstaff in *The Merry Wives*. Nor is there (as a result of the trick played upon them) to Benedick and Beatrice; for from the outset we are made to see, despite their banter and wrangling, and indeed because of it, that they decidedly take to one another. In the case of verbal deception, on the other hand, for a purpose purely comic, as that practised by the Prince and Poins and by the Merry Wives upon Falstaff, or by Sir Toby and Maria upon Malvolio, such precautions to preserve the victim's reputation as we have taken notice of in *Othello* would, by the very nature of the purpose, be much out of keeping. As in Plautus and Terence, Chapman and Jonson, this is a practical joke, a comic reprisal, or an exposure of folly; and openly the victim is made a butt or gull.

2. Tragedy and Comedy Together

I

Comedy and tragedy, then, both were and are alike, as counterparts; and they must now at the close be viewed together, particularly in the light of to-day. In either genre this unpsychological method — by misrepresentation or misunderstanding — is, when rightly handled and simply accepted, richer than the psychological in effect. In tragedy it is more tragic, in comedy more comic. And that is evident when at this point we compare the ancients, tragic and comic, or else Shakespeare and Molière, with those contemporary dramatists who derive the action more strictly from the character.

These are superficially more plausible but, other things being equal, fundamentally less potent, whether read or played.

They move us less, by character or situation, by what is said or done. Their verisimilitude is greater, but their contrasts are weaker. The opposition lies less in what is human and emotional and more in what is intellectual — not so much at the centre of the play and more at the circumference. Mere character does not suffice for it. It must be eked out by ideas and problems. And there is a tragi-comic irony, not within the *Master Builder* or *Rosmersholm*, but encircling and engulfing it; and another irony, comic or fairly poignant, round about *Candida* or the *Well of the Saints*. Either appears less at the play than after it; and often as much in the stage directions as in the dialogue and action. The text, really, must be both played and read.

And what is missing in modern tragedy and comedy alike is for the most part (naturally enough) what in Shakespeare is now misapprehended. The bolder strokes are wanting, the free spirit is not precipitated, and a new and autonomous (though mimic) world is not conjured into being, as it is by Shakespeare, Jonson, and Congreve, Aristophanes and Molière. Often in the mere difference of this from the actual world resides much of the comic effect, as not of the tragic. For this is needed the illusion of reality; for that, satire or burlesque, exaggeration or transformation: but for neither, anything of a transcript. Concerning the Restoration Comedy of Manners, Charles Lamb was undoubtedly right. It is not 'a veracious picture of actual English manners and morals', but 'a world of itself almost as much as fairy-land'. A wand is waved and what is gross, licentious, and heartless is transmuted by wit and mirth; or what is dark and seamy slinks into the background, and only what is bright and gay steps before us. The only defect in Lamb's criticism is his failure constantly to remember what lurks behind. 'It is altogether a speculative scene of things, which has no reference whatever to the world that is'. If that were so, this new world would not be funny — if by this merry but significant 'transposition and transformation' (as Proust calls it) we were not remotely reminded of the original, our own or others' practical and conjugal relations, in the world that is; though these, of course, must not be thrust upon us, any more than Emilia's native perspicacity in *Othello*, or they would break the charm. Sometimes, indeed, Lamb does remember, as when in the preceding essay, *On Some of the Old Actors*, he speaks of the 'playful selections and specious combinations rather than strict metaphrases of nature'. A *strict* metaphrase — a transcript — is, he implies, not art.

For the preservation of the comic illusion, as of the tragic, certain distinctions or manipulations have commonly been employed. As presented in their earlier intensity, and even as nowadays, the two illusions are mutually exclusive — only in the hands of the greatest masters does one with impunity encroach upon the other, and then it is in due subordination. In regular comedy, that is, the ancient and that of Jonson, Congreve, and Molière, noble passion or emotion is suppressed; even in the Romantic it is subdued; and for the purely comic effect in either, sympathy is unfavourable. In tragedy there are passion and emotion in abundance, to arouse both pity and fear. Indeed, the situation is deliberately manipulated to awaken sympathy otherwise not forthcoming; as in the case of Macbeth influenced by his lady and the Weird Sisters, and slaying the King behind the scenes, not on the boards. In comedy, on the other hand, the situation is manipulated so as to isolate the duped or cheated, the beaten or betrayed, only their follies being kept before us, the causes and extenuating circumstances ignored. Sir Toby, Maria, and the Clown tease the Steward and crack jokes at his expense under our eyes; Malvolio himself begs and wails in the dark, off-stage. Shylock is suffered to plead his injuries as a justification only in bloodthirsty triumph, craving a revenge which 'betters the instruction', but to the cost of his own avarice and compassed about by hatred, on the one hand, and by derision on the other. How they came to be what they are, what the world had done to them, is no more to be considered in the case of the Jew and the Steward in comedy than in that of the villains in tragedy. And so it is with awkward suitors and jealous husbands, stingy fathers and unsophisticated provincials, in Plautus and Terence, Congreve and Molière. Though not sympathetically or approvingly, we are ranged on the side of them that rob or cheat, like Tranio and Scapin; or boast, lie, and run away, like Falstaff, who, though he is guilty of all these misdemeanours, is funny. He is *not* so funny when, with some Romantic critics, we consider his hopeful youth and disappointed age, or take his misdoings for make-believe. Sometimes in Shakespeare, however, just as comedy encroaches upon tragedy, tragedy encroaches upon comedy, the isolation is incomplete and sympathy creeps in; and consequently the comic effect is not so consistent and emphatic as in Jonson, Molière, and Plautus. Shylock, as we have seen above, is a case. Falstaff, guilty of more venial offences, both the object and the inexhaustible fountain of mirth, enjoys plenary indulgence; and comedy and sympathy nearly merge.

Such is the mimic comic world — such are its order and economy — but what of the entrance to it? That, as to the tragic has by bold strokes and a precipitation been often best, and certainly most expeditiously, effected. It has been by the avenue of these various devices of misunderstanding and deception, or of some particular assumption, all of which nowadays are (as threadbare or improbable, or both together) commonly considered taboo. In principle (though less in practice, as will appear) we grimly insist on what is both probable and original: such devices or assumptions, in Shakespeare and still more in the other Elizabethans, who lack his authority, we, when we stop to consider, refuse to accept or fail to understand. There is the swindling in *Volpone*. 'Cupidity goes with parsimony', cries William Archer as he turns away; 'and who ever heard of avarice staking large sums on a problematical post-obit'? Yet even as mere matter of fact, whereon Mr. Archer is here insisting, this logic of his is not that of common human nature. Often the most avaricious, though with a pang — and there, in reality itself, is a contrast and conflict of which Jonson fully avails himself — take to the highest play. Scotchmen I have known who, shortly after the close of the War, put as much as half their patrimony into paper German marks. And are not the French, the Italians, the Spanish, the very Hebrews with whom parsimony is both the racial vice and the racial virtue, the most insatiate and inveterate gamblers? That fact of itself is enough to warrant, in a satirical comedy whereof the scene is laid in a far-away and fantastic Venice, the assumption that cupidity may override parsimony, when the assumption is skillfully presented at the beginning. There, as in *King Lear* and the *Oedipus* and according to the precept of Aristotle, is the place for the improbability — as a postulate, a basic premise. Mr. Archer, so hard on Jonson, will not lay a finger on Shakespeare; but in *his* Venetian comedy, romantic instead of satiric, there are postulates still more improbable — that one friend should permit another to give his enemy his bond, valid in law, with a forfeiture of a pound of flesh of the creditor's own choosing; and that a young woman should by the will of a sensible parent be left at the mercy of the wooer cleverest at conundrums. These last assumptions, to be sure, lead to what is serious rather than comic or tragic; and it is the deception — the disguises, and the turning of the tables on Shylock — that more directly conduces to the comic. But all alike offer in comedy that advantage which we have noted in tragedy, an opportunity and warrant for the character to do and say what, quite of himself or psychologically, he would not do or say. The avaricious dupes in *Volpone* enrich the swindler and impoverish themselves, gloating over the bright prospects for a timely inheritance from him and so from the others; much as the miserly Harpagon is it made to keep horses and servants, woo a beautiful young woman, and even give a banquet — that he may stint man, woman, and beast as he does it. And what they say is more finely incongruous still. Shylock complacently pities Launcelot as he lets him quit his service, both to spare his own and to help waste Bassanio's borrowed purse, not knowing that the lad is at this moment helping to cheat him out of both ducats and daughter — 'The patch', he mutters, 'is kind enough'; and so Sganarelle pities Valère as, after giving him the ambiguous message from Isabelle, he watches him go off apparently heartbroken but really elated —

> Ce pauvre malheureux trop rempli d'arnitié.

(The first-named comic effect has, in our sentimental times, been stifled or muffled.) And it is only from out of such premises of deception that proceed such dramatic conclusions as when Corvino in *Volpone* (who, to outdo the doctor reported to be competing with his daughter, offers up his own wife, of whom he has been savagely jealous) calls him, in a paroxysm of avarice, *Wretch, Covetous wretch*", or as when Ford, in *The Merry Wives*, impatient of uncertainty after the fatuous Falstaff's confidences and the trustful Page's assurances and misled by what he has learned of the Merry Wives' intrigues, cries out, choosing to be right though at a cuckold's cost, 'I will prevent this, detect my wife, be reveng'd on Falstaff, and *laugh at Page*'. By a more reasonable and more nearly normal process of development, such a clash of contrast and consequent explosion of merriment could scarcely, and certainly less speedily, be attained.

II

Therefore, strange to say, the best comic and tragic writers are now falling back upon what is a modern and contemporary equivalent of misunderstanding or deception, disguise or feigning, and the accompanying aside or soliloquy; that is, appearances as the natural cloak over reality (or all the reality there is), and consciousness itself as a veil. The one is in Pirandello, the other in O'Neill and the Vanguard. There is a prolonged contrast between speech and thought, or between thought conscious and half-conscious, as in the *Strange Interlude* and *The Adding-Machine*; there are actual masks, as in *The Great God Brown*, and virtual ones, as in *Mourning Becomes Electra*; and continually there are furtive, covert motives — mothers hating daughters or jealous of sons, and fathers hating sons and jealous of daughters — in opposition to the honest, acknowledged ones. Or else, renouncing originality and recurring to Ancient and Renaissance example, the dramatists take to the old stories again, those of Greek tragedy or the fabliaux, as do O'Neill and Synge. (The Shakespeare critics are a little behind the times!) Even before this, something of the duplicity of effect in *Othello*, *Hamlet*, and *Macbeth* was secured by a modern destiny, as heredity or family tradition, in plays such as *Rosmersholm* and *Ghosts*; and by a modern disguise, as the outer man masking the inner — what he or the world thinks he is overlying what he is at heart — in plays such as *The Doll's House* and *Candida*. At bottom the methods, tragic or comic, ancient or modern, are the same. Fate and the *fallax servus*, Iago and Iachimo, Viola in a doublet and Hamlet playing mad, and the numerous varieties of fatality and double personality, unconscious deception and self-deception, in current use among us, all perform, with different degrees of verisimilitude and plausibility, of philosophic significance and emotional potency, one unchanging function.

And what is that? It is to make a situation rather than develop one, to frame a plot and precipitate an action, rather than to hold the mirror up to nature. It is to imitate life, not truly and faithfully but, as with all art, in such a fashion — within the limits of medium and tradition, of the *mores* and the imagination — as to force us to think and feel. And this is the function of poetry itself — 'to heighten consciousness', as Miss Sitwell says. For that effect in drama there must be irony and conflict and, therefore, contrast or parallel — and for any of these, in turn, there must be accumulation and compression. And for that effect at its simplest, in mere poetry, there must be metaphor.[3] The language of poetry, and particularly the greatest, is, unlike that of prose, charged as with electricity, 'changeable' as silk. Of itself, life (or the plain statement) will not do. Even if it were different and itself afforded such good situations as those of ancient myth or poetic invention, still it would not do. In great drama they would therefore have to be better, that is (again) improbable — though not *within* the drama, of course, even as such situations are not now. In tragedy and comedy both, life must be, as it has ever been, piled on life, or we have visited the theatre in vain.

And if not in vain, what then? To make us think and feel, to heighten and widen our consciousness, and nothing more? The Greeks, at their great period, the classical French at theirs, strove in tragedy for a purgation, in comedy for a castigation, and in both for some measure of justice (not perfect or 'poetic', but tragic or comic) in the lot meted out to men. Shakespeare and the moderns, whatever their efforts in either direction, fall much farther short of these. They have no religious philosophy like that of the ancients; and in tragedy they do not attain as the ancients did to any reassuring adjustment of human suffering to the will of Heaven. For faith is now broken; life is more intricate and mysterious : the notions not only of the benevolence of Heaven or Nature, but of the responsibility of man, are undermined.

3. See Max Eastman, *The Literary Mind* (1931), p. 84, &c. For the surcharged quality of poetic language, carrying a meaning with many facets, but all within the compass of the poet's mind, not imparted by the modern reader's, see W. Empson, *Seven Types of Ambiguity* (1930), save where he is, now and then, led by his ingenuity astray.

[4]How far this was with Shakespeare the case we cannot know, so little do his characters venture upon speculation, so seldom does he appear himself. Certainly he offers no solution to the problem. Though as a man a Christian and a Protestant, as a dramatist he has no theology or theodicy, no philosophy or 'message'. By some characters the gods are declared to be just; by others, to be unjust; and the only consolation in the presence of the bitter mystery is in patience, acceptance. Instead of the austere but poignant serenity of Sophoclean tragedy at the end, there is, on the one hand, the spirit of quiet sorrow, on the other, a practical concern for the punishment of the offenders and the restoration of the State; and the passionate symphony closes quietly, on a rest-tone. A note of reconciliation has, by Professors Dowden and Bradley, been discerned in the superiority of the character of his heroes and heroines to the fate which befalls them — in some distant reverberate intimation that what happens to Cordelia does not matter, all that matters is what she is — and the more senseless and monstrous her fate, the less does it concern her. But that idea is really a transcendental inference of the critics' own, not anything which finds a basis in the text.[5] There the beauty of the hero's and heroine's natures makes their tragic fate only the more lamentable, not irrelevant. Why should a dog, a horse, a rat have life, and *thou* no breath at all? Or, again, a note of reconciliation has been found in Shakespeare's sense of the dreaminess and unreality of life. But the most notable expression of this is on the lips of the bloodstained and unrepentant Macbeth and the blameless Prospero, in which cases, though for different reasons, it does no tragic service. Still less does Shakespeare put before us the terrestrial, social problems of an Ibsen or an Hervieu, which, however little in the solution they may purge our emotions, impart to the tragic spectacle a little meaning, though not much. And all that I can discover to alleviate our dismay when for the last time the curtain falls, is, apart from the life-giving spirit of poetry moving and hovering over the stage, the breadth and fairness, the exaltation and pity, in the presentation. (These are no matters of inference but of

4. In this paragraph I am somewhat indebted to Professor Frye, though at many points I differ with him.
5. See my *Shakespeare Studies,* pp. 182-3 for the Hegelianism.

direct imaginative or emotional effect.) There is no cynicism, no pessimism — the vision is too clear and broad. Good and evil are not, as to-day, confused or merged, but are, as Croce says, 'as light opposed to darkness'.[6] Evil is not negative or incidental; but while under suffering it may grow worse as in Macbeth, good, on the other hand, may grow better as in Lear. And by evil good is not in the long run triumphed over or overshadowed. If, on one side there are Goneril, Regan, and Cornwall, Edmund and Oswald, on the other there are Lear, Cordelia, and the Fool, Kent, Gloucester, Edgar, Albany, and the true-hearted retainers and servants. If many people do ill by those who have done well by them, many others do well by those who have done ill by them. The earth trembles; but the verities are unshaken, the moral values and even the social sanctions are unbroken. Justice is administered, not only in the end to the villains, but (though in a disproportionate measure) to the hero and heroine. That is, the causal connexion is observed and recognized; and in this tragedy too, once the situation is attained, character becomes its own destiny. The postulate once posited and granted in the case of Othello and Macbeth, Hamlet and Lear, what befalls them is for the most part brought upon them, in the natural course of events, by themselves. And though our sympathies are elicited for them by artifice and manipulation; and even in a measure for the villains also, as Richard and Macbeth Iago and Edmund, by endowing them with 'energy of intellect, dauntless versatility of daring, invincible fertility of resource', and appareling them (though with a difference) like the heroes themselves in poetry, or bejeweling them with wit and humour : yet by all these claims upon our admiration our judgements are not weakened, nor are the issues confused. In fine, the poetically and dramatically transmuted and transformed material of life still retains life's proportions and values; and Shakespeare's tragedy wears the steadying, though not comforting, aspect of truth. We are made (and all along, as well as at the close) to feel deeply and rightly, and to think sanely, if not to any definite ultimate purpose or upshot; and as by no other tragedy our consciousness is heightened, our imagination widened. There is,

6. *Ariosto*, *Shakespeare*, and *Corneille*, p. 143 f.

however, no piercing of the veil. Of Shakespeare the words of Hazlitt are truer than of Wordsworth : 'He sees nothing loftier than human hopes; nothing deeper than the human heart'. Philosophy, transcendentalism does not here apply. But when Professor Bradley reads with the same spirit as the author writ, he speaks admirably and to the purpose.

'Its final and total result', he says of *King Lear*, 'is one in which pity and terror, carried perhaps to the extreme limits of art, are so blended with a sense of law and beauty that we feel at last, not depression and much less despair, but a consciousness of greatness in pain, and of solemnity in the mystery we cannot fathom'.

Or perhaps Croce describes the result, though more dryly, more adequately:

'He knows no other than the vigorous, passionate life upon earth, divided between joy and sorrow, with, around and above it, the shadow of a mystery'.

4
Principles of Emendation in Shakespeare[1]

W.W. Greg

The Professor of Latin in the University of Cambridge[2] has said what is perhaps the last word on the subject of emendation, in a passage that runs as follows: 'A textual critic engaged upon his business is not at all like Newton investigating the motions of the planets: he is much more like a dog hunting for fleas. If a dog hunted for fleas on mathematical principles, basing his researches on statistics of area and population, he would never catch a flea except by accident'. I do not believe that this is a fair account of textual criticism in general, but so far as emendation is concerned it comes extraordinarily near the truth. The fact is that there is only one general principle of emendation, which is that emendation is in its essence devoid of principle. At its finest it is an inspiration, a stirring of the spirit, which obeys no laws and cannot be produced to order. In other words, emendation is an art. Yet even as such there should be some conditions which by its very nature it must obey, for it is surely no idle dream of scholars to be 'learned in searching principles of art'. And if we can do nothing to help great critics in making brilliant emendations, we may at least hope to discover some rules that should prevent little critics from making foolish ones.

As a starting-point for our search let us consider one or two famous emendations, not necessarily in Shakespeare, that have won general acceptance. There is one that may be called

1. Shakespeare Lecture of the British Academy (1928).
2. A.E. Housman.

Theobald's emendation *par excellence*, though it was not entirely his own. Mistress Quickly (that was) describes Falstaff's death:

> after I saw him fumble with the Sheets, and play with Flowers, and smile vpon his fingers end, I knew there was but one way: for his Nose was as sharpe as a Pen, and a Table of greene fields.

So the folio, which is our only relevant authority. To-day all editions of Shakespeare read: 'for his nose was as sharp as a pen, and a' babbled of green fields'. When we remember that 'babbled' would very likely be written 'babld', and that in the hands of the time 'b' and 't', and final 'd' and 'e' are often difficult to distinguish, there need be no hesitation in accepting what many readers feel to be a particularly Shakespearian turn of phrase.

My next instance is linked no less closely with the name of that great and modest scholar Arthur Bullen. Marlowe's Faustus in his study tosses the unprofitable Aristotle aside with the words:

> Bid *Oncaymœon* farewell, *Galen* come:

according to the earliest edition. The second substitutes '*Oeconomy*' That this is wrong is clear from the metre (which was first doctored in the fourth edition) but it was the guess of someone with enough learning to know that one of Aristotle's works was the *Oeconomica*, hardly, one would suppose, a compositor. Bullen, pondering the passage, perceived that there was really no error at all, but only a rather misleading spelling of the Aristotelian phrase *ὂν kaì* μὴ *ὄν*,'being and not being'.

Lest the glamour of great names and famous lines should sway your judgement to an over-ready acceptance of what I would make the basis of my argument, I will add by way of challenge an emendation of my own. It is one of which I am rather proud, for it is in Latin, and my classical attainments are thoroughly Shakespearian. In an appallingly bad text of a very inferior play of Greene's there are some lines which have been printed by editors, after minor emendation, thus:

> O vos qui colitis lacusque locosque profundos,
> Infernasque domus et nigra palatia Ditis!

On which one editor remarked that no emendation could relieve the verses of the false quantity in 'lacus' — which shows that Classical Greats is not always a sufficient training for textual criticism. For it is evident that in this passage 'locos profundos' has no meaning: what we want is 'lucos' for the sense, and for the metre the inversion 'lucosque lacusque'. The line is based on a phrase of Cicero, 'lacus lucosque colitis'. The change from 'lucos' to 'locos' is a mere printer's error, but the inversion must be laid to the charge of the author, for it is due to too close a following of the prose original.

I think that a careful consideration of these three examples will teach us something in respect to the principles — or shall I say the limiting conditions? — of emendation, and I propose to use them as illustrations in seeking answers to certain questions. In the first place: What makes an emendation acceptable? I do not, of course, mean the appeal to sentiment or commonplace that pleases by removing a phrase jarring to the feelings or calling for mental effort at comprehension. One critic would have Hamlet 'hot' instead of 'fat', another 'faint', another 'fey'; and when Collier forged in the Perkins folio the emendation 'blankness', for the line, Nor heaven peep through the blanket of the dark, an eminent actor, so I have heard, declared that he had happily removed what had always been a stumbling-block in *Macbeth*. Such things are mere folly. By an acceptable emendation I mean, of course, one that strikes a trained intelligence as supplying exactly the sense required by the context, and which at the same time reveals to the critic the manner in which the corruption arose. Most readers of *Henry V* feel instinctively the justness of Theobald's emendation, and few would question the appropriateness of Bullen's; the third is supported by the detection of the source. That this source at once explains the harder part of the corruption is my excuse for thrusting the trifle on your consideration; *ὂν καὶ* μὴ *ὂν* is rather a brilliant interpretation than a strict emendation; the change from 'babld' to 'table' is perhaps more obvious to us than it was to Theobald.

The criterion of acceptance is high, and it is necessary that criticism should insist rigorously upon the conditions, for unless they are fulfilled there can be no certainty about the emendation, and there may be half a dozen, or half a hundred, with claims upon our attention. But of course comparatively few emendations really satisfy the test. This is a point I wish to stress, because I do not think that criticism has always faced the implications of its own methods. It is apt to forget two facts which it would nevertheless not dispute. One is that even the most careful authors do sometimes write sentences which it is impossible to regard as affording a perfectly satisfactory sense: the other is that corruption must sometimes occur through agencies that by their nature it is impossible to trace. Even Milton has 'Hermione' where he should have had 'Harmonia', but no one now follows Bentley in therefore dismissing the passage as spurious. And if we were to cast out of Shakespeare's text all phrases which we should hesitate to admit into it as emendations, I think that we should leave some considerable gaps in the canon. On the other hand, who shall say what chance words overheard in the printing-house may have found their way into a compositor's brain and so out at his fingers? In all likelihood there are on record more — perhaps many more — actually correct emendations that fail to pass the test, than there are that emerge successful : they are correct but we can never know that they are. This comes out clearly, I think, in a textual study of Massinger. We are so fortunate as to possess several hundred corrections made with his own hand in the original editions of his plays, but among those of any consequence I think there are not very many that an editor would feel bound to accept on strictly critical principles. And it is significant that several correct emendations proposed by Massinger's early editors were subsequently rejected in what remains the standard edition. Meanwhile, if we demand that a true emendation shall explain the corruption, we are left wondering how in one place the word 'Constantinople' came to be substituted for the word 'Court'.

A second consideration suggested by the emendations with which I started brings me to what is the real subject of my address. It is this. When we have satisfied ourselves that an emendation is acceptable, the next question we ought to ask is what it implies with respect to the history and origin of the text. We may find that it implies something that is contrary to known fact, or at least something that conflicts with the implications of other emendations, or with evidence from some different source. Thus Theobald's emendation, though he may not have realized it, implies that the folio text of *Henry V* was set up from a manuscript written in the ordinary English hand of the period. In the circumstances this is, of course, what we should expect. But, had we reason to suppose that the copy supplied to the printer was prepared in modern spelling on a typewriter, the emendation would lose most of its plausibility. Again, if there were independent evidence that the second edition of *Doctor Faustus* was a naïve print from the same manuscript that served as copy for the first, we should have seriously to consider whether '*Oeconomy*' was not original, and '*Oncaymœon*' but a freakish misreading. Lastly, the seemingly trivial emendation 'lucosque lacusque', or rather the whole reconstruction of the passage in which it occurs, bears quite a formidable weight of implication. It implies an illiterate compositor and a singular absence of proof correction; it implies, on the other hand, some scholarly revision of the copy, for below a superficial layer of printer's errors this Latin is in better order than, for instance, a corresponding passage of Italian in the same play; and lastly it implies an author whose composition was governed more by the *Gradus* than by an instinct for metre. In fact it implies, or at least suggests, something like a complete history of the text.

The central point at which I am aiming is this: that no emendation can, or ought to be, considered *in vacuo*, but that criticism must always proceed in relation to what we know, or what we surmise, respecting the history of the text. True, we surmise more often than we know, and a sufficient number of acceptable emendations would form a good enough ground for the revision of any textual theory. But we ought to realize clearly whither an emendation is leading us. It is no use proposing emendations in the hope that upon *some* theory they may prove possible. There are texts whose data are so simple, or whose history is so unknown, that a minimum of restraint is placed upon the invention of the critic. But where the available evidence is at all full, no one has a right to ask us to accept any emendation without attempting to show that its implications are not inconsistent with known facts or contrary to common sense. And if a critic is so bold as to propose several emendations in the same text, he may fairly be challenged to prove that they do not involve mutually contradictory theories of its origin.

I shall devote the remainder of the hour your kindness has placed at my disposal to grouping Shakespeare's plays in accordance with what is usually assumed to be their textual history, and to considering very briefly the limits which the conditions in each group impose upon the freedom of emendation, and what in fact the practice of editors has been.

In doing so I shall confine my attention to the canon of the first folio, leaving out of account *Pericles*, the textual history of which is anomalous without being very enlightening. We are left then with thirty-six plays, which I propose to divide into four groups. The first class consists of seventeen plays which were printed for the first time in the folio of 1623. They are, *The Tempest, The Two Gentlemen of Verona, Measure for Measure, The Comedy of Errors, As You Like It, All's Well that Ends Well, Twelfth Night*, and *The Winter's Tale* among the comedies; *King John*, 1 *Henry VI*, and *Henry VIII* among the histories; and *Coriolanus, Timon of Athens, Julius Caesar, Macbeth, Antony and Cleopatra*, and *Cymbeline* among the tragedies. In my second class each play had been previously issued in a separate edition and it was from this quarto that the folio text was printed. Nine plays belong here; I give them in the chronological order of their appearance: *Titus Andronicus, Richard II, Richard III*, 1 *Henry IV, Love's Labour's Lost, The Merchant of Venice, Much Ado about Nothing, A Midsummer Night's Dream*, and *King Lear*. The third class consists of three plays which the folio printed, not from the previous quarto text, but from an independent manuscript representing substantially the same version: namely, 2 *Henry IV, Troilus and Cressida*, and *Othello*. Lastly, we have a fourth class, each play of which survives in two different versions, one an authoritative text, whether quarto or folio, and the other a bad text, which, whatever its precise nature, may be fairly described in the famous phrase as 'stolen and surreptitious'. This class, which of course offers by far the best hunting to the textual detective, has seven members, to wit:

The Taming of the Shrew, 2 and 3 *Henry VI, Romeo and Juliet, Henry V, The Merry Wives of Windsor*, and finally *Hamlet*.

I wish to make it clear that in this classification I am not giving you results of my own investigations or even expressing my own views. I am merely gathering the best critical opinion on various points that I can find, in order to use it as a basis for certain further inquiries. It does not matter much, if at all, whether the assumptions are in every case correct: I think, however, that when a critic has had the opportunity of considering and comparing the views of investigators such as the Cambridge editors, P. A. Daniel, Mr. Pollard, and Mr. Dover Wilson, he should be in a fair position to form at least a provisional judgement. It is true that in respect to Class IV I have taken into consideration some comparatively recent speculation: I do not, however, ask you to accept this as certain, but only to consider what follows supposing it to be true.

Class I, in which we have but a single text of each play, is the least interesting from our present point of view, for the textual data impose the minimum of restriction on conjecture. It is the happy hunting ground of the irresponsible editor, since his fancy can seldom be shown to conflict with textual logic. Yet even here there are some critical decencies to be observed. Emendation should be relative to the general nature and preservation of the text: a conjecture that was plausible in a corrupt text such as *Macbeth* might be inadmissible in a play like *The Tempest*, which may have been set up from Shakespeare's own manuscript. Of positive guides, beyond general suitability, there are perhaps only two: a knowledge of the errors a compositor is likely to make in setting the type, and a knowledge of those he is likely to make in reading his copy. There may be more to be discovered with respect to the first of these: our only appreciable advance of late has been the recognition of the fact that apparent errors of the ear are often due to the compositor trying to carry too many words in his mind at once. On the other hand much attention has recently been given to the problem of misreading, and though the study of manuscript forms may not have quite made good the promise held out by some enthusiasts, there can be no question as to its importance. Every critic of the texts with which we are concerned ought in the first place to make himself thoroughly familiar with the various contemporary styles of writing, which is easy enough; with the type of hand which Shakespeare must have written, a matter not seriously in doubt; and, if possible, with the hand Shakespeare actually wrote, about which the less said on this occasion the better. But though excellent use has sometimes been made of the *ductus literarum*, I incline to think that, while the method should always be ready to the critic's hand, it cannot often be paraded with effect. Its value is greater as a hint than as a proof. Now and then, indeed, a consideration of manuscript forms may cast a sudden light upon the obscurities of type. One of Heywood's printed plays has the startling peculiarity that in place of 'Actus 4' and '5' we have 'Actus 46' and '56'. If, however, we turn to his manuscript plays and observe the symbols he used for 'quartus' and 'quintus', we shall wonder, not that they were once misprinted '46' and '56', but that they were ever printed as anything else. But it is seldom that we meet such an illuminating example as this.

I shall for the moment pass over Class II and consider Class III, consisting of those plays for which we have two basic texts printed from independent manuscripts but representing essentially the same version. Here then quarto and folio are independent witnesses to a common tradition, a fact that puts a fairly tight curb on emendation. As a rule one text may be expected to correct the other. In cases of failure the two may have a common error, or different errors. If the latter, emendation is specifically limited by the necessity of accounting for both corruptions. Common errors must be supposed to go back to the author's original or very near it. This is, of course, not unlikely, but it should make us scrutinize rather closely the evidence on which error is assumed. And even when we are satisfied that corruption is present, it will be well to consider what interpretation was placed upon the text, as preserved, by the compositors and scribes who transmitted it, and by the actors who probably used it.

In 2 *Henry IV* there are a number of errors common to the two texts. Perhaps the most striking is where a speech that undoubtedly belongs to Bardolph is assigned to Poins. And since the quarto is clearly derived from a prompt-copy and the folio represents a further stage-revision of the play, we cannot but wonder into what actor's part the speech was copied and who actually spoke it at the Globe. Not all the alleged errors are equally certain, but if editors have thought themselves obliged to resort to a considerable amount of conjecture, it has not been without some show of reason. Indeed, their practice appears to me less consistent with a belief in two independent witnesses, than with the assumption that the folio text is somehow based with revision upon that preserved in the quarto. And in this connection it is possibly significant that I have been unable to find a good instance of divergent error in the two.

In *Troilus and Cressida* there is at least one instance in which the quarto and the folio have different readings, both certainly wrong, and there may be others. And although I cannot think that editors have always been right in the common errors they have supposed, it is difficult to avoid the conclusion that these are by no means uncommon. This and certain curious agreements in spelling and punctuation seem to me to raise a difficulty in the way of supposing that the only relation between the texts is that of a common source to the manuscripts used as copy. Uncertainty on this point has important consequences. Take for example the wonderful speech of Cressida:

> Sweet, bid me hold my tongue;
> For in this rapture I shall surely speak
> The thing I shall repent. See, see, your silence,
> Cunning in dumbness, from my weakness draws
> My very soul of counsel! Stop my mouth.

'Cunning' is Pope's emendation for the original 'Comming', but the expression 'coming' was quite usual in the sense of forward, apt. The emendation does give a more perfect sense, and if the text rested upon a single witness we could be content to accept it, if, however, the reading has double authority it should, I think, be retained.

Othello, the remaining play of this group, stands textually in sharp contrast to those we have just been considering. Among readings of any importance I think there are only four in which the Cambridge editors felt constrained to emend a reading supported by the two authorities, and in not one of these cases is it certain that they were right. A typical instance is seen in Iago's words:

> My wife must move for Cassio to her mistress;
> I'll set her on;
> Myself awhile to draw the Moor apart,
> And bring him jump when he may Cassio find
> Soliciting his wife: . . .

Instead of 'awhile' Theobald proposed to read 'the while'. This does, indeed, give a slighly better construction and has, I believe, been generally accepted. Yet it is clearly impossible to say that Shakespeare cannot have written the text as it stands. In the case of *Othello*, therefore, there is every reason to suppose that quarto and folio are independent witnesses to the author's original, and conversely that the original came near to being textually perfect. It is useful to bear this fact in mind when considering such controverted lines as :

> A fellow almost damn'd in a fair wife;

and:

> Put out the light, and then put out the light. . . .

I must now revert to our second group of plays, which really forms a transition class between I and III. Its nine members agree in this, that a quarto and not an independent manuscript served as copy for the folio text, but they differ widely in the extent to which that copy was corrected and revised from some other source. At one end of the scale we have 1 *Henry IV*, for which a quarto was reprinted almost without alteration, at the other end *King Lear*, the copy for which was so extensively revised and expanded that many critics have been led to believe that the folio text was printed from an independent manuscript. Between these extremes lie *Love's Labour's Lost*, *Much Ado about Nothing*, *A Midsummer Night's Dream*, and *The Merchant of Venice*, in all of which the folio contains corrections and stage-directions derived from the playhouse; *Richard II* and *Richard* III which have quite definitely been revised; and *Titus Andronicus*, in which a whole new scene has been added. In 1 *Henry IV* the textual problem is essentially the same as in Class I. But even here, and progressively through the other members of the class, there is always the possibility that a folio variant may be a fragment of an independent textual tradition, and moreover one which an editor, working within a few years of the author's death and in close touch with his fellow actors, thought superior to that of the quarto. This is no ground why we should necessarily prefer the folio reading, but it is a ground for giving it respectful consideration. In *Lear* we reach a critical position almost analogous to that in *Othello*. Divergence between quarto and folio will imply divergence of textual tradition. On the other hand agreement between the two cannot (as in Class III) be assumed to mean fidelity to the original, since it is certain that not all the variants of the independent manuscript will have been transferred to the copy used for the folio.

Both the fact that the folio text of *Lear* was printed from the first quarto, and that the revision of this quarto by comparison with the playhouse manuscript was not perfect, are proved by an interesting bibliographical accident. For certain sheets of the first quarto exist both in a corrected and an uncorrected state, and some of these uncorrected readings survive in the folio, only partially assimilated to the corrected form. Thus the end of one line was originally set up in the quarto as 'come and tends seruise', but was later corrected to 'commands her seruice'. Here the folio prints 'commands, tends, seruice', showing that the compositor had before him an originally uncorrected copy which had been brought only partially into agreement with the true reading. Moreover, imperfect correction of the copy can be traced in a number of other passages. Since Theobald, Lear has said:

> What, have his daughters brought him to this pass?

But the quarto reads 'What, his daughters', and the folio 'Ha's his Daughters'. Evidently the corrector, intending to insert 'has' after 'What', accidentally substituted it for that word. (Theobald's 'have' is a mere sophistication.)

But if these inferences are correct, as I believe they are, it is extraordinary how seldom editors have agreed in rejecting readings of any consequence warranted by both texts. In one place '*Historica passio*' is an obvious twin error for '*Hysterica passio*' and there are certainly some similar mistakes in punctuation, but the collection is a small one and even so includes some doubtful examples. A crucial instance is in Edmund's speech, which the more conservative editors print as follows:

> Well, my legitimate, if this letter speed
> And my invention thrive, Edmund the base
> Shall to the legitimate. I grow; I prosper:
> Now, gods, stand up for bastards!

For my own part I cannot quite reconcile myself to this, though at the same time I do not feel certain of the admirable emendation 'shall top the legitimate', first proposed by Edwards and adopted into the text by Capell and the Cambridge editors. Be this as it may, it seems to me that the text of *King Lear* is considerably better than on our textual theory it has any right to be, and I think there still remains a problem for investigation.

We now come to our fourth class, that highly important group of plays that have reached us in two quite different versions. The view of the older critics, that one of these versions represented an early draft subsequently remodelled, has gradually given place to the theory that it is a mangled text based somehow upon an actual representation and superseded by one published with authority. According to the former view the inferior version is chronologically antecedent to the other; according to the latter it is derivative, presupposing the other, though the possibility of subsequent revision is not excluded. This may be taken to represent in general the current opinion as regards *Romeo and Juliet*, *Henry V*, *The Merry Wives of Windsor*, and *Hamlet.* It is only of late, and mainly through the investigations of Mr. Peter Alexander, that the theory has been extended to cover *The Taming of the Shrew* and the two later parts of *Henry VI.* It has not yet passed into the mortmain of orthodoxy; and I do not ask you to accept it as more than a provisional hypothesis. Neither would I suggest that a single history applies, except perhaps in barest outline, to all seven plays. Indeed it is plain upon the face of it that the critical data are not at all points analogous. If the quarto *Taming of a Shrew* is a derivative text based substantially upon *The Taming of the Shrew*, as we know it in the folio, there has been far more elaborate writing up of the derived material than is found, for example, in *Henry V.* Certain features in *The Merry Wives* suggest that the quarto text may have been vamped up by the actor of a particular part, and the same theory has been applied to some other plays. On the other hand, if an actor played the traitor in *The Merry Wives* it is clear that he relied on memory alone, whereas in *Hamlet* he may have made use of his written part. This possibility suggests that the first quarto of *Hamlet* at least may be a very composite text, and that, though undoubtedly a bad egg, it is of the curate's variety. The choruses of *Henry V*, which to some extent mark the act structure in the folio, find no place in the quarto: on the other hand *A Shrew* preserves the conclusion of the framework-action which it is natural to suppose must once have been present in *The Shrew*, though there is no trace of it in the folio.

But great as is the diversity of individual cases there are, if the modern theory is correct, certain fundamental features in common. In all seven plays we have on the one hand an authoritative text derived by transcription or printing from the author's original, and on the other a vamped text at least one step in the transmission of which is memorial. The critical implications of these assumptions are obvious. Where the texts differ, one possesses vastly greater authority than the other : where they agree, we not only have direct transcriptional witness to what the author wrote, but we know, subject to certain possible exceptions, that this was what was actually spoken on the stage. In the latter case, before resorting to emendation, we shall be not only justified but bound to go to lengths of interpretation which would be altogether fantastic in Classes I and II, and would be doubtful even in Class III.

The seven plays of our fourth group fall into two divisions. In *Romeo and Juliet* and *Hamlet* the bad quarto was superseded after about a couple of years by a good quarto containing a text substantially identical with that later printed in the folio. For these, therefore, we possess three several authorities, and to them I shall return. In the other five plays the bad quarto was only superseded by the good text printed in the folio. These present a rather simpler problem. Although, of course, each has features of its own, we can only on this occasion examine a single play as more or less representative of its class. *Henry V* will serve as well as any.

There are, of course, a number of errors in the folio text, and it is only to be expected that in some instances the correct reading should survive in the quarto. Editors have indeed made pretty free use of the latter, sometimes with full justification, sometimes perhaps indiscreetly. When, according to the folio, Corporal Nym says:

> It must be as it may, though patience be a tyred name,
> yet shee will plodde,

he is talking nonsense, and when for 'name' the quarto has 'mare', the graphic similarity suggests that it preserves the correct reading. On the other hand we may take such a passage as this:

> *Boy.* Doe you not remember a saw a Flea sticke vpon *Bardolphs* Nose, and a said it was a blacke Soule burning in Hell.
>
> *Bard.* Well, the fuell is gone that maintain'd that fire: that's all the Riches I got in his seruice.

In place of 'Hell' Capell introduced 'hell fire' from the quarto, and in view of Bardolph's reply all later editors seem to have felt constrained to accept the alteration. They may have been right, but I do not think they were justified.

In one place the quarto supplies a speech of Nym's that seems necessary to the sense, and this perhaps justifies the insertion from the same source of a line in Henry's great speech on the feast of Crispian, though it is certainly not indispensable. I think the most interesting case is the passage which stands in the folio as follows:

> *Belf*[*ord*]. Farenwell good *Salisbury*, & good luck go with thee:
>
> And yet I doe thee wrong, to mind thee of it,
> For thou art fram'd of the firme truth of valour.
> *Exe*[*ter*]. Farewell kind Lord: fight valiantly to day.
> *Bedf.* He is as full of Valour as of Kindnesse,
> Princely in both.

The quarto gives the second and third lines in the mangled form:

> And yet in truth, I do thee wrong,
> For thou art made on the [t]rue sparkes of honour

and also alters the speakers; but what is significant is that it tacks these lines on to the words spoken in the folio by Exeter; and in so doing it is clearly right. How, then, did they get misplaced in the folio? One naturally supposes that they were a marginal addition in the manuscript, the position of which the compositor mistook. If so they afford further evidence that the quarto is dependent on the final version of the play, and not on an earlier draft.

As regards emendation, I cannot find that any reading rejected by editorial consensus is supported by a clear agreement of the original texts. But there are three cases of what I may call disguised agreement, and in each of these I think that editors have been wrong. I can only call attention to one now; the most interesting and perhaps the most doubtful. On the eve of Agincourt, Fluellen and Gower meet in the English camp, and the folio reads:

> *Gower*. Captaine *Fluellen*.
> *Flu*. 'So, in the Name of Iesu Christ, speake fewer: . . .

Malone and modern editors alter this to 'speak lower'. But 'lower', which comes from the third quarto, is merely a compositor's emendation for 'fewer' in the first quarto, and this would seem to be a misprint for 'fewer' as in the folio. There is no difficulty in the reading 'fewer' itself, in the sense of less, 'fewer words'; the supposed necessity of reading 'lower' arises from Gower's subsequent promise 'I will speake lower', and from Holinshed's report of an order 'that no noise or clamor should be made in the host'. It would be interesting to write a full commentary on the passage, but here it must suffice to observe that Fluellen does not censure Gower for shouting but for 'tiddle tadle' and 'pibble bable', and that the humour of it is that all the time it is Fluellen who babbles, while Gower can hardly get a word in edgeways.

In *Henry V* at least the textual phenomena are what we should expect from the assumed history. I may, however, repeat the warning that we must not expect the phenomena to be altogether constant throughout the group, and that in every particular play editorial practice should be governed by a detailed examination of the textual data.

Our last two plays agree in possessing three several authorities for the text. But they differ markedly as to the nature of these authorities. In both cases we have a bad quarto superseded by a good one, but whereas in *Hamlet* the folio was printed from a manuscript and shows important differences, in *Romeo and Juliet* it was set up almost without alteration from the authorized quarto text. The latter, therefore, presents a comparatively simple problem, for the relation of the good quarto to the folio is that of the simplest cases of Class II, and need not further concern us, while the relation of the quartos to one another is essentially the same as in *Henry V.*

There is, however, one peculiarity of *Romeo and Juliet* which gives it a unique interest for the critic, namely that the bad quarto of 1597 served to some extent as copy for the good quarto of 1599. This fact was first observed by a German writer half a century ago, but it has only recently shown signs of creeping into critical consciousness. The evidence is supplied by a number of bibliographical peculiarities, the most obvious being that certain speeches are printed in italic in both quartos, and it is to my mind conclusive. But it applies to only a small part of the play, namely the first two sheets of the first quarto. It seems clear that some editor was commissioned to prepare the copy for an authorized quarto, and for this purpose was provided with the 1597 edition and a playhouse manuscript. He began by taking the printed text and elaborately correcting and expanding it by comparison with the manuscript, but when he got to the end of sheet B he decided that it would be less trouble to make a transcript of the latter. This he proceeded to do through the remainder of the play, though I will not say that he may not have used other fragments of the printed text, and I am certain that he consulted it on occasions when the manuscript was obscure.

This bibliographical induction is borne out in a rather remarkable way by the textual evidence of a number of corruptions common to the two quartos. When Romeo meets Capulet's servant he asks him whither the guests are invited, and the conversation proceeds:

> *Serv.* Up.
> *Rom.* Whither?

Serv. To supper; to our house.

This is Theobald's arrangement of the text, and it is very likely correct: the quartos make the words 'to supper' part of Romeo's speech. There are two other common errors within a few lines of this, and the next scene is marked by an agreement of the texts in several peculiar spellings, the most notable being 'a leauen' (or 'a leuen') for eleven. All these occur in sheet B. In the remainder of the play, eight sheets, there is one common error (to which I shall return), and one, or possibly two, partial agreements in abnormal spellings. The conclusion is obvious.

This peculiar textual history should prepare us for something unusual in the readings. We find it in the frequent use which editors have made of the bad quarto in their endeavour to emend the good one. The cases are ten or twelve times as numerous as in *Henry V* and mostly of much greater importance. The Cambridge editors are fairly conservative in the matter, but I have counted 118 instances (trivialities apart) in which they have replaced a reading of the second quarto by what is substantially that of the first, or about one in every twenty-five lines. Of course nothing like all these are really needed, but I think that about a third are inevitable; and if it is once admitted that the first quarto is right in two score cases, there is no particular reason to jib at six score.

The most certain corrections supplied by the first quarto are not as a rule the most interesting, though they include such readings as 'chaples' (*i.e.* chapless) for 'chapels' and 'pay' for 'pray'. But there seems no reason to question the correctness of the line:

Hence will I to my ghostly father's cell,

which editors have taken mainly from the first quarto, for the reading of the second, 'my ghostly Friers close cell', can only have originated, one supposes, in inability to decipher the playhouse manuscript. At the same time there are a few passages in which I think editors have done wrong to desert the primary authority, for instance in the Friar's reproof to Romeo:

O she knew well,
Thy loue did reade by rote, that could not spell :

where most editors since Pope have printed the less pregnant reading of the first quarto, 'and could not spell'.

The one common error in the later sheets of the play appears in a passage that raises a number of textual problems. Mercutio's conjuring of the invisible lover, so far as it can with decency be quoted, which happily will serve our turn, is printed by the Cambridge editors as follows:

> Romeo! humours! madman! passion! lover!
> Appear thou in the likeness of a sigh :
> Speak but one rhyme, and I am satisfied;
> Cry but 'ay me'! pronounce but 'love' and 'dove';
> Speak to my gossip Venus one fair word,
> One nick-name for her purblind son and heir,
> Young Adam Cupid, he that shot so trim
> Then King Cophetua loved the beggar-maid!

I am not going to argue whether 'Adam Cupid' is right, though I think it may be: the point is that it is an emendation for '*Abraham*: *Cupid*' a reading in which the two quartos agree *literatim et punctuatim*. Now, two things are evident, namely that this as it stands cannot be correct, and that the second quarto must have copied it from the first. Is this, then, a passage for which the editor in 1599 used a fragment of the printed edition? The suggestion is ruled out by other readings which prove that the compositor of the second quarto had manuscript copy before him. Thus the fourth line is substantially taken from the first quarto; the second quarto reads:

> Crie but ay me, prouaunt, but loue and day,

where 'prouaunt' and 'day' are certainly graphic errors. It is clear that the editor was having unusual difficulties with the playhouse copy in this passage — it must have been mutilated or defaced — and that when he came to young Cupid he boldly turned to the printed text for guidance. But if this is so, we shall do well to examine very carefully the readings in which the second quarto differs from the first. Already, apart from the fourth line, editors have borrowed from the first quarto 'shot so trim' and 'son and heir', but they have followed the second quarto in the first line, where the first quarto has:

> *Romeo*, madman, humors, passion, liuer, . . .

Noting the slight change of order, which emphasizes the descent from man to his complaints, there seems a good deal to be said for the reading 'liuer', this being, of course, the seat of the disease of love. And again in the last line we may wonder whether 'begger wench', as in the first quarto, is not more in accord with Mercutio's humour than the more conventional 'beggarmaid'. The latter, familiar from the ballad, would no doubt have come more readily from the editor's pen.

Among the plays of Class IV *Romeo and Juliet* is remarkable in that the bad text seems a good deal better, and the good text a good deal worse, than we are accustomed to find. I fancy it offers opportunities of critical exploration which have not yet been exhausted.

Discussion of Shakespeare usually comes round in the end to *Hamlet*; and for us too the wheel is come full circle. *Hamlet* is not only, from the literary point of view, the most discussed play in the canon, it is also the one that presents the most complex problem to the textual student. It is the only play for which we possess three ostensibly independent authorities. And the earliest of these texts, the bad egg, appears to be of a more complex or variable badness than the other members of that addled sitting : or else its quality has been submitted to more minute examination. This is a topic upon which I cannot enter now. The theory which I wish to examine, without necessarily accepting, is that the good second quarto was printed direct from Shakespeare's autograph, that the folio was printed from a playhouse manuscript copied from that autograph, which had undergone certain alteration in the course of two decades of constant use as a promptbook, and that the bad first quarto is in the main based upon a representation of the play, the actors' parts for which had been transcribed from the same prompt-copy in its original state. The actual textual history must be a good deal more complicated than this, but I wish at present merely to inquire how far this theory will 'work' in view of the variant readings found in the authorities and the emendations that have found favour with editors. In this investigation I have had the benefit of studying an important essay by Professor Dover Wilson on 'Spellings and Misprints in the Second Quarto of *Hamlet*'.

There are five classes of readings that throw light on our problem, namely : agreements of the first quarto and the folio against the second quarto, agreements of the two quartos against the folio, agreements of the second quarto and the folio which editors have rejected in favour of the first quarto, agreements of the second quarto and the folio which editors have rejected without seeking help from the first quarto, and agreements of all three texts which editors have rejected.

It is a curious fact that where the second quarto and the folio differ the support of the first quarto is almost exactly balanced between them : in fifty-five instances it agrees with the other quarto, in fifty-seven with the folio. If our theory is correct its agreements with the folio are not of much significance, since both go back ultimately to the prompt-book; all that the first quarto can show is that the folio reading is not due to the compositor and that it could pass muster on the stage. Analysis seems to show that the great majority of instances (44 out of 57) are due either to misprints in the second quarto or to small variants introduced in transcribing the prompt-copy. There are also three definite errors originating in that operation. The most interesting result is that the prompt-copy seems to have undergone some authoritative revision before the copying of the actor's parts, for there are ten passages or so in which readings of the autograph appear to have been deliberately altered. If Mr. Dover Wilson is right, one of the prompt-book errors was the substitution of snatches of old 'tunes' for 'lauds' through a misreading of Shakespeare's writing. The corrections or alterations are all instructive: I have only space to mention that Shakespeare seems originally to have written 'fearful Porpentine', and that 'fretfull' was a happy second thought.

The variants in which the first quarto supports the second against the folio are of much greater importance, since on our theory agreement of the quartos establishes the reading of the prompt-book. Apart from chance coincidence, of which there may be a few examples, variation in the folio implies either a misprint in that text or an alteration subsequent to the preparation of the actors' parts. Misprints account for nearly half the cases; the rest are divided about equally between small editorial tinkerings, very likely made in preparing the playhouse manuscript for press, and alterations made in it in the course of its twenty years of use as a prompt-book. The distinction of these classes is of course conjectural. The most interesting misprint is the substitution of 'Landlesse' for 'lawelesse' resolutes, due, it would seem, to the easy misreading of 'lawe' as 'land'. Among editorial changes there are a couple that suggest that the speech with which Hamlet leaves Ophelia, after consigning her to a nunnery, had become partly obliterated in the manuscript. The dozen or so major alterations are important. Shakespeare himself, it would seem, altered 'quietly interr'd' to 'quietly enurn'd', and perhaps made the necessary correction in the 'dayly Cast of Brazon Cannon', where 'cost' had got into the acted version. But he surely had no hand in the 'too too solid Flesh'. A vision of Burbage's waist-band should suffice to prove that, editors notwithstanding, Shakespeare can never have meant to write 'solid' here. It is a desperate guess for the unintelligible 'sallied' of the quartos. The problem is therefore one of emendation and I shall return to it.

There are eight passages in which the Cambridge editors have adopted a reading of the first quarto to the exclusion of one supported by the second quarto and the folio. One of these is clearly necessary, but the error is an easy one and may well have arisen independently in the two more authoritative texts. The other seven should be rejected. Three or four are mere mischievous normalizations; one is an exceedingly ingenious conjecture, for which the editors have not been given the credit they deserve, but which is at the same time rather hazardous. Of the rest the most crucial is in the Play scene, where in reply to Ophelia's 'Still better, and worse', Hamlet snaps:

> So you must take your husbands.

Here 'must take' was introduced by Pope from the first quarto in place of 'mistake' as in the other texts. But surely Capell was right in printing 'mis-take': Hamlet means: 'For better or worse! Why, that's the silly way you choose husbands'.

There are ten instances, where the first quarto affords no help, in which the Cambridge editors have rejected a reading certified by both the second quarto and the folio. Some are trivial; once or twice Shakespeare and the prompter were both certainly nodding; but 'good kissing carrion' I am inclined to believe is correct, and 'cauiary' should not be altered to 'caviare', a form very rare in Shakespeare's day. Only one is of first-rate interest. Polonius hides behind the arras with the words : 'I'll silence me even here.' Hanmer emended 'silence' to 'sconce'. But, as Dowden remarked, only in death could Polonius be really silent, and it is just because he cannot 'silence' him that he dies. The emendation destroys the dramatic irony of the phrase.

There are even three cases in which the editors have rejected a reading which has the warrant of all three authorities. In one they did not venture on any emendation, and I propose to return to it in a moment. One is a trivial matter, a second-folio spelling adopted in the teeth of textual evidence. The last is very significant.

> White his shroud as the mountain snow,
>   Larded with sweet flowers;
> Which bewept to the grave did go
>   With true-love showers.

So Ophelia sings, at least according to Pope, and such no doubt were the words of the song she had in mind, supposing it to have been traditional. But in the third line all three texts read 'did not go', and we are bound to believe that not only is this what Shakespeare wrote, but what Ophelia actually sang on the stage. It is idle to talk of printers and their intrusive negatives; it would be equally idle to point out that Massinger once committed this very error in his own manuscript : the present case cannot be accidental, nor could it escape notice. Ophelia is suddenly struck by the inappropriateness of the words she is singing and alters them to a harsh discord.

This completes what I have to say of the practice of editors considered in relation to the textual theory of *Hamlet* with which we began. If that theory is true it is clear that editors will have to modify their practice considerably. That it is true I will not assert, but we have found nothing in the textual evidence that necessarily contradicts it, and a good deal that is doubtful in editorial practice where this conflicts with it.

I wish in conclusion to consider two or three emendations or explanations of emendations suggested by Professor Dover Wilson in the paper already mentioned. As is well known he has based his work chiefly upon an analysis of Shakespeare's supposed handwriting and spelling, but he has pursued this line of inquiry in conjunction with textual theory. For example he argues that where the second quarto gives us what may be a misreading of Shakespeare's autograph it is a facile abdication of critical function to accept instead a makeshift reading from the folio. Take for instance:

> The terms of our estate may not endure
> Hazard so near us as doth hourly grow
> Out of his lunacies.

The last word is supplied by the folio; the quarto has 'browes'. This of course is impossible, and we may suppose that it is just because it is impossible that the folio started guessing, but we are bound to do our best with it. Mr. Dover Wilson suggests a misreading of 'brawls'. I do not know whether his conjecture is right, but I am sure that his method is sound.

So with the 'too too solid flesh' already glanced at. The folio's 'solid' is a guess we must reject: the 'sallied' of the quartos is unintelligible. But 'sallies' occurs elsewhere in the second quarto as a misprint for 'sullies', showing that the words could be easily confused in Shakespeare's hand. Thus, when he intended 'sullied' flesh, it was twice misread as 'sallied' and finally misemended to 'solid'. Of this explanation I have little doubt.

Lastly, what are we to make of the threefold witness to Polonius's words? —

> And they in France of the best rank and station
> Are of a most select and generous chief in that.

Mr. Dover Wilson tells us that 'of a' is a misreading of Shakespeare's attempt to write 'often'. I cannot discuss the details, but the emendation does not present any insuperable difficulty either graphic or metrical. What, however, are its textual implications? Granted that Shakespeare wrote 'often' in such a way that it would naturally be read 'of a': then we have to assume that the compositor of the second quarto so printed it, that the scribe of the playhouse manuscript so wrote it, that the scribe of the actors' parts accepted the reading, and likewise the actors who performed along with Shakespeare on the stage, the reporter of the representation, and the printer of his version; that meanwhile the reading remained unaltered in the prompt-copy, and passed muster with the editor and compositor of the folio. It would be idle to pretend that such a chain of error and persistence in error is not improbable; but where the facts are themselves unreasonable we need not be surprised if the explanation seems fantastic. It is the implications that are important, and it is Professor Dover Wilson's chief merit that he has courageously faced the consequences of his proposals. That renders his work significant even where it may prove mistaken, and I make no excuse for dwelling upon it here.

Thus I come back at the end to the point with which I started, the interdependence of emendation and textual theory. We have considered the many aspects that the editorial problem assumes with the shifting relations of particular texts, but this interdependence is the one general principle that has emerged from, I fear, an o'er-lengthy discussion. To be fruitful the task of emendation must be pursued in relation to a clear perception of the possibilities of textual history; otherwise it is as a bow drawn at a venture. It is no revolutionary doctrine that I am preaching, and if, so far, it has been little reflected in the practice of editors, this has been perhaps less through deliberate neglect than because the data for its application have been insufficient. For of one thing at least the preparation of this lecture has made me more than ever conscious, the need for a fresh and thorough investigation into the bibliographical history of the authorities for Shakespeare's text.

Note

Dr. J. W. Mackail tells me that this instance of error in Milton (p. 81), which I lifted from his Warton Lecture, is a bad example. It appears that the mistake is found in the only authorities that were accessible when Milton wrote.

5
King Lear[1]
H. Granville-Barker

'Lear is essentially impossible to be represented on a stage' — and later critics have been mostly of Charles Lamb's opinion. My chief business in this Preface will be to justify, if I can, its title there.

Shakespeare meant it to be acted, and he was a very practical playwright. So that should count for something. Acted it was, and with success enough for it to be presented before the king at Whitehall. (Whatever his faults, James I seems to have had a liking for good drama.) And Burbage's performance of King Lear remained a vivid memory. At the Restoration it was one of the nine plays selected by Davenant for his theatre. He had in mind, doubtless, its 'reforming and making fit' — all of them except *Hemlet* and *Othello* were to suffer heavily from that. But Downes, his prompter, tells us that it was '. . . *Acted* exactly as Mr. *Shakespear* wrote it . . .' — several times apparently — before Nahum Tate produced his version in 1681. This hotch-potch held the stage for the next hundred and fifty years and more, though from Garrick's time onwards it would generally be somewhat re-Shakespeareanized.[2] One cannot prove Shakespearean stage-worthiness by citing Tate, but how far is it not Tate rather than Shakespeare that Lamb condemns?

1. *Prefaces to Shakespeare* (1927); this extract from the *King Lear* preface was revised in 1935 for the present collection.
2. Elliston and Kean, after a little hesitation, went so far as to restore the tragic ending. Then, in 1838, Macready acted Shakespeare's play again. But even he tampered with its structure, and — by much omission — with its text.

He has Shakespeare's play in mind, but he had never seen it acted. Part of his complaint is that '. . . Tate has put his hook in the nostrils of this Leviathan, for Garrick and his followers, the showmen of the scene, to draw the mighty beast about more easily'. And he never considers Shakespeare's play in relation to Shakespeare's stage. He came near to doing so; for, later in the essay, with *The Tempest* for theme, he speaks of '. . . the elaborate and anxious provision of scenery, which the luxury of the age demands . . .' which '. . . works a quite contrary effect to what is intended. That which in comedy, or plays of familiar life, adds so much to the life of the imitation, in plays which appeal to the higher faculties positively destroys the illusion which it is introduced to aid'. Had he followed out this argument with *King Lear* for an example, giving credit to Shakespeare the playwright as well as to Shakespeare the poet — I do not say that he would have reached a different conclusion, for there is still the plea to be met that here, for once, Shakespeare the playwright did overreach himself, but he must at least have recognized another side to the question. Lamb's essay should be read, of course, as a whole. He loved the drama; the theatre alternately delighted and exasperated him. The orotund acting of his day, its conventional tricks, can have been but a continual offence to his sensitive ear and nicety of taste. He here takes his revenge — and it is an ample one — for many evenings of such suffering. He never stopped to consider whether there might not be more even to the actor's despised art than that.

A profounder and a more searching indictment of the play's stage-worthiness comes from A. C. Bradley in the (for me) most remarkable of those remarkable lectures on Shakespearean Tragedy. To him it seems '. . . Shakespeare's greatest achievement, but . . . *not* his best play'. The entire argument should be read; but this, I think, sums it up not unfairly : 'The stage is the test of strictly dramatic quality, and *King Lear* is too huge for the stage. . . . It has scenes immensely effective in the theatre; three of them — the two between Lear and Goneril and between Lear, Goneril and Regan, and the ineffably beautiful scene in the Fourth Act between Lear and Cordelia — lose in the theatre very little of the spell they have for imagination; and the gradual interweaving of the two plots is almost as masterly as in *Much Ado*. But (not to speak of defects due to mere carelessness) that which makes the *peculiar* greatness of *King Lear*, — the immense scope of the work; the mass and variety of intense experience which it contains; the interpenetration of sublime imagination, piercing pathos, and humour almost as moving as the pathos; the vastness of the convulsion both of nature and of human passion; the vagueness of the scene where the action takes place, and of the movements of the figures which cross this scene; the strange atmosphere, cold and dark, which strikes on us as we enter this scene, enfolding those figures and magnifying their dim outlines like a winter mist; the half-realised suggestions of vast universal powers working in the world of individual fears and passions, all this interferes with dramatic clearness even when the play is read, and in the theatre not only refuses to reveal itself fully through the sense but seems to be almost in contradiction with their reports.' And later: 'The temptation of Othello and the scene of Duncan's murder may lose upon the stage, but they do not lose their *essence*, and they gain as well as lose. The Storm-scenes in *King Lear* gain nothing, and their very *essence* is destroyed.' For this essence is poetry and, he concludes, '. . . such poetry as cannot be transferred to the space behind the foot-lights, but has its being only in imagination. Here then is Shakespeare at his very greatest, but not the mere dramatist Shakespeare'.

Notice, first of all, how widely Bradley's standpoint is removed from that — we may venture to surmise it — of 'the mere dramatist Shakespeare' and his fellows the actors. To say of certain scenes that they were 'immensely effective in the theatre' and add that they lost there 'very little of the spell they have for imagination', to argue that 'the temptation of Othello and the scene of Duncan's murder may lose upon the stage, but they do not lose their *essence*, and they gain as well as lose' — it would have sounded to them queer commendation. For in whatever Shakespeare wrote was the implied promise that in the theatre it would gain. Bradley passes easily to : 'the Storm-scenes in *King Lear* gain nothing, and their very *essence* is destroyed.' The mere dramatist, on his defence, would rightly refuse to follow him. The premises to the argument are not the same.

Bradley and Lamb may be right in their conclusions. It is possible that this most practical and loyal of dramatists did for once — despite himself, driven to it by his unpremeditating genius — break his promise and betray his trust by presenting to his fellows a play, the capital parts of which they simply could not act. Happily for them, they and their audiences never found him out. But if Bradley is right not the most perfect performance can be a fulfilment, can be aught but a betrayal of *King Lear*. There is the issue. The thing is, of course, incapable of proof. The best that imperfect human actors can give must come short of perfection, and the critic can always retort to their best that his imagination betters it. Bradley's argument is weighty. Yet — with all deference to a great critic — I protest that, as it stands, it is not valid. He is contending that a practical and practised dramatist has here written a largely impracticable play. Before condemning these 'storm scenes' he should surely consider their stagecraft — their mere stagecraft. For may not 'the mere dramatist' have his answer hidden there? But this — starting from his standpoint of imaginative reader — he quite neglects to do.

Ought we, moreover, to assume — as Bradley seems to — that a play must necessarily make all its points and its full effect, point by point, clearly and completely, scene by scene, as the performance goes along? Not every play, I think. For the appreciation of such a work as *King Lear* one might even demand the second or third hearing of the whole, which the alertest critic would need to give to (say) a piece of music of like calibre. But leave that aside. No condoning of an ultimate obscurity is involved. And comedy, it can be admitted, demands an immediate clarity. Nor is the dramatist ever to be dispensed from making his story currently clear and at least provisionally significant. But he has so much more than that to do. He must produce a constant illusion of life. To do this he must, among other things, win us to something of a fellow-feeling with his characters; and even, at the play's critical moments, to identifying their emotions with our own.

Now the significance of their emotions may well not be clear to the characters themselves for the moment. There are devices enough by which if the dramatist wishes, this significance can be kept currently clear to the audience. There is the Greek chorus; the earlier Elizabethans turned Prologue and Presenters to account; the *raisonneur* of nineteenth-century comedy has a respectable ancestry. Shakespeare uses the *raisonneur* in varying guises. And in this very play we detect him in the Fool, and in Edgar turned Poor Tom. But note that both they and their 'reasoning' are blent not only into the action but into the moral scheme, and are never allowed to lower its emotional temperature — indeed they stimulate it. For here may be the difficulty in preserving that 'dramatic clearness' which Bradley demands; it may cost — and repeatedly be costing — dramatist and actors their emotional hold upon their audience. Not so much when the interest is centred upon such a character as Hamlet, himself ever oscillating between thought and emotion, or upon the struggle between intellect and passion of Iago and Othello, or upon the inward tragedy of Macbeth. In these cases the contrasting threads can at least be closely and firmly woven. But Lear's progress — dramatic and spiritual — is through a dissipation of egoism; submission to the cruelty of an indifferent Nature, less cruel to him than are his own kind; to loss of himself in madness. Consider the effect of this, of the battling of storm without and storm within, of the final breaking of that Titan spirit, if Shakespeare merely let us look on, critically observant. For, so considered, Lear is an intolerable tyrant. Regan and Goneril have a good case against him. We should not side with them; but our onlooker's sympathy might hardly be warmer than, say, the kindly Albany's.[3] We do see him in his suffering through Kent's faithful eyes; but not all his honesty makes Kent spiritually discerning. Shakespeare besides needs to give us more than sympathy with Lear, something deeper than understanding. If the verity of his ordeal is really to be brought home to us, we must, in as full a sense as may be, pass through it with him, must make the experience and its overwhelming emotions momentarily our own.

3. Whom — not to admit any Laodicean view of the matter — Shakespeare carefully keeps out of the angry scenes which lead to Lear's self-banishment to the wild and the storm.

Shakespeare may have set himself an impossible task; but if he is to succeed it will only be by these means. In this mid-crisis of the play he must never relax his emotional hold on us. And all these things of which Bradley complains, the confusion of pathos, humour, and sublime imagination, the vastness of the convulsion, the vagueness of the scene and the movements of the characters, the strange atmosphere and the half-realized suggestions — all this he needs as material for Lear's experience, and ours. Personally, I do not find quite so much vagueness and confusion. To whatever metaphysical heights Lear himself may rise, some character (Kent and Gloucester through the storm and in the hovel, Edgar for the meeting with the blinded Gloucester), some circumstance, or a few salient and explicit phrases will always be found pointing the action on its way. And if we become so at one with Lear in his agony that for the time its full significance escapes us, may not memory still make this clear? For that is very often true of our own emotional experiences. A confusion of suffering or joy at the time; only later do we realize, as we say, 'what it all meant to us'. It is, I suggest, this natural bent which Shakespeare turns to his account in these larger passages of *King Lear.* In the acting they move us profoundly. The impression they make remains. And when the play is over they, with the rest of it, should cohere in the memory, and clarify; and the meaning of the whole should be plain. Shakespeare, I protest, has not failed; he has — to the degree of his endeavour — triumphantly succeeded. But to appreciate the success and give effect to it in the play's performance we must master and conform to the stagecraft on which it depends.

In this hardest of tasks — the showing of Lear's agony, his spiritual death and resurrection — we find Shakespeare relying very naturally upon his strongest weapon, which by experiment and practice he has now, indeed, forged to an extraordinary strength, and to a suppleness besides : the weapon of dramatic poetry. He has, truly, few others of any account. In the storm scenes the shaking of a thunder-sheet will not greatly stir us. A modern playwright might seek help in music — but Shakespeare's music is not of that sort; in impressive scenery — he has none. He has, in compensation, the fluidity of movement which the negative background of his stage allows him. For the rest, he has his actors, their acting and the power of their speech. It is not a mere rhetorical power, nor are the characters lifted from the commonplace simply by being given verse to speak instead of conversational prose. All method of expression apart, they are *poetically conceived*; they exist in those dimensions, in that freedom, and are endowed with that peculiar power. They are dramatic poetry incarnate.

Thus it is that Shakespeare can make such calls upon them as here he must. In the storm scenes they not only carry forward the story, revealing and developing themselves as they do so, they must — in default of other means — create the storm besides. Not by detachedly describing it; if they 'lose themselves' in its description, they will for that while lose something of their own hold on us. The storm is not in itself, moreover, dramatically important, only in its effect upon Lear. How, then, to give it enough magnificence to impress him, yet keep it from rivalling him? Why, by identifying the storm with him, setting the actor to impersonate both Lear and — reflected in Lear — the storm. That, approximately, is the effect when — the Fool cowering, drenched and pitiful, at his side — he launches into the tremendous:

> Blow, winds, and crack your cheeks! rage! blow!
> You cataracts and hurricanoes, spout
> Till you have drench'd our steeples, drown'd the cocks
> You sulphurous and thought-executing fires,
> Vaunt-couriers of oak-cleaving thunder-bolts
> Singe my white head! And thou, all-shaking thunder,
> Strike flat the thick rotundity of the world!
> Crack nature's moulds, all germens spill at once
> That make ungrateful man.

This is no mere description of a storm, but in music and imaginative suggestion a dramatic creating of the storm itself; and there is Lear — and here are we, if we yield ourselves — in the midst of it, almost a part of it. Yet Lear himself, in his Promethean defiance, still dominates the scene.

But clearly the effect cannot be made by Lamb's 'old man tottering about the stage with a walking-stick'; and by any such competitive machinery for thunder and lightning as Bradley quite needlessly assumes to be an inevitable part of the play's staging it will be largely spoilt. What actor in his senses, however, would attempt to act the scene 'realistically'? (I much doubt if any one of Lamb's detested barnstormers ever did.) And as to the thunder and lightning, Shakespeare uses the modicum to his hand; but it is no dramatic consequence, and his stagecraft takes no account of it.[4] Yet if the human Lear seems lost for a moment in the symbolic figure, here is the Fool to remind us of him:

> O nuncle, court holy water in a dry house is better than this rain-water out o' door. Good nuncle in, ask thy daughters' blessing; here's a night pities neither wise men nor fools;

— and to keep the scene in touch with reality. Yet note that the fantasy of the Fool *mitigates* the contrast, and the spell is held unbroken. It is not till later — when Lear's defiant rage, having painted us the raging of the storm, has subsided — that Kent's sound, most 'realistic' common sense, persuading him to the shelter of the hovel, is admitted.

But Shakespeare has other means of keeping the human and the apocalyptic Lear at one. Though the storm is being painted for us still —

> Rumble thy bellyful! spit, fire! spout, rain!
> Nor rain, wind, thunder, fire are my daughters:
> tax not you, you elements, with unkindness;
> I never gave you kingdom, call'd you children,
> You owe me no subscription: then let fall
> Your horrible pleasure; here I stand, your slave;
> A poor, infirm, weak and despis'd old man . . . .

— both in the sense of the words and the easier cadence of the verse the human Lear is emerging, and emerges fully upon the sudden simplicity of

> . . . here I stand, your slave;
> A poor, infirm, weak and despis'd old man.

4. Bradley argues in a footnote that *because* Shakespeare's 'means of imitating a storm were so greatly inferior even to ours' he could not have 'had the stage-performance only or chiefly in view in composing these scenes'. But this is, surely to view Shakespeare's theatre and craft with modern eyes. The contemporary critic would have found it easier to agree that just *because* your imitation storm was such a poor affair you must somehow make your stage effect *without* relying on it.

But the actor is not, therefore, suddenly to drop from trenchant speech to commonplace, present us a pathological likeness of poverty, infirmity, and the rest, divest himself of all poetic power, become, in fact the old man with a walking-stick. For if he does he will incontinently and quite fatally cease to be the Lear that Shakespeare has, as we said, conceived and embodied in poetry. In poetry; not, one must again insist, necessarily or simply in verse. And it is no more, now or later, a mere question of a method of speaking than of form in the writing. Verse, prose, and doggerel rhyme, in those strenuous scenes, each has its use, each asks an appropriate beauty of treatment, and the three in harmony are, by dramatic title, poetry.

The actor has then, not simply or chiefly to speak poetically, but, for the while, somehow to incarnate this poetry in himself. He can do so — paradoxically — by virtue of an exceptional self-sacrifice. Physically, Shakespeare's Lear must surrender to *him*; he makes himself in return an intellectual and emotional instrument for its expression. That is the way of all honest acting. If the actor's personality is the richer, a character will be absorbed in it. In a play of familiar human commerce actor and character may collaborate, so to say, upon equal terms. But give the character the transcendent quality of poetry, the actor can no longer bring it within the realistic limits of his personality. He may — obtusely — try to decompose it into a realism of impersonation, decorated by poetic speech. It is such a treatment of Lear which produces Lamb's old man with a walking-stick, and, for Bradley, dissipates the poetic atmosphere. But what Shakespeare asks of his actor is to surrender as much of himself as he can — much must remain; all that is physical — to this metaphysical power.

The thing is easier to do than to analyse. Children, set to act Shakespeare, will fling themselves innocently at the greatest of the plays; and, just because they do not comprehend and so cannot subdue the characters to their own likeness, they let us see them — though diminished and feeble — as through a clear glass. For the accomplished actor it is not quite so easy. He must comprehend the character, identify himself with it, and then — forget himself in it. Yet in this play and these very scenes he will find the example of Lear's own relation to the storm; in the reflection of its grandeur upon him, and the force lent by his fellowship with it to the storm devouring his mind. One must not push the comparison too far, nor is the psychology of acting a subject to be compassed in a sentence or two. But very much as the storm's strength is added to Lear's when he abandons himself to its apprehension, may the Lear of Shakespeare's poetry and dramatic art be embodied in the actor if he will but do the same. And *there* should be the Lear of Lamb's demand, great 'not in corporal dimension but in intellectual'. Upon a 'realistic' stage the thing cannot be done. With Shakespeare made to delegate half his privileges to scene-painter and property-man a like dissociation will be forced upon the actor. And it is not only that the apparently real heath and hovel and the all but real thunder and lightning will reduce the characters which move among them to mere matter of fact also, but that by the dissociation itself, the appeal to our imagination — upon which all depends — is compromised. For the strength of this lies in its unity and concentration. It is the unity of the appeal that allows Shakespeare to bring so much within its scope. Yet, with time, place and circumstance, night, storm and desolation, and man's capacity to match them in despair all caught into a few lines of poetry, it should not be so hard to absorb besides — he willing — the ego of the actor who speaks them. Then he will stand before us not physically ridiculous by comparison with them, but invested with their radiant quality.

Shakespeare contrives within this harmony the full range of the effects he needs. There are not two Lears — the Titan integrating the storm and the old man breaking under it. In the accommodating realm of dramatic poetry they can remain one. Those contrasted aspects of them are shown in the swift descent we noted from magniloquence to simplicity, from rivalry with the elements to the confession of

> . . . here I stand, your slave;
> A poor, infirm, weak and despis'd old man.

Or there, we may say, are the two Lears in one: the old man pathetic by contrast with the elements, yet terribly great in our still immediate sense of his identity with them.

At best, of course, the actor can be but a token of the ideal Lear; and, thanking him, we may still feel that in the rarefied spaces of our imagination we come unaided nearer to Shakespeare's imaginings — though what have we after all but a token of words upon paper to measure these by? But does the actor only remove us a stage farther from our source? I think not. He gives the words objectivity and life. Shakespeare has provided for his intervention. He can at least be a true token.

The Method of the Dialogue

The dialogue of *King Lear* is remarkable for its combination of freedom and power. Of the plays that neighbour it, the sustained melodies of *Othello* may give greater dignity. In *Macbeth* there are passages that seem to wield a sort of secret sway. *Antony and Cleopatra* has ease and breadth for its normal virtues as *Coriolanus* has strength; and, thereafter, Shakespeare passes to his last period of varied and delightful ease. But the exact combination of qualities that distinguishes the writing of *King Lear* we do not find again; nor indeed should we look to, for it is the product of the matter and the nature of the play. Shakespeare was in nothing a truer artist than in this, that, having mastered his means of expression, journeyed from the rhymed couplets and fantastic prose of *Love's Labour's Lost* to the perfected verse and balanced prose of *Henry V* and the mature comedies, he yet fettered himself in no fixed style. He may write carelessly; here and there amid the poetic splendours we find what seem to be clap-trap couplets and lines flatter than a pancake. But, his imagination once fired, the idea seldom fails of the living vesture it needs. This, it may be said, it is any writer's business to discover. But Shakespeare's art lies in the resource, which can give individual expression to a thought or emotion within the bounds, for instance, of a stretch of formal verse if his first need is for the solid strength of this; or, more often, in the moulding of verse and prose into such variety of expressive form that it is a wonder any unity of effect is kept at all — yet it is. It lies in the daring by which, for a scene or two, he may dispense with all unity of form whatever, if his dramatic purpose will so profit. Witness such a seemingly haphazard mixture of verse, prose, and snatches of song as we find in the scenes between Lear, Kent, Gloucester, the Fool, and Poor Tom. Yet the dramatic vitality of these scenes lies largely in this variety and balance of orchestration; their emotional strain might be intolerable without it. But the root of the matter, of course, is in the imaginative vitality with which he dowers the characters themselves. It is always instructive to watch Shakespeare getting his play with its crew under way, to see him staring his subject, setting his characters in opposition. Some lead off, fully themselves from the start, some seem to hang on his hands, saying what they have to say in sound conventional phrase, some he may leave all but mute, uncertain yet, it would seem, of his own use for them. Not till the whole organism has gathered strength and abounds in a life of its own is the true mastery to be seen. Even so, in *King Lear* there is more to be accounted for. In no other of the plays, I think, unless it be *Macbeth*, are we so conscious of the force of an emotion overriding, often, a character's self-expression, and of a vision of things to which the action itself is but a foreground. And how this and the rest of the play's individuality is made manifest by the form as well as the substance of the dialogue, by the shaping and colour of its verse and prose, it is, of course, of primary importance for producer and actors to observe. There is no one correct way of speaking Shakespeare's verse and prose, for he had no one way of writing it. One way grew out of another with him. Little of the method of *Romeo and Juliet* will be left in *King Lear*, much of the method of *Hamlet* still may be. But the fresh matter of a play will provoke a fresh manner, and its interpretation must be as freshly approached.

For more reasons and in more directions than one, Shakespeare seeks strength in simplicity in the writing of *King Lear.* The noble conventional speech of its beginning will not serve him long, for this is the language of such an authority as Lear discards. There is needed an expression of those fiercer, cruder strengths which come into play when a reign of order ends and a moral code is broken. Edmund begins glibly, but is indulged neither with subtle thought nor fine phrases. Goneril becomes like a woman with a fever in her: 'I'll not endure it . . . I will not speak with him . . . the fault of it I'll answer . . . I'd have it come to question . . . I would breed from hence occasions, and I shall. . . .' Mark how broken is the eloquence of Lear's appeal to Regan; mark the distraction of his

> No, you unnatural hags,
> I will have such revenges on you both
> That all the world shall — I will do such things,
> What they are yet I know not, but they shall be
> The terrors of the earth. You think I'll weep;
> No, I'll not weep:
> I have full cause of weeping, but this heart
> Shall break into a hundred thousand flaws
> Or ere I'll weep.

Here, one would say, is verse reduced to its very elements.

Shakespeare has, besides, to carry us into strange regions of thought and passion, so he must, at the same time, hold us by familiar things. Lear, betrayed and helpless, at an end of his command of self or circumstance, is dramatically set above the tyranny and logic of both by being made one with the storm, and by his harmonizing with the homely fantasies of the Fool and the mad talk of Poor Tom, till his own 'noble anger' breaks the bounds of reason too. Without some anchorage in simplicity, this action and these characters would range so wide that human interpretation could hardly compass them. Kent does something to keep the play's feet firm on the ground; Gloucester a little; the Fool was to Shakespeare's audience a familiar and sympathetic figure. But Lear himself might escape our closer sympathy were it not for his recurrent coming down from the heights to such moments as

> No, I will be the pattern of all patience;
> I will say nothing;

as

> My wits begin to turn.
> Come on, my boy. How dost, my boy? Art cold?
> I am cold myself. Where is this straw, my fellow?

as

> No, I will weep no more. In such a night
> To shut me out! Pour on, I will endure.
> In such a night as this!

or as

> Make no noise, make no noise; draw the curtains; so,
> so, so.
> We'll go to supper i' the morning; so, so, so.

This final stroke, moreover, brings us to the simplest physical actualities; Lear's defiance of the elements has flickered down to a mock pulling of the curtains round his bed. Later, when he wanders witless and alone, his speech is broken into oracular fragments of rhapsody; but the play of thought is upon actuality and his hands are at play all the time with actual things; with the flower (is it?) he takes for a coin, with whatever serves for a bit of cheese, for his gauntlet, his hat, for the challenge thrust under Gloucester's blind eyes. Let us note, too, how one of the finest passages of poetry in the play, Edgar's imaginary tale of Dover cliff, consists of the clearest-cut actualities of description. And when Lear wakes to his right senses again, simplicity is added to simplicity in his feeling the pin's prick, in his remembering not his garments. The tragic beauty of his end is made more beautiful by his call for a looking-glass, his catching at the feather to put on Cordelia's lips, the undoing of the button. These things are the necessary balance to the magniloquence of the play's beginning and to the tragic splendour of the storm.

Amid the sustained magnificence of the first scene we find the first use of an even more simple device, recurrent throughout the play.

> . . . what can you say to draw
> A third more opulent than your sisters? Speak.
> Nothing, my lord.
> Nothing?
> Nothing.
> Nothing will come of nothing; speak again.

Again and again with varying purpose and effect Shakespeare uses this device of reiteration. Note Edmund's

> . . . Why brand they us
> With base? with baseness? bastardy? base, base?
> . . . Well, then
> Legitimate Edgar, I must have your land.
> Our father's love is to the bastard, Edmund,
> As to the legitimate: Fine word, — legitimate!
> Well, my legitimate, if this letter speed,

> And my invention thrive, Edmund the base
> Shall top the legitimate.

The repetition itself does much to drive in on us the insistent malice of the man.

Lear summons Oswald with

> O! you sir, you sir — come you hither, sir.
> Who am I, sir?

and the tragic counterpart of this is

> Hear, Nature, hear! dear goddess, hear.

Gloucester's grieved refrain falls casually enough:

> O, madam, my old heart is crack'd, is crack'd.
> . . . O lady, lady, shame would have it hid.
> . . . I know not, madam, 'tis too bad, too bad.

And for a rounded elaboration of the effect, we have Lear's

> O, reason not the need; our basest beggars
> Are in the poorest thing superfluous:
> Allow not nature more than nature needs,
> Man's life is cheap as beast's. Thou art a lady;
> If only to go warm were gorgeous,
> Why, nature needs not what thou gorgeous wear'st
> Which scarcely keeps thee warm. But, for true need —
> You heavens, give me that patience, patience I need!

Half a dozen other such instances, more or less elaborate, of major and minor importance, can be found; till we come to the effect at its crudest in

> Howl, howl, howl, howl! O, you are men of stones
> . . . and to the daring and magic of
>   Thou'lt come no more.
> Never, never, never, never, never.

It is a simple device indeed, but all mature artists tend to seek strength in simplicity of expression. It is, at its simplest, a very old device, and older than drama. Iteration casts, of itself, a spell upon the listener, and the very sound of that echoing 'Never' can make us sharers in Lear's helplessness and despair. Bradley says of this last speech that it leaves us 'on the topmost peaks of poetry;' and so, surely, it does. Rend it from its context, the claim sounds absurd; but dramatic poetry is never to be judged apart from the action it implies.

King Lear — are we still to think? — cannot be acted. The whole scheme and method of its writing is a contrivance for its effective acting. This contrast and reconciliation of grandeur and simplicity, this setting of vision in terms of actuality, this inarticulate passion which breaks now and again into memorable phrases — does not even the seeming failure of expression give us a sense of the helplessness of humanity pitted against higher powers? All the magnificent art of this is directed to one end; the play's acting in a theatre.

The Characters and their Interplay

Lear

Lear himself is so dominant a figure that the exhaustion of his impetus to action with the play's end barely in sight leaves Shakespeare a heavy task in the rallying of its forces for what is still to do. The argument has been raised by then, moreover, to such imaginative heights that any descent from them — even Lear's own — must be precarious. They are heights that Shakespeare himself, perhaps, did not clearly envisage till the soaring had begun. Not that there is anything tentative in the presentation of Lear. Never was character in play, one exclaims, so fully and immediately, so imminently and overwhelmingly set forth! But in this lies the actor's first difficulty.

With the dividing of the kingdom and Cordelia's rejection the trend of the action is clearly foreshadowed:

> So be my grave my peace, as here I give
> Her father's heart from her.

By all the rules of drama we know within a little what the retribution for that must amount to; and Shakespeare will not disappoint us. But equally it would seem that for this massive fortress of pride which calls itself Lear, for any old man indeed of eighty and upwards, there could be no dramatic course but declension. Who would ever think of developing, of expanding, a character from such overwhelming beginnings? Yet this is what Shakespeare does, and finds a transcendent way to do. So the actor's difficulty is that he must start upon a top note, at what must be pretty well the full physical stretch of his powers, yet have in reserve the means to a greater climax of another sort altogether. It is here, however, that the almost ritual formality of the first scene will help him. The occasion itself, the general subservience to Lear's tyranny (Kent's protest and Cordelia's resolution only emphasize this), Lear's own assertion of kingship as something not far from godhead, all combine to set him so above and apart from the rest that the very isolation will seem strength if the actor takes care to sustain it. There need be, there must be, no descent to petulance. Lear marking the map with his finger might be marking the land itself, so Olympian should he appear. The oath by the sacred radiance of the sun is one that only he may swear. That Kent should call him an 'old man' is in itself a blasphemous outrage.

> Come not between the dragon and his wrath . . . .
> The bow is bent and drawn, make from the shaft . . . .
> Nothing: I have sworn; I am firm.

Lines like these mark the level of Lear, though their fatality may be a trifle mitigated by the human surliness of

> Better thou

Had'st not been born than not to have pleased me better; by the grim humour which lies in

> Nothing will come of nothing: speak again;

in the ironic last fling at Kent of

> Away! By Jupiter,
> *This* shall not be revoked;

and in the bitter gibe to Burgundy:

> When she was dear to us we did hold her so,
> But now her price is fall'n;

even, one would like to suspect, in the reason given for his fast intent to shake all cares of State from him, that he may

> Unburden'd crawl toward death

— for our next sight of his Majesty will show him back from hunting with a most impatient appetite for dinner! Note, too, the hint of another Lear, given us in the music of three short words — the first touch in the play of that peculiar verbal magic Shakespeare could command — when, sated with Goneril's and Regan's flattery, he turns to his Cordelia with

> Now, our joy . . .

But Lear must leave this first scene as he entered it, more a magnificent portent than a man.

He has doffed his kingship; free from its trappings, how the native genius of the man begins to show! It flashes on us as might the last outbursts of some near-extinct volcano. He is old and uncertain; but a mighty man, never a mere tyrant divested of power. He has genius, warped and random genius though it may be, and to madness, as will appear, very near allied. And Shakespeare's art lies in showing us this in nothing he does — for what he does now is foolish — but in every trivial thing that he is, All the action of the scene of the return from hunting, all his surroundings are staged to this end. The swift exchanges with the disguised Kent and their culmination:

> Dost thou know me, fellow?
> No, sir, but you have that in your countenance which
> I would fain call master.
> What's that?
> Authority

— his encounter with the pernickety jack-in-office Oswald, and with the frail, whimsical Fool who mockingly echoes his own passionate whimsies; all this sets off and helps set in motion a new and livelier, a heartier Lear. Not that Shakespeare bates us one jot of the old man's stiff-necked perversities. He no more asks our sympathy on easy terms for him than will Lear yield an inch to Goneril's reasonable requests. A hundred useless knights about the house — even though, from their master's point of view, they were men of choice and rarest parts — must have been a burden. Lear's striking Oswald really was an outrage; after due complaint Goneril would doubtless have reproved his impertinence — for all that she had prompted it! Even with the petted Fool, and in the very midst of the petting, out there snaps

> Take heed, sirrah, the whip!

We need look for no tractable virtues in him.

The play's adopted story has its appointed way to go, but here begins the way of Lear's soul's agony and salvation as Shakespeare is to blaze it. The change in him shows first in the dialogue with the attendant knight and the delicate strokes which inform it. The knight, dispatched to bid that mongrel Oswald come back, returns only to report the fellow's round answer that he would not. 'He would not!' flashes Lear at the unbelievable phrase. But when, picking his words — as, if you were not a Kent (and there had been room at best for but one Kent at Court), no doubt you learned to do with Lear — the knight hints hesitatingly at trouble, the quiet response comes:

Thou but remember'st me of mine own conception: I have perceived a most faint neglect of late; which I have rather blamed as mine own jealous curiosity, than as a very pretence and purpose of unkindness: I will look further into't. But where's my fool? I have not seen him these two days.

Since my young lady's going into France, sir, the fool hath much pined away.

No more of that; I have noted it well. Go you, and tell my daughter I would speak with her. Go you, call hither my fool. O! you sir, you, sir, come you hither, sir!

— this last to the mongrel Oswald who has appeared again. But Lear — can this be the Lear of the play's first scene? — to be turning his knight's 'great abatement of kindness' to 'a most faint neglect,' and' blaming, even so, his own jealous curiosity for noting it! But the Fool's grief for Cordelia he has noted well. Lest it echo too loudly in his proud unhappy heart, with a quick turn he brings the old Lear to his rescue, rasps an order here, an order there, and — takes it out of Oswald.

From now on the picturing of him is lifelike, in that it has all the varied, unexpected, indirect, and latent eloquence of life. Shakespeare is at his deftest, his medium at its freest and most supple. Let the interpreter be alert too. This Lear is as quick on the uptake as it is his Fool's business to be. An unnatural quickness in an old man, is it, and some sign of a toppling brain? His silences are as pregnant. He listens and finds cheer in the Fool's chatter and song, throws him an answer or so to keep it alive, snarls now and then like an old lion if a sting goes too deep. Yet his thoughts, we can tell, are away. We must visualize this scene fully and accurately; the Fool carolling, his poor heart being heavy with Cordelia's loss he carols the more; the old king brooding; and Kent ever watchful, with a dog's eyes. Mark the effect of Goneril's appearance before her father, in purposed, sullen muteness; the Fool's speech points it for us, should we be unobservant; then her break into the prepared formality of verse, as this verse will seem, capping the loose prose of the scene and the Fool's rhyming. Mark, too, the cold kingliness of Lear's four words, all his response to her careful address:

> Are you our daughter?

He resorts to irony, the fine mind's weapon, which blunts itself upon the stupid — for Goneril is stupid, and she has stupidity's stubborn strength. But when the storm of Lear's wrath does break, I think she inwardly shakes a little.

> You strike my people, and your disordered rabble
> Make servants of their betters . . .

sounds like scared bravado. She can wait, though, for the storm to pass; and, for the moment, it does pass in senile self-reproaches. A few more such futile outbursts, she is confident, and the extravagant old tyrant will be spent and tame enough. But, suddenly, the servants are dismissed and she is alone with husband and father. And her father, rigid, transformed, and with slow, calm, dreadful strength, is calling down the gods' worst curse upon her.

> Hear, Nature, hear! dear goddess, hear!
> Suspend thy purpose if thou didst intend
> To make this creature fruitful . . . .

The actor who will rail and rant this famous passage may know his own barnstorming business, but he is no interpreter of Shakespeare. The merely superficial effect of its deadlier quiet, lodged between two whirlwinds of Lear's fury, should be obvious. But its dramatic purpose far out passes that. Not indifferently did Shakespeare make this a pagan play, and deprive its argument of comfortable faith in virtue rewarded, here or hereafter. And it is upon this deliberate invocation of ill that we pass into spiritual darkness. The terror of it moves Albany rather than Goneril, whom, indeed, nothing is ever to move. But as he rouses himself to plead against it Lear is gone.[5]

---

5. The 'Away, away,' is thus spoken to the propitiatory Albany, and has no reference to the servants, who have already been sent off, nor, I think, to Lear's own departure. The point is disputable, no doubt, and I would not go to the stake for my reading of it. The Quartos have 'Go, go, my people' repeated as if his first order had not been obeyed. I must leave it to better judges of their origin and value to say whether this is mere muddlement of text. But, even if it is not, the Folio's change of phrase might cover a change of meaning too.

Now havoc begins in him. We have his raging, distracted return, tears of helpless despair punctuating hysterical threats; later the stamping, muttering impatience of his wait for his horses. We know that he sets out on a long hard ride, dinnerless after his hunting. Later we learn that the journey was wasted; he had to post on to Gloucester's. Did he ride through the night without rest or pause? Shakespeare is hunting both Lear and the play's action hard and using every device to do it.

Yet the next day when he reaches Gloucester's house — this old man past eighty, and physically we should suppose near exhaustion — he is master of himself, is his most regal self again.[6] We are given the scene with Kent awaked in the stocks to show it.

> Ha!
> Makest thou this shame thy pastime?

All the old dignity in this; there follows the brusque familiar give and take which true authority never fears to practise with its dependents; then again the majestic

> Resolve me, with all modest haste, which way
> Thou might'st deserve, or they impose, this usage
> Coming from us.

and the iron self-control in which the shameful tale is heard. When the tale is ended he still stands silent, while the Fool pipes for us an artless mockery (the art of this!) of his bitter and ominous thoughts. Regan too, Regan too! The grief of disillusion has now become physical pain to him,

> O, how this mother swells up toward my heart;
> Hysterica passio! down, thou climbing sorrow.

But he masters it.

> Where is this daughter? . . .
> Follow me not; stay here.

And, solitary in his pride, he goes to face and prove the worst.

If the play, with the invocation of the curse upon Goneril, entered an arena of anarchy and darkness, Lear himself is to pass now from personal grievance to the taking upon him, as great natures may, of the, imagined burden of the whole world's sorrow — and if his nature breaks under it, what wonder! And

6. But the outward signs of exhaustion must begin to be upon him.

Shakespeare brings about this transition from malediction to martyrdom, with great art, by contrivance direct and indirect, by strokes broad and subtle; nor ever — his art in this at its greatest — does he turn his Lear from a man into an ethical proposition. The thing is achieved — as the whole play is achieved — in terms of humanity, and according to the rubric of drama.

Lear comes back with Gloucester; the well-meaning Gloucester, whose timid tact is the one thing least likely to placate him. He is struggling with himself, with the old tyrannic temper, with his new-found knowledge of himself, with his body's growing weakness. He is like a great oak-tree, torn at the roots, blown this way and that. When the half-veiled insolence of Regan's and Cornwall's greeting must, one would think, affront him, a pathetic craving for affection peeps through. When he once more finds refuge in irony, it is to turn the edge of it against himself. But with four quick shocks — his sudden recall of the outrage upon his servant, the sound of a trumpet, the sight of Oswald, the sight of Goneril — he is brought to a stand and to face the realities arrayed against him. The confronting must be made very plain to us. On the one side stand Goneril and Regan and Cornwall in all authority. The perplexed Gloucester hovers a little apart. On the other side is Lear, the Fool at his feet, and his one servant, disarmed, free but a minute, behind him. Things are at their issue. His worst errors, after all, have partaken of nobility; he has scorned policy. He has given himself, helpless, into these carnal hands. He will abide, then, as nobly the fate he has courted. Note the single touch of utter scorn for the cur Cornwall, who, the moment looking likely, takes credit for those stocks.

> I set him there, sir; but his own disorders
> Deserved much less advancement.
>
> You! Did you!

But all consequences he'll abide, even welcome, he'll abjure his curses, run from one ingrate daughter to the other, implore and bargain, till the depth is sounded and he stands at last surrendered, and level in his helplessness and deprivation with the least of his fellowmen.

> *Goneril* Hear me, my lord,
> What need you five-and-twenty, ten, or five

To follow in a house where twice so many
Have a command to tend you?
Regan. What need one?

Lear. O! reason not the need; our basest beggars
Are in the poorest thing superfluous:
Allow not nature more than nature needs,
Man's life is cheap as beast's. . . .
But, for true need —
You heavens, give me that patience, patience I need!
You see me here, you gods, a poor old man
As full of grief as age, wretched in both!

'O! reason not the need . . .'! This abandoning of the struggle and embracing of misfortune is a turning point of the play, a salient moment in the development of Lear's character, and its significance must be marked. He is now at the nadir of his fortunes; the tragic heights are at hand.

It may be thought that by emphasizing so many minor points of stagecraft the great outlines of play and character will be obscured. But while Shakespeare projects greatly, asking from his interpreters a simplicity of response, lending them greatness by virtue of this convention that passes the play's material through the sole crucible of their speech and action, he yet saves them alive, so to speak — not stultified in an attempt to overpass their own powers nor turned to mere mouthpieces of mighty lines — by constant references to the commonplace (we noted more of them in discussing the methods of the dialogue). He invigorates his play's action by keeping its realities upon a battleground where any and every sort of stroke may tell.

Thus there now follows the tense passage in which Goneril, Regan, and Cornwall snuff the impending storm and find good reason for ill-doing. What moralists! Regan with her

O! sir, to wilful men,
The injuries that they themselves procure
Must be their schoolmasters.

Cornwall, with his

Shut up your doors, my lord; 'tis a wild night:
My Regan counsels well; come out of the storm.

This is surely the very voice — though the tones may be harsh — of respectability and common sense? And what a prelude to the 'high engender'd battles' now imminent! Before battle is joined, however, the note of Kent is interposed to keep the play's story going its more pedestrian way and to steady us against the imaginative turmoil pending. This use of Kent is masterly; and, in the storm scenes themselves, the contrasting use of the Fool, feeble, fantastic, pathetic, a foil to Lear, a foil to the storm — what more incongruous sight conceivable than such a piece of court tinsel so drenched and buffeted! — is more than masterly.

But it is upon Lear's own progress that all now centres, upon his passing from that royal defiance of the storm to the welcomed shelter of the hovel. He passes by the road of patience:

> No, I will be the pattern of all patience;
> I will say nothing,

of — be it noted — a thankfulness that he is at last

> . . . a man
> More sinn'd against than sinning,

to the humility of

> My wits begin to turn.
> Come on, my boy. How dost, my boy? Art cold?
> I am cold myself. Where is this straw, my fellow?
> The art of our necessities is strange
> That can make vile things precious. Come, your hovel,

and, a little later yet, mind and body still further strained towards breaking point, to the gentle dignity, when Kent would make way for him — to the more than kingly dignity of

> Prithee, go in thyself: seek thine own ease.
> This tempest will not give me leave to ponder
> On things would hurt me more. But I'll go in:
> In, boy; go first.[7]

Now comes the crowning touch of all:

> I'll pray, and then I'll sleep.

---

7. There are practical reasons for postponing the entering of the hovel by a scene. For Kent to lead Lear elsewhere fits both with the agitated movement of the action and the freedom of Elizabethan stage method. It enables Shakespeare both to relieve the high tension of the storm scenes and to provide for the continuity of the Gloucester-Edmund story. And he takes advantage of all this to show us some further battering at Lear's sanity. Note in particular the ominously broken thoughts and sentences of the end of the speech to Kent just before the hovel is reached; and these, as ominously, are set between connected, reasoned passages.

In the night's bleak exposure he kneels down, like a child at bedtime, to pray.

> Poor naked wretches, wheresoe'er you are,
> That bide the pelting of this pitiless storm,
> How shall your houseless heads and unfed sides,
> Your loop'd and window'd raggedness, defend you
> From seasons such as these? O, I have ta'en
> Too little care of this! Take physic, pomp;
> Expose thyself to feel what wretches feel;
> That thou mayst shake the superflux to them,
> And show the heavens more just.

To this haven of the spirit has he come, the Lear of unbridled power and pride. And how many dramatists, could they have achieved so much, would have been content to leave him here! Those who like their drama rounded and trim might approve of such a finish, which would leave us a play more compassable in performance no doubt. But the wind of a harsher doctrine is blowing through Shakespeare. Criticism, as we have seen, is apt to fix upon the episode of the storm as the height of his attempt and the point of his dramatic defeat; but it is this storm of the mind here beginning upon which he expends skill and imagination most recklessly till inspiration has had its will of him; and the drama of desperate vision ensuing it is hard indeed for actors to reduce to the positive medium of their art — without reducing it to ridicule. The three coming scenes of Lear's madness show us Shakespeare's art at its boldest. They pass beyond the needs of the plot, they belong to a larger synthesis.[8] Yet the means they employ are simple enough; of a kind of absolute simplicity, indeed.

The boldest and simplest is the provision of Poor Tom, that living instance of all rejection. Here, under our eyes, is Lear's new vision of himself.

> What! have his daughters brought him to this pass?
> Could'st thou save nothing? Did'st thou give them all?

Side by side stand the noble old man, and the naked, scarce human wretch.

8. It is worth noting that the Folio cuts out the lunatic trial of Regan and Goneril. Was it, by chance, this episode that Shakespeare's actors failed to make effective, while the scenes of the storm were of no particular difficulty to them?

Is man no more than this? Consider him well. Thou owest the worm no silk, the beast no hide, the sheep no wool, the cat no perfume. Ha! here's three on's are sophisticated; thou art the thing itself; unaccommodated man is no more but such a poor, bare, forked animal as thou art. Off, off, you lendings! Come; unbutton here.

Here is a volume of argument epitomized as only drama can epitomize it, flashed on us by word and action combined. And into this, one might add, has Shakespeare metamorphosed the didactics of those old Moralities which were the infancy of his art.

What! hath your grace no better company?

gasps poor Gloucester, bewailing at once the King's wrongs and his own, as he offers shelter from the storm. But Lear, calmness itself now, will only pace up and down, arm in arm with this refuse of humanity:

Noble philosopher, your company.

— nor will he seek shelter without him. So they reach the outhouse, all of his own castle that Gloucester dare offer. What a group! Kent, sturdy and thrifty of words; Gloucester, tremulous; the bedraggled and exhausted Fool; and Lear, magnificently courteous and deliberate, keeping close company with his gibbering fellow-man.[9]

They are in shelter. Lear is silent; till the Fool — himself never over fitted, we may suppose, in body or mind for the rough and tumble of the world — rallies, as if to celebrate their safety, to a semblance of his old task. Edgar, for his own safety's sake, must play Poor Tom to the life now. Kent has his eyes on his master, watching him — at what new fantastic trick? The old king is setting two joint stools side by side; they are Regan and Goneril, and the Fool and the beggar are to pass judgment upon them.

The lunatic mummery of the trial comes near to something we might call pure drama — as one speaks of pure mathematics or pure music — since it cannot be rendered into other terms than its own. Its effect depends upon the combination of the sound

9. And Kent is unknown to Lear and Edgar to his father, as we shall sufficiently remember.

and meaning of the words and the sight of it being brought to bear as a whole directly upon our sensibility. The sound of the dialogue matters almost more than its meaning. Poor Tom and the Fool chant antiphonally; Kent's deep and kindly tones tell against the higher, agonized, weakening voice of Lear. But the chief significance is in the show. Where Lear, such a short while since, sat in his majesty, there sit the Fool and the outcast, with Kent whom he banished beside them; and he, witless, musters his failing strength to beg Justice upon a joint stool. Was better justice done, the picture ironically asks, when he presided in majesty and sanity and power?

But what, as far as Lear is concerned, is to follow? You cannot continue the development of a character in terms of lunacy — in darkness, illuminated by whatever brilliant flashes of lightning. Nor can a madman well dominate a play's action. From this moment Lear no longer is a motive force; and the needs of the story — the absolute needs of the character — would be fulfilled if, from this exhausted sleep upon the poor bed in the outhouse, he only woke to find Cordelia at his side. But Shakespeare contrives another scene of madness for him, and one which lifts the play's argument to a yet rarer height. It is delayed; and the sense of redundancy is avoided partly by keeping Lear from the stage altogether for a while, a short scene inter posed sufficiently reminding us of him.[10]

His reappearance is preluded — with what consonance! — by the fantastically imaginative episode of Gloucester's fall from the cliff. There also is Edgar, the aura of Poor Tom about him still. Suddenly Lear breaks in upon them.[11] The larger dramatic

10. In the Quarto another preceding scene is also concerned with him.

11. *Mad,* says the stage direction, and no more; the usual *fantastically dressed with wild flowers* is Capel's addition. But something of the sort is justified by Cordelia's speech in the earlier scene. And the dramatic purpose of them is plain: to emphasize the contrast between this and our last sight of him amid the barren wildness of the heath and the storm.
There are signs, it may be noted, that this Gloucester-Lear encounter is a second thought on Shakespeare's part. Apart from its redundance to the action, the Gloucester-Edgar scene is complete without it; and originally, one would guess, Gloucester's

I'll bear . . . henceforth
Affliction till it do cry out itself

value of the ensuing scene can hardly be overrated. For in it, in this encounter between mad Lear and blind Gloucester, the sensual man robbed of his eyes, and the despot, the light of his mind put out, Shakespeare's sublimation of the two old stories is consummated. No moral is preached to us. It is presented as it was when king and beggar fraternized in the storm and beggar and Fool were set on the bench of justice, and we are primarily to *feel* the significance. Yet this does not lack interpretation; less explicit than when Lear, still sane, could read the lesson of the storm, clearer than was the commentary on the mock trial. Edgar sets us an example of sympathetic listening. His asides enforce it, and the last one:

> O matter and impertinency mixed,
> Reason in madness!

will reproach us if we have not understood. The train of fancies fired by the first sight of Gloucester, with its tragically comic

> Ha, Goneril with a white beard!

(Goneril, disguised, pursuing him still!) asks little gloss.

They flattered me like a dog . . . . To say 'Ay' and 'No' to everything I said ! . . . When the rain came to wet me once and the wind to make me chatter, when the thunder would not peace at my bidding, there I found 'em, there I smelt 'em out. Go to, they are not men o' their words; they told me I was everything; 'tis a lie, I am not ague-proof.

Gloucester's dutiful

> Is't not the king?

begins to transform him in those mad eyes. And madness sees a Gloucester there that sanity had known and ignored.

> I pardon that man's life: What was thy cause?
> Adultery?
> Thou shalt not die: die for adultery! No:
> The wren goes to't, and the small gilded fly
> Does lecher in my sight.
> Let copulation thrive; for Gloucester's bastard son
> Was kinder to his father than my daughters
> Got 'tween the lawful sheets.

'Enough, enough!' and die. (lines 75-77)
was followed directly by Edgar's
Well, pray you, father! (line 224)

Gloucester knows better; but how protest that to an erratic voice? Besides which there is only the kindly stranger-peasant near. A slight unconscious turn of the sightless eyes toward him, a simple gesture in response from Edgar, patiently biding his time, will illúminate the irony and the pathos.

Does the mad mind pass logically from this to some uncanny prevision of the ripening of new evil in Regan and Goneril? Had it in its sanity secretly known what lay beneath the moral surface of their lives, so ready to emerge?

> Behold your simpering dame
> Whose face between her forks presageth snow;
> That minces virtue and does shake the head
> To hear of pleasure's name;
> The fitchew, nor the soiled horse, goes to't
> With a more riotous appetite.[12]

But a man — so lunatic logic runs — must free himself from the tyrannies of the flesh if he is to see the world clearly:

> Give me an ounce of civet, good apothecary to sweeten my imagination.

And then a blind man may see the truth of it, so he tells the ruined Gloucester:

> Look with thine ears: see how your justice rails upon yond simple thief. Hark in thine ear : change places, and, handy-dandy, which is the justice, which is the thief? Thou hast seen a farmer's dog bark at a beggar? . . . And the creature run from the cur. There thou might'st behold the great image of authority; a dog's obeyed in office.

It is the picture of the mock trial given words. But with a difference! There is no cry now for vengeance on the wicked. For what are we that we should smite them?

---

12. The (superficial) inappositeness of this passage is quoted now-a-days as evidence of Shakespeare's morbid occupation, about now, with the uncleaner aspects of sex. But it is by no means inapposite to the larger moral scheme of the play. Goneril's lust has become an important factor in the action. Shakespeare cannot give much space to its developments, nor does he care to set the boys acting women to deal directly and elaborately with such matters. So he uses, I think, this queer intuition of the mad mind as a mirror in which the vileness is reflected and dilated.

Thou rascal beadle, hold thy bloody hand!
Why dost thou lash that whore? Strip thine own back;
That hotly lust'st to use her in that kind
For which thou whip'st her. The usurer hangs the cozener.
Through tattered clothes small vices do appear;
Robes and furr'd gowns hide all. Plate sin with gold,
And the strong lance of justice hurtless breaks;
Arm it in rags, a pigmy's straw doth pierce it.

Shakespeare has led Lear to compassion for sin as well as suffering, has led him mad to where he could not hope to lead him sane — to where sound common sense will hardly let us follow him:

None does offend, none, I say, none.

To a deep compassion for mankind itself.

I know thee well enough; thy name is Gloucester;
Thou must be patient; we came crying hither:
Thou know'st the first time that we smell the air
We wawl and cry. I will preach to thee: mark . . . .
When we are born, we cry that we are come
To this great stage of fools.

This after-part of Lear's madness may be redundant, then, to the strict action of the play, but to its larger issues it is most germane. It is perhaps no part of the play that Shakespeare set out to write. The play that he found himself writing would be how much the poorer without it!

The simple perfection of the scene that restores Lear to Cordelia one can leave unsullied by comment. What need of any? Let the producer only note that there is reason in the Folio's stage direction:

Enter Lear in a chair carried by servants.

For when he comes to himself it is to find that he is royally attired and as if seated on his throne again. It is from this throne that he totters to kneel at Cordelia's feet.[13] Note, too, the pain of his response to Kent's

In your own kingdom, sir.
Do not abuse me.

13. Shakespeare kept — and transformed — this piece of business from the old play; for Cordelia kneels, too, of course. It should be given its full value.

Finally, Lear must pass from the scene with all the ceremony due to royalty; not mothered — please! — by Cordelia.

Cordelia found again and again lost, what is left for Lear but to die? But for her loss, however, his own death might seem to us an arbitrary stroke; since the old Lear, we may say, is already dead. Shakespeare, moreover, has transported him beyond all worldly issues. This is, perhaps, why the action of the battle which will seemingly defeat his fortunes is minimized. What does defeat matter to him — or even victory? It is certainly the key to the meaning of the scene which follows. Cordelia, who would 'out-frown false fortune's frown', is ready to face her sisters and to shame them — were there a chance of it! — with the sight of her father's wrongs. But Lear himself has no interest in anything of the sort.

> No, no, no, no! Come let's away to prison
> We two alone will sing like birds i' the cage:
> When thou dost ask me blessing, I'll kneel down,
> And ask of thee forgiveness:[14] so we'll live
> And pray, and sing, and tell old tales and laugh
> At gilded butterflies, and hear poor rogues
> Talk of court news . . . .

He has passed beyond care for revenge or success, beyond even the questioning of rights and wrongs. Better indeed to be oppressed, if so you can be safe from contention. Prison will bring him freedom.

> Upon such sacrifices, my Cordelia,
> The gods themselves throw incense. Have I caught thee?
> He that parts us shall bring a brand from heaven
> And fire us hence like foxes. Wipe thine eyes;
> The good years shall devour them, flesh and fell;
> Ere they shall make us weep; we'll see 'em starve first.

Lear's death, upon one ground or another, is artistically inevitable. Try to imagine his survival; no further argument will be needed. The death of Cordelia has been condemned as a wanton outrage upon our feelings and so as an aesthetic blot upon the play. But the dramatic mind that was working to the tune of

> As flies to wanton boys are we to the gods;

14. That scene in the old play haunted Shakespeare.

They kill us for their sport,

was not likely to be troubled by niceties of sentiment or aesthetics. The main tragic truth about life, to the Shakespeare that wrote *King Lear*, was its capricious cruelty. And what meeter sacrifice to this than Cordelia? Besides, as we have seen, he must provide this new Lear with a tragic determinant, since 'the great rage . . . is kill'd in him', which precipitated catastrophe for the old Lear. And what but Cordelia's loss would suffice?

We have already set Lear's last scene in comparison with his first; it will be worth while to note a little more particularly the likeness and the difference. The same commanding figure; he bears the body of Cordelia as lightly as ever he carried robe, crown and sceptre before. All he has undergone has not so bated his colossal strength but that he could kill her murderer with his bare hands.

. . . I kill'd the slave that was a-hanging thee.
'Tis true, my lords, he did.

— says the officer in answer to their amazed looks. Albany, Edgar, Kent, and the rest stand silent and intent around him; Regan and Goncril are there, silent too. He stands, with the limp body close clasped, glaring blankly at them for a moment. When speech is torn from him, in place of the old kingly rhetoric we have only the horrible, half human

Howl, howl, howl, howl!

Who these are, for all their dignity and martial splendour, for all the respect they show him, he neither knows nor cares. They are men of stone and murderous traitors; though, after a little, through the mist of his suffering, comes a word for Kent. All his world, of power and passion and will, and the wider world of thought over which his mind in its ecstasy had ranged, is narrowed now to Cordelia; and she is dead in his arms.

Here is the clue to the scene; this terrible concentration upon the dead, and upon the unconquerable fact of death. This thing was Cordelia; she was alive, she is dead. Here is human tragedy brought to its simplest terms, fit ending to a tragic play that has seemed to out leap human experience. From power of intellect and will, from the imaginative sweep of madness,

Shakespeare brings Lear to this; to no moralizing nor high thoughts, but just to

> She's gone for ever.
> I know when one is dead and when one lives;
> She's dead as earth. Lend me a looking-glass;
> If that her breath will mist or stain the stone,
> Why, then she lives.

Lacking a glass, he catches at a floating feather. That stirs on her lips; a last mockery. Kent kneels by him to share his grief. Then to the bystanders comes the news of Edmund's death; the business of life goes forward, as it will, and draws attention from him for a moment. But what does he heed? When they turn back to him he has her broken body in his arms again.

> And my poor fool is hang'd. No, no, no life!
> Why should a dog, a horse, a rat, have life,
> And thou no breath at all? Thou'lt come no more,
> Never, never, never, never, never!
> Pray you undo this button; thank you, sir.
> Do you see this? Look on her, look, her lips,
> Look there, look there![15]

---

15. Bradley has an admirable note upon this passage, just such a fine piece of perception as we expect from him. Lear, he says, at the very last, thinks that Cordelia lives, and dies of the joy of it.

6

Direct Self-Explanation[1]

L.L. Schücking

1. The Relations between Actors and Audience

The primitive and popular features of Shakespearian art described in the Introduction have demonstrated the close connexion which existed between the stage and the audience. It is necessary, however, to become quite clear on this point, in order properly to estimate its influence on dramatic technique. We must remember that our illusion in the theatre is entirely different from that of the Elizabethans, as has been excellently shown by Kilian (*Shak Jahrbuch,* 39, p. xiv *seg.*). Our drama is enacted under the tacit agreement that there are no spectators present. Only one wall, that in front of the audience, is wanting to the scene. In, contrast to this, Shakespeare's stage is surrounded by the spectators on three sides. The actor may be said to stand in the midst of the audience; he is always mindful of this while he is acting, and evidently in many cases directly addresses his spectators. Kilian proves how strikingly this relation is evidenced by the monologue, in which the speaker, so to say, fraternizes with the audience, and how the whole dramatic composition and the illusion connected with it may in this manner be absolutely destroyed. It is no longer a monologue in the proper sense — *i.e.,* the expression of an individual who, thinking aloud, renders account of his most intimate thoughts and feelings — but a means which the author uses in order to instruct his audience about the events, or about the plans and character of the personage speaking. Such instruction and explanation is

1. *Character Problems in Shakespeare's Plays* (1922).

further emphasized by the form in which the actor delivering the monologue addresses the audience; *e.g.*, 'And mark how well the sequel hangs together', or 'To say the truth', or 'Mark me now'. Kilian shows how this use of elements which according to our present view contradict the essence of the monologue forms a peculiar feature of Shakespeare's monologues in every period of his art, and most clearly appears in the latest products of his riper years.

2. Self-explanation in Harmony with the Character (Remarks on the Characters of Hamlet, Falstaff, &c.)

In drawing attention to the simplicity of the soliloquizing actor who allows his audience to look behind his mask, we have taken only a partial, though very characteristic, aspect of this technical device. It is not true that the Shakespearian drama shows the traces of a more primitive time only in this one respect, while closely resembling the modern drama in all others. The primitiveness and a certain childishness manifested in the traits with which we have so far become acquainted is apparent, less distinctly, perhaps, but recognizable on closer scrutiny, in the whole mechanism of the Shakespearian drama. All the details of the technique are more harmless, simple, unsophisticated, than we are inclined to imagine. The monologue is not the only and not the most important among the naïve devices used for enlightening the audience. In the course of the play — that is, in the actual dialogue — the characters on the stage supply the audience with the most important information about themselves and reveal the innermost secrets of their nature. In a number of cases, it is true, most people will not regard this practice as a clumsy technical device, but rather look upon it as a tendency of the author to endow his figures with an inclination toward introspection, most probably without any conscious intention of throwing light upon the mental features of his personages for the spectators' benefit. Where this inclination is unobtrusive and incorporated in other similar traits, as, for example, the habit of self-reproach, it will at once escape the suspicion of being merely a primitive and intentional device. Nevertheless, these instances also are worthy of note. A case in point is to be found in *Hamlet*. The great majority of serious critics are agreed on the necessity of conceiving Hamlet not as a man of action, but essentially as a man of reflection. This reflection, however, is not only directed upon the world but also upon himself. The utterances of Hamlet in this latter respect are usually regarded as chiefly characterizing the subjective state of his soul. Indeed, who would take the railings and self-accusations, the insults with which he tries to spur himself to action, the doubts of himself, for Gospel truth? But while taking this view, we must not overlook that in this character too we can discern Shakespeare's tendency to make his figures explain themselves in a manner which must be taken very seriously and which far transcends mere self-accusation and doubt.

A fundamental feature of Hamlet's character is a fanatical sense of truth. The reference to this quality contained in one of Hamlet's first utterances in the play, 'I know not "seems" (I. ii), may be regarded as a necessary product of the situation and a proper and natural detail of the dialogue. This explanation, however, will not hold good in regard to the passage where he mentions his weakness. He describes it by saying that King Claudius is 'no more like my father than I to Hercules' (I. ii). This means that he is the very opposite of the embodiment of bodily strength. Further, when he speaks of 'my weakness and my melancholy' (II. ii, towards the end), these allusions, according to the more or less clearly outlined conceptions which his contemporaries had of the 'melancholy' type of character in the drama, point to a group of qualities not in any way contradictory to those of which he accuses himself in other places. Especially of his ambition he speaks on various occasions, once mentioning it in plain words (III. i. 126), and also later on showing several times that the accession of his uncle had disappointed his hopes (V. ii. 65, &c.). His pride, which he mentions to Ophelia in the same passage, often appears, and who would deny that his behaviour shows some of that vindictiveness of which he accuses himself on the same occasion? This trait too is clearly worked out, especially by contrasting Hamlet with his friend. When he explains to Horatio the clever trick which has helped him to get rid of Rosencrantz and Guildenstern for ever, the good fellow, otherwise accustomed to go with him through thick and thin, is unable to suppress a certain uneasiness, and replies: 'So Guildenstern and Rosencrantz go to't.' Hamlet, almost offended, makes a firm stand against all scruples: 'Why, man, they did make love to this employment'. Whoever allows himself to be employed against him must suffer the consequences; he feels no pity for him, as Polonius also was to find out.

The effect of self-explanation is thoroughly natural in all cases where it is put into the mouth of an introspective character like Hamlet. He strives for truth at any cost, and his state of mind makes it conceivable that in his self-revelation he should not shrink even from cruelty against his own personality. Being so natural and comprehensible, this trait in the Prince's character does not attract any undue attention in this passage. Indeed, there can be no denying that the question as to the respective claims of self-explanation and self-reproach occasionally requires a careful investigation. This trait, however, has evidently become so much second nature to Shakespeare in his dramatic work that he bestows it even upon characters who are anything but fanatical worshippers of truth. This applies to a certain extent even to Falstaff himself. It is true a great part of the comic effect which radiates from this figure is due to the opposite trait, viz., the endeavour of the fat knight to create for himself a character which he does not possess, as, for instance, when he makes himself out to be a hero or succeeds in wrapping himself up in an atmosphere of uprightness which is of only very doubtful quality and is excellently fitted for inducing the kind-hearted hostess to part with her last penny. In case of need, when driven into a position of self-defence, he changes his character as he might do a mask, and on being driven from one cover he immediately finds another just as favourable. The masks, of course, fit him so ill and protect him so little that everybody sees through them at once, and he himself dares only to put them on with a humorous twinkle of his eye. The comic effect is all the greater when the stupidity of Justice Shallow prevents him from recognizing the bad moral disguise and makes him regard the fat knight as an influential lord at Court, or when the hostess, after having been cheated a thousand times, is once more taken in by his protestations.

Falstaff, though his is a character nor at all given to self-analysis, nevertheless finds very shrewd and apt expressions to throw light upon certain sides of his personality and its relation to his environment: 'I am not only witty in myself, but the cause that wit is in other men' (1 *Henry IV,* II. i). These words give the briefest possible formula for the part he has to play in the drama, and clearly describe the category to which he belongs. To be witty himself and to stimulate laughter and wit in others is the business of the clown. Indeed, Falstaff is not principally a swaggerer and blusterer, as certain misguided literary critics would have him be, but is the prince and grand master of all dramatic clowns, and belongs to the dramatic tradition which makes the clown the centre of the comic under-plot in the serious drama. Falstaff's definition of himself also suggests an excellent reason for the magic attraction exerted by the Boar's Head Tavern: he is a witty carouser and boon companion who indulges every one of his whims, and whose humour irresistibly infects his company, calls forth their good spirits, and provides them with an inexhaustible source of merriment by allowing them to use him with impunity as the target of their wit.

The fact that he is old and they are young makes no difference, for — here again his own remark throws light upon the character — 'The truth is,' he says to the Lord Chief Justice, 'I am only old in judgment and understanding' (2 *Henry IV,* I. ii).

This hits the nail on the head. Falstaff, while possessing the soundest experience of old age, is also endowed with the mercurial versatility, the unbounded elasticity, the light-heartedness and power of enjoyment found only in the young man of eighteen who takes no thought of the morrow, and in the blind confidence of youth pays little heed to the consequences of his actions. The old greybeard utters only his most heartfelt conviction when on the occasion of the robbery, whipping up his own courage with violent words, he roars at the frightened travellers, 'What! ye knaves, young men must live' (1 *Henry IV,* II. ii).

The objection may be made that this youth is artificial and owes its origin to drink, the indispensable stimulant to Falstaff's humour. Certainly no actor would give a correct representation of Falstaff who did not use this sort of drunken good-humour as a key to his character. Moreover, the meekness and the cheap compassion for his own condition is that of the old toper. There is a vein of youthfulness in him, however — the hilarious mood of the eighteen-year-old student on the spree, itching for practical jokes. It breaks out when, in an advanced stage of jollity, his riotous imagination prompts him to impersonate the King in a 'comedy extempore', making the armchair his throne, the leaden dagger his sceptre, clapping a 'cushion' on his head for a crown, and mimicking with stilted pomposity and ridiculous affectation of pathos the reproachful father and King.

A similar importance must be attached to the assertions which King Lear makes about himself. All Shakespeare's kings, even his crowned rascals, are surrounded by a certain halo of prestige. Shakespeare's fervent royalism is seen in his preference for one in particular of all the forms of the sentiment of veneration — namely, reverence for superiors and its obverse, princely pride. Pride, in Shakespeare's eyes, is a necessary attribute of the great. In *All's Well that Ends Well* an eminent man is praised for possessing pride without contempt, and although his 'humility' is lauded he is admired because

> who were below him
> He us'd as creatures of another place.

So the idea of 'service' has nothing repugnant to him. 'You have that in your countenance', Kent says to Lear, 'which I would fain call master.' His Lear has a greater endowment of this kind of majesty than any other figure in his plays. For this reason the blows of Fate that inflict such cruel wounds on his pride are infinitely more painful to him than acts of ingratitude and baseness would be to an ordinary mind. But the more his pride is wounded, the more clearly does it show its unconquerable nature; it will perish only with the life of the King himself. Even in his madness this pride remains unshaken. He arises more majestic where others would be in danger of lapsing into ridicule. Thus we may indeed say of Lear, applying the Shakespearian conception of kingliness, that he is 'every inch a king'. This characteristic phrase, again, is uttered by the King *with reference to himself* (IV. vi. 110). The significance of these words is not greatly affected by the fact that they are spoken in a state of madness.

3. Ambiguous Self-explanation (Rascals and Heroes; Julius Caesar)

On proceeding further in our inquiry, we begin to see certain difficulties in the application of this technical device. It must be admitted that this trait, according to our modern conceptions, can be approved only in passages where the action gives warrant for it and where it has no disturbing influence on the characterization. In most cases, however, it will prove unsuitable because of its psychological impossibility or because of the conflict which it produces between the direct and the indirect methods of characterization.

As regards the first difficulty, it would clearly be an absolute self-contradiction if, for instance, anybody were to explain in long-winded speeches, and with great wealth of vocabulary, that he is remarkable for his gift of silence, and it would be equally absurd to endeavour to prove stupidity by a great display of clever arguments, or superficiality[2] by means of heartrending complaints, or to express a matter-of-fact disposition in highly poetical language. Common experience will show that cleverness consists in properly recognizing what is stupid, that nobody can be superficial who suffers from a sense of his own deficiencies, and that beauty of language is a sure sign of artistic talent. Shakespeare's transgressions of this law will be dealt with later on.

The second difficulty may be regarded as almost more important than the first one. In ordinary life an utterance of a person made in order to draw attention to supposedly praiseworthy or reprehensible sides of his character allows us to infer his real character by way of indirect characterization; and we believe we can apply the same kind of reasoning to persons in a play, since we know that to recognize the good or evil in oneself, and even to go so far as to show them in the presence of others, requires special characteristics. Most interpreters following the traditional method have seen no difficulties here. Utterances of criminal personages in which they openly describe

2. Like Browning's Andrea del Sarto, who deeply moves us by confessing that unfortunately his superficial character prevents him from being a good painter!

their deeds as wicked were unquestionably taken for Gospel truth and hardly ever regarded as serving as a means of indirect characterization. Lady Macbeth (I. v), looking at her own behaviour from an outside point of view calls it 'cruelty', and describes her murderous intentions as 'fell'. A man like Iago, for example, terms his own behaviour villainy. ''Tis here, but yet confused', he says, after hatching the devilish plot of destroying Othello, his master; '*Knavery's* plain face is never seen till used' (II. i. *c.* 320). Cloten, in *Cymbeline*, the villain of the piece, quite glibly talks of the villainous orders he has given (III. v. 113). A person who is so little weighed down with the recognition of his own wickedness we usually style a cynic. This appellation might possibly fit a real rascal like Edmund in *King Lear*, who describes himself as 'rough and lecherous' (I. ii. 145). But this would be to regard these matters from an entirely erroneous point of view. This kind of self-characterization should not be considered as in any way an attempt at realism. Wetz (*Die Menschen in Shakespeares Dramen,* p. 184) seriously states that '*Shakespeare's wretches and villains are perfectly clear about the criminal nature or their actions*'. This flatly contradicts the truth of life. A more recent investigator, Wolff, tries to explain this trait by observing that in the Renaissance period people were far more frank and open, whereas 'under the stronger pressure of modern public morality they never abandon their hypocrisy and refuse to lift the mask of dissimulation even in their own private thoughts'. In point of probability we should rank this line of argument about as highly as an attempt to explain the five-legged lions of the Assyrians by asserting that lions with five legs had actually existed at that time, or to account for the primitive drawings of prehistoric men, in which faces are represented in profile, yet having two eyes, by declaring that in those days a man's two eves were both on the same side of his face. The source of the error here is a misconception of the art-form, which itself is primitive. The Assyrians wished the lion to have four legs from whichever side it was looked at. In the drama the villain is to be a villain, the noble character is to appear noble, from whichever side we look at them. This mode of representation has never been true to facts, neither in the Renaissance nor before; in all probability even Cain did not lack a very good reason for killing Abel (though this may not have been, as Byron asserts, his extreme dullness). The reason for this departure from reality is to be looked for in the careful regard which Shakespeare everywhere pays to the limited mental capacity of the public. The poet desires above all to avoid misapprehension of the main outlines of the action and the characters, to prevent the spectators from confusing the ethical values and from taking pleasure in the vices represented and the situations produced by them. In short, the public was an influential factor in determining the art-form.

We have long been accustomed, by a tacit agreement, not to take offence at this aspect of Shakespearian technique, but to regard it as a primitive trait impossible nowadays, and therefore not exposed to misinterpretations. When the villains talk of their villainy we do not on that account consider them as cynics. Numerous critics of *Othello*, for example, find in certain speeches of Iago, in spite of the utterance cited above, an endeavour to palliate his wickedness, a thing which no cynic ever does. This kind of characterization turns out to be entirely traditional. Just in the same way the Jew of Malta, notwithstanding the very special reasons for his action, says of himself, on entering upon his villainous course: 'Now will I show myself to have more of the serpent than the dove; that is, more knave than fool'.

In this inquiry we are too apt to overlook the question that might be raised: What are we to think of utterances just the opposite of these, containing references to praiseworthy qualities? If Shakespeare's art-form is still so imperfect that it does not allow us, as we do nowadays, to interpret the calm description given by a person of his own baseness as a sign of cynicism, are we then forbidden to perceive in self-revelations regarding the possession of valuable moral qualities nothing but conceit, boastfulness, or arrogance? Here we may remember the ghost of Hamlet's father, who thinks himself so superior to his brother Claudius, a person 'whose natural gifts were poor to those of mine' (I. v. 51 *seq.)*. This description in point of fact perfectly agrees with that which Hamlet gives of his father; nevertheless, spoken by the father himself, these words strike us as somewhat self-complacent. Did Shakespeare mean this?

There does not seem to be any sense in thus showing up a weak side in the character of the ghost. Let us further consider the account which Prospero in *The Tempest* gives of himself, how he designates himself as

> the prime duke, being so reputed
> In dignity, and for the liberal arts
> Without a parallel.
>
> (I. ii. 73)

Cordelia, too, in *King Lear* may serve as an illustration. In the exposition she describes herself as wanting

> that glib and oily art
> To speak and purpose not, since *what I well intend,*
> *I'll do't before I speak* . . . .
> . . .[I lack] that *for which I am richer,*
> A still-soliciting eye, and such a tongue
> That I am glad I have not.

Here her air of knowing perfectly well what she is doing in presenting her advantages in their true light strikes a false note in the infinite harmony of her being, so that Kreyssig thinks he can discover a ring of something like 'sauciness' in 'the reply with which the daughter of the old Lear cannot quite disguise her race'. We may regard it as absolutely certain, however, that Shakespeare had not the slightest intention of endowing with any trait of vanity the touching figure of Cordelia, whom we see on other occasions, overpowered by her emotions, standing speechless, unable to articulate a word or even to produce a single sound.

We may also think of Brutus in *Julius Caesar,* a personage much given to self-clearacterization, which, however, is adroitly interwoven with the action. Sometimes we seem to perceive traits in him which make us doubt whether they are intentional or not. It does sound like a boast when he describes himself as 'arm'd so strong in honesty'. It is evident, however, that this was not Shakespeare's intention. He merely overdoes the emphasis in order not to miss being clearly understood; hence the false impression we receive. Brutus acts without any selfish motives — his morality seems even to surpass that of his model in Plutarch — he only follows his duty, obeying that which he calls his 'honour'. He is meant to possess dignity, self-esteem, and well-merited pride. In expressing these qualities, however, he seems to us to transgress the limit which divides self-esteem from vanity and boastfulness. Any other personage might say, for example, that it would be an honour to be slain by Brutus; from his own mouth (V. i. 59) this remark strikes us as in bad taste, and as a sign of arrogance.

The attempt may be made to explain this practice here as due to Shakespeare's opinion that this manner of praising oneself was a Roman custom. There is little ground, however, for this supposition. We find the same trait in other characters who are not Romans; for example, when Henry V, giving audience to the French ambassadors and seeing them hesitate to deliver the arrogant message of their Dauphin, praises his kingly self-command in the words:

> We are no tyrant, but a Christian king,
> Unto whose grace our passion is as subject
> As are our wretches fetter'd in our prisons.
>
> (*Henry V*, I. ii. 241.)

It is just this monarch who proves himself to be anything but a braggart.

A more difficult question is presented by the objection that possibly at that time self-praise was not considered as a moral defect, at least so long as it did not overstep the limits of truth, that the expression of pride in one's own achievements and ability was less hampered by moral restraint than in later times. In that case the dramatist's conception would be true to the life of his time, and ours would be based upon a false, anachronistic conception. One glance, however into the history of the manners of that time, a short perusal of some of those modest speeches with which high functionaries, like the Speakers of Elizabeth's Parliament, entered upon their offices, suffice to show us that here we are no longer in the Homeric age, and that modesty in speaking of one's own person is by no means foreign to Elizabethan times. So we shall probably have to be satisfied with the conclusion that we are here face to face with a mere dramatic tradition, very liable to misinterpretation. On the other hand, Shakespeare may have been influenced in endowing his figures of sovereigns with this trait by the pompous style in which the crowned dignitaries of his as well as of our own time speak of themselves in royal edicts, though no personal qualities are implied here.

All this is much less significant for the characterization of Brutus than of Julius Caesar himself. Caesar is one of those Shakespearian figures who have almost without exception been misunderstood by an anachronistic school of criticism, most flagrantly perhaps by Brandes. In the light of his investigation Shakespeare's Caesar has become a contemptible wretch; he goes so far as to call him a caricature, 'the sum-total of all unpleasant qualities. He makes the impression of an invalid. Stress is laid on his suffering from falling-sickness. He is deaf of one ear. He is no longer in possession of his old vigour. He swoons when the crown is offered to him. He envies Cassius, who is a better swimmer than himself. He is as superstitious as any old crone. He enjoys flattery, talks pompously and haughtily, boasts of his firmness, and is changeable and inconsistent. He acts imprudently, unreasonably, and does not recognize the dangers threatening him, whereas all others see them'. In another passage Brandes calls him puffed up with conceit, always ceremonious, starched, and stilted, and adds that nobody really believes his assertion that he is ignorant of fear. Other critics have further reproached him with being theatrical.

It is undoubtedly true that for a number of these traits evidence can be found in the play. When Caesar, for example (I. ii), asks Antony to touch his wife at the feast of the Lupercal because 'our elders say' that this is a cure for barrenness he shows himself to be superstitious. This trait, however, Shakespeare found in Plutarch, where it is referred to as a common Roman belief, and, reading in the same source of Caesar's belief in omens, he rightly transferred it to Caesar. Moreover, this is one of those small touches which he employs to produce in the drama the true colour of antiquity. Plutarch also tells us of the imperator's epilepsy and headache; Shakespeare converts these diseases into the falling-sickness and deafness of one ear. As regards this last point, we must admit that we cannot explain why he has represented Caesar as deaf. There is no authority either for his description of Caesar's ambiguous attitude towards flattery, and his conviction that he himself is inaccessible to it (MacCallum, p. 223). Brandes' reproach, however, that Caesar is 'always changeable and inconsistent' greatly overshoots the mark. The scene which Brandes chiefly uses to justify this accusation is the one in Plutarch where Caesar, on the morning of his assassination, moved by the prayers of his wife, who is frightened by her dream, has decided not to go to the senate-house, and is induced to change his mind by the cunning interpretation which Decius, one of the conspirators, gives of the dream. It is impossible, however, to infer from this scene that Caesar is inconsistent or timid; only when his wife goes down on her knees to implore him does he yield and abandon his decision. After her fears have been lulled and silenced by the treacherous eloquence of Decius there is no further reason to prevent him from going.[3] The other traits also, with the exception of Caesar's boastfulness, are all in a very similar manner drawn from Plutarch.

The fact that Shakespeare borrowed these traits from his source would not suffice in itself to disprove Brandes' representation. Supposing each of them to be historically correct, their combination might nevertheless be effected in a one sided and biased manner amounting almost to a falsification. By methodically utilizing less sympathetic traits related by Plutarch the figure of Brutus too might have been radically altered. We must ask ourselves, however, what reason Shakespeare could have had for giving such a caricature of Julius Caesar. This would be all the more astonishing as in various passages of his dramas he speaks of him with the greatest respect, and unswervingly follows the well-known tradition which saw in him one of the greatest of men, perhaps *the* greatest of all times. Most Shakespearian critics have answered this question by asserting that he found it advisable not to make Caesar too

3. It may also be that even before yielding to his wife he has been a little unnerved by her terrible anxiety. But the way in which some critics, and especially M.W. MacCallum in his excellent book, *Shakespeare's Roman Plays and their Background* (London, 1910, p. 221 *seq.*), construe a disagreement between this scene and Caesar's declaration in the senate that his resolutions are as unshakable as the polar star strikes one as almost ludicrous. Caesar in no way loses his character by doing his wife a favour which, after all, is very insignificant.

great, as otherwise the conspirators would have appeared too insignificant in comparison. Dramatic necessities, therefore, above all the prominent importance assigned to Brutus, the moral hero of the play, are said to have thrown the figure of Caesar into the background. This explanation has been rejected by Brandes, who saw its unsoundness without himself being able to substitute a better one. He flatly denies the necessity of belittling Caesar, and insists that Shakespeare might have improved the play by representing him as great; indeed, as the conflict is based on a political contrast, the drama could only have been rendered more tragic by the purely human greatness of the person sacrificed. There are thus important dramatic reasons why the limitations to which the part of Caesar is subjected can affect only the amount of space allotted to it and its share in the action, not the human proportions of his personality. We must not lightly suppose that Shakespeare, who knew very well how to represent historical or legendary poetic figures, like Henry V, Cressida, and Cleopatra, of whom his contemporaries had a vivid impression, would have dared to put before them a Julius Caesar whose great qualities had been consciously and purposely suppressed. This being ruled out as quite impossible, why then should such an inflated 'invalid', as Brandes styles him, be shown on the stage in the place of Julius Caesar?

The answer is not difficult. Shakespeare's Caesar, if we refuse to read the drama with the eyes of the critics mentioned above, will appear to us in a very different light. It is true many of the enumerated traits are actually there, but they do not *show* much. That they obtrude so little is due to the impression which we receive of Caesar. His greatness is shown less in his own person than in the enormous influence which he exercises upon his environment. He is the centre of everything. The very first scene shows the town full of jubilation over his triumph, which entices even the artisan from his honest work. His enemies are seen to be possessed by a kind of impotent fury against the gigantic power of that influence which lays the world at his feet. Even the words uttered, with gnashing of teeth, by the most relentless of his enemies, the irreconcilable Cassius, echo the admiration of the whole world:

This man
Is now become a god.
. . . he doth bestride the narrow world
Like a colossus.

(I. ii. 114)

Also the reverence which Brutus feels for him in his soul is boundless: 'We all stand up against the spirit of Caesar' (II, i. 167). They all know, even when killing him, that he is 'the foremost man of all this world' (IV. iii. 22). In this manner an atmosphere is created in which Caesar appears surrounded by a magic light which after his fall adds a still greater lustre to his memory. It is therefore quite absurd to suppose that Shakespeare diminishes the importance of Caesar. Rather must we say that *the vastness of his figure is tacitly or openly presupposed in all the happenings of the play.*

The question now arises whether his demeanour in the play corresponds to the great opinion generally entertained of him. We know that occasionally in Shakespeare's works a contradiction may appear between these two things, as, for example, in the characterization of King Claudius (*vide infra*). But here we can speak only very conditionally of such a contradiction. Caesar is represented as a born ruler of men, an imperious character in every sense of the term. His very first speeches consist of a succession of commands. One after the other Calpurnia, Antony, the procession, the soothsayer, the musicians, &c., are given their orders; even Antony, himself an important personage, is at his beck and call like a schoolboy. When he is furious his entourage, even if a Cicero be among them, look 'like a chidden train' (I. ii. 182), and they dwindle down to the size of mere retainers the moment he shows himself. With unerring penetration he reads their characters; of the lean Cassius especially he expects nothing good. But though he professes to be ignorant of fear he yields to the urgent requests of his wife, who is anxious to keep him at home on that fateful morning until her care is dispelled; nevertheless, he goes out with the conspirators, chatting gaily with them. On his way he encounters the last chance of saving himself in the person of a well-wisher who tries to warn him. But as the conspirators at the same time present him with a petition the attempt to warn him fails, chiefly because of the clumsiness of his friend, who, urged by the fullness of his heart, presses his paper upon him with the remark that it contains a matter touching him personally. This is only a reason, however, for Caesar in his sublime impartiality to defer the perusal until the other matter has been transacted, and he angrily rebukes the petitioner, who, in his anxiety, refuses to obey. No trace of small-mindedness is perceivable in all these actions, nothing that could lower his dignity or be at variance with his greatness. Some of his words, like the famous and profound remark,

> He thinks too much; such men are dangerous,
>
> (I. ii. 192)

bear the stamp of genius. Moreover, his behaviour in the assassination scene does not betray the invalid of Brandes. No cry of fear, no lamentation from his lips, interrupts the terrible catastrophe.

This being the true picture of Caesar, how did the critics come by the impression described above? The reason evidently is that Shakespeare has endowed his hero with a number of small human traits which are indispensable for enlivening the portrait and rendering it truly individual. The excessive reverence in which he is held by all probably assured the dramatist that by making him human he did not risk destroying that impression of greatness on which the whole play rests. Thus he gave him the historically interesting traits of the falling-sickness, of a certain superstition, allowed his mortal enemy sneeringly to relate the story (invented by Shakespeare, but here to be taken as true to the character of Caesar) about his bodily weakness, and made another conspirator remark that he was not inaccessible to flattery. All these details, however, are of little significance. They show him to be human after all, but they do not reduce the gigantic dimensions of his personality. Shakespeare even makes him appear nobler than does Plutarch, who, for example, expressly states that his reasons for not wishing to go to the senate-house on the day of assassination were suspicion and apprehension. In the drama, however, it is only Calpurnia for whose sake he decides to remain at home. Much the same may be said of the coronation scene, which fails in such a curious manner. Here Shakespeare, true to his usual practice, almost exactly reproduces what is related in Plutarch, and thus, in a way, makes him responsible for the psychological probability of the whole occurrence. The importance of this scene, however, is not so great as to merit closer attention.

We have now shown that the traits mentioned are in no way at variance with Caesar's greatness. It would be too much, however, to maintain that they all serve to express it in the best possible manner. We witness none of the deeds which render Caesar immortal, or which only he can perform. To represent them was certainly not Shakespeare's intention, because Caesar's greatness appears sufficiently without them. The play does not treat of the 'famous victories of Julius Caesar', and according to its original plan — it is probable that this external plan is not due to Shakespeare himself, but was taken over by him — it can represent him as crowned with laurel wreaths, but cannot show how these were gained. His *Coriolanus* later on is arranged according to an essentially different plan, and begins by showing the hero engaged in the greatest undertaking of his life, so that we are not required, during the whole succession of scenes, to trust implicitly to the author for the hero's greatness. Coriolanus was unknown to his audience. In the case of Julius Caesar such a procedure was unnecessary; his greatness was proclaimed loudly enough in universal history.

All objections raised against the characterisation of Caesar have now been dealt with and refuted, with one exception. That which remains is apparently the strongest of them all, and the only one which explains our treatment of this whole question in this connexion. It is the opinion that Caesar is drawn as the type of the braggart, a theatrical, bombastic, pompous, puffed-up, conceited, and boastful person. Here we encounter a gross misunderstanding of Shakespeare's art-form which characterizes all Shakespearian criticism of the last hundred years. It is true people of our times who read or hear Caesar's words without having a connected idea of Shakespeare's methods of characterization will undoubtedly receive an unsympathetic impression of the kind just described. Thus, for example, we are astonished by the frequent repetition of his assurance that he is ignorant of fear. Of Cassius he says:

. . . I fear him not:
Yet if my name were liable to fear,
I do not know the man I should avoid
So soon as that spare Cassius . . . .
I rather tell thee what is to be fear'd
Than what I fear, for always I am Caesar.

(I. ii. 195)

He remarks to Calpurnia:

Of all the wonders that I yet have heard,
It seems to me most strange that men should fear;
Seeing that death, a necessary end,
Will come when it will come.

(II. ii. 34)

And again:

. . . danger knows full well
That Caesar is more dangerous than he:
We are two lions litter'd in one day,
And I the elder and more terrible.

(II. ii. 44)

The same high opinion of himself which animates these last words he voices in the lines:

. . . the things that threaten'd me
Ne'er look'd but on my back; when they shall see
The face of Caesar, they are vanished.

(II. ii. 10)

The scene which best shows his self-esteem is that in the Capitol, before his assassination. When Metellus Cimber, according to the arrangement of the conspirators, kneels before him and addresses his entreaties to him, Caesar, without the least suspicion of the danger which is now hanging immediately over his head, indignantly replies:

These couchings and these lowly courtesies,
Might fire the blood of ordinary men,
And turn pre-ordinance and first decree,
Into the law of children. Be not fond,
To think that Caesar bears such rebel blood
That will be thaw'd from the true quality
With that which melteth fools . . . .

(III. i. 36)

Still more clearly he draws a line between the others and himself in the last words which are directed towards the whole body of the conspirators:

> I could be well moved if I were as you;
> If I could pray to move, prayers would move me;
> But I am constant as the northern star,
> Of whose true-fix'd and resting quality
> There is no fellow in the firmament.
> The skies are painted with unnumber'd sparks,
> They are all fire and every one does shine,
> But there's but one in all doth hold his place:
> So in the world; 'tis furnish'd well with men,
> And men are flesh and blood, and apprehensive;
> Yet in the number I do know but one
> That unassailable holds on his rank,
> Unshaked of motion : and that I am he,
> Let me a little show it, even in this. . . .
>
> (III. i. 58)

When the petitioner, regardless of all refusals, once more besieges him with solicitations, he sums up all that he has said of himself, rising to a climax in his angry exclamation :

> Hence! Wilt thou lift up Olympus?
>
> (III. i. 74)

The answer is given by the daggers of the conspirators.

Those are the words on which the accusation against Caesar is founded that he is a puffed-up, theatrical boaster. 'With too much levity of mind and without scruples in his very deficient knowledge of the facts he set out to portray Caesar,' says Brandes, 'and as he made Jeanne d'Arc a witch, he made Caesar a braggart!' We have already indicated that in a modern play this kind of self-contemplation, rising almost to self-worship, could justify this inference. We also know that he who talks so much of his courage generally arouses the suspicion of being a coward.

Against this view, even if for the moment we leave out of consideration Shakespeare's specific kind of dramatic technique, which all this is intended to point out, we must raise the objection that it does not explain how Shakespeare could represent the great Caesar as a vain and cowardly boaster while making the world resound with his praises. For his arrogance, which critics have also found in the lines

> What is now amiss
> That Caesar and his senate must redress?
>
> (III. i. 32)

a passage of Plutarch has been adduced which tells of Caesar's occasionally treating this body with disdain; and for the self-assurance, bordering on conceit, which appears in his words about his sublime position among men a remark made by Suetonius — whom Shakespeare never drew upon — has been held responsible which says that he had declared 'his words should be regarded as laws' (cf. Mich. MacMillan's introduction to the 'Arden' Shakespeare, p. xxv *seq.*). But what is the significance of these scanty data in comparison with the information about Caesar which Shakespeare could gather from Plutarch? Still less importance can we attach to the reference to Caesar (already brushed aside by Brandes) made by Rosalind in *As You Like It,* where in her usual roguish manner she calls the famous 'I came, saw, and overcame' 'Caesar's thrasonical brag', for this remark is, of course, made in a quite jocular sense and connexion. We might as well here throw into the balance the words of good old Falstaff, who, having had a success quite unexpected by himself on the field of battle in capturing a live prisoner, expresses his pride in the words : 'I may justly say with the hook-nosed fellow of Rome : I came, saw, and overcame' (2 *Henry IV,* IV. iii). Further, we shall have to ask why Shakespeare, if he really intended to depict Caesar as a coward or boaster, does not make a single one of the conspirators (who are so eager to discover his weaknesses) utter the slightest word about these qualities. Why does even Cassius, his most deadly enemy, call him a lion (even though he uses this expression only because his hatred makes him regard the others as deer)? Brutus goes so far as to testify, in plain words:

> . . . to speak truth of Caesar
> I have not known when his affections sway'd
> More than his reason.
>
> (II. i. 19)

This, coming from Shakespeare's own mouth, is extraordinary praise, as many parallel passages show.

All these circumstances seem to indicate that we are on the right track in regarding the self-characterization of Julius Caesar as not dissimilar to the other cases in which the dramatic self-explanation bears a much more primitive character than the more advanced sides of Shakespearian art would at first make us inclined to suspect. In these instances we may even see survivals of the primitive conventionalized art, in which the figures have scrolls with the so-called 'legend' ('I am . . .') hanging out of their mouths. In this case there was a special reason for relapsing so signally from a realistic to a conventionalized art-form. The American scholar Ayres[4] has shown that there exists a dramatic tradition in the representation of Julius Caesar which originates from a Caesar-drama in Latin by Muret (1544). In it Caesar is clearly drawn after the figure of the Hercules Œtaeus of Seneca. The vainglorious language is the same in both cases. Muret's example has been followed by the later Caesar-dramas, of which that by the Italian Pescetti (Verona, 1594) contains such striking analogies to Shakespeare's play that a connexion between them by means of a common source is clearly recognizable. We may therefore assume that Shakespeare had before him an older play which also followed the tradition just mentioned, and which made Caesar use the same kind of language. Shakespeare, by accepting it, intermingled with the realism of his representation an alien element, which at least in his case should not be interpreted realistically, for the reasons already adduced. No doubt the information which Caesar gives of himself is meant by Shakespeare to correspond exactly with his real character. It would not surprise us if we heard it uttered by another person about Caesar. It perfectly agrees with what we are told in other passages about the man who has become a god, the 'colossus' who

> should get the start of the majestic world,
> And bear the palm alone.

Evidently, however, there is no intention of charging Caesar with the odium of vanity or vainglory because he says these things. There is as little reason for regarding Caesar as a braggart on account of the praises he applies to himself as there is to style

4. Publications of the Modern Language Assoc of America, xxv (1910), p. 183 sq.

Iago or Cloten in *Cymbeline* (III. v. 113) cynics merely because they talk of their own behaviour as 'knavery' or 'villainy'. Here again we reach the limits of realism and are faced by a dramatic tradition of an unrealistic type similar to that which allows the villain to take the audience into his confidence. At the same time there is no denying that Caesar is meant to show self-esteem and pride. Above all, Shakespeare cannot imagine this great figure without a great measure of pathos in his speeches, the same kind of pathos which is frequently associated in his mind with the idea of classical antiquity. Here it appears in a peculiarity of Caesar's diction in passages which undoubtedly are due to Shakespeare's own invention. He likes to speak of himself in the third person ('Caesar shall forth', and other similar expressions). This circumstance has induced serious students of Shakespeare to regard it as possible that Shakespeare has naïvely followed Caesar's book on the Gallic War, where he always speaks of himself in the third person and calls himself by name. A glance into the historical plays, however, would have been sufficient to show that Shakespeare also makes other great figures, who have not written any historical treatises in the third person, speak of themselves in the same manner whenever they grow pathetic, as, for example, Richard II:

> What must the king do now? Must he submit?
> The king shall do it: must he be deposed?
> The king shall be contented: must he lose
> The name of king?
>
> (III. iii. 143)

Or:

> Long mayst thou live in Richard's seat to sit,
> And soon lie Richard in an earthy pit!
>
> (IV. i. 218[5])

The difference between these cases and that of Caesar is that in him this trait is more strongly emphasized, just as his self-characterization, compared with the instances mentioned above, is more obtrusive. We may perhaps add that from this trait we can infer the manner in which Caesar ought to be

5. Similarly, *King Lear* (I. iv. 276 *seq.*), *Antony and Cleopatra* (IV. xiii. 14 *seq.*), &c.

acted. He is not conceivable without an extraordinary display of pathos. This adherence to tradition can in many cases be secured only by avoiding the realistic style, a departure which would strike us nowadays as highly artificial. But be this as it may, the example shows that if we wish to know how the author himself wants us to understand his characters we must in every case look closely at what they say about themselves, and we ought to take these utterances far more seriously, and see in them a more direct expression of the author's intention, than our modern dramatic technique would allow us to do.

7
'Henry V'
Charles Williams

With *Henry V,* therefore, Shakespeare reached the climax of exterior life; it is at once a conclusion and a beginning. It is not primarily a patriotic play, for the First Chorus knows nothing of patriotism nor of England, but only of a *Muse of fire which would ascend the brightest heaven of invention* by discovering a challenge between mighty monarchies. Patriotism certainly keeps breaking in, but rather like the army itself: the mass behind Henry is dramatically an English mass, and as the play proceeds he becomes more and more an English king. So much must be allowed to the patriots; it is, however, for them to allow that he becomes something else and more as well, and it is in that something more that his peculiar strength lies.

Before defining that, however, and his own words define it, it may be well to remark a few of the differences between *Henry V* and its precedent *Henry IV.* The newer manner of the blank verse itself is accentuated; it gains in speed. Less even than in *Henry IV* are there any involutions or adornments, its movements, like the action of the persons, admit of no delay. It has lost superfluity, though it has not yet gained analysis. No word blurs, but each word does not yet illuminate, as each was to illuminate in that later play of action and vision, *Antony and Cleopatra.* Here it is equivalent to the King's desire and the King's deed and equals the one with the other. But there is, at first, no variation between the King and other characters, as there is variation between the Prince and Hotspur and Falstaff in *Henry IV*: what the King is, he is, and the others are apart from him. In fact, the next differences between the two plays are (i) the omission of Hotspur, and (ii) the omission of Falstaff. It will be said that Hotspur is dead before *Henry TV* ends and Falstaff dies soon after *Henry V* begins. But whatever historical necessity or moral convenience compelled those two deaths, the result is to leave the stage free not only for King Henry himself, but for something else — for the development of the idea of honour. In *Henry IV* honour had been peculiarly the property of Hotspur, and it had seemed like being his property in a narrower sense. He had regarded it almost as if it were something he owned as he owned his armour, something that he could capture and possess.

> By heaven methinks it were an easy leap
> To pluck bright honour from the pale-fac'd moon,
> Or dive into the bottom of the deep,
> Where fathom-line could never touch the ground,
> And pluck up drowned honour by the locks;
> So he that doth redeem her thence might wear
> Without corrival all her dignities:

Against this splendid and egotistical figure is the figure of Falstaff. Up to the last act of *2 Henry IV* the distinction of Falstaff had been that, though he may want a lot for his comfort, he does not need it for his complacency. Hotspur, without a sense of his own honour, feels himself deficient; it is why he rebels. Falstaff, without the same sense, feels himself free; it is why he runs away or fights as circumstances and his own common sense dictate. Henry V might have been made like either of them; in fact, he was made like neither. Neither Hotspur nor Falstaff could suit the Muse of fire or the brightest heaven. Honour must for Henry in his own play be something consonant with that brightness, and that invention discovered a phrase which made honour more than reputation — whether for possession or repudiation.

> And those that leave their valiant bones in France,
> Dying like men, though buried in your dunghills,
> They shall be fam'd; for there the sun shall greet them,
> And draw their honours reeking up to heaven,
> Leaving their earthly parts to choke your clime.

Their bodies are dead; their honours live, but not as fame upon earth. The heaven of invention is to suggest this other heaven; the honour of poetry is to show the honour of the spirit in challenge. It is a little reminiscent of *Lycidas*; where also Fame is transmuted into something pleasing to 'all-judging Jove'. The honours which so live are the spirits and souls of the righteous — anyhow, of the righteous at Agincourt. It is to Henry that the identification is given; it is for him that honour is now a name for man's immortal part. If that venture of war which is the result of the challenge between two great worldly powers, two mighty monarchies, is defeated, this end at least is left to those who carry themselves well in that venture.

As far as the war itself is concerned, the play did not attempt any illusion. It put war 'in the round'. The causes of it are there; dynastic claims are the equivalent of the modern prestige of governments. The force of the verse carries the sincerity of the intention, and the tennis-balls are part of the cause of the war; that is, the other monarchy is also involved. Any insincerity is part of the way of things, but insufficient to cloud the glory of the change. In this sense Shakespeare threw over the diplomatic advice of the King in *Henry IV* as well as the martial egotism of Hotspur.

Besides the causes of war there is, in the first Harfleur scene, what a soldier-poet called 'Joy of Battle'; so, with a horrid faithfulness, in the second Harfleur scene, is the usual result of Joy of Battle. So, finally, in the field before Agincourt, is a kind of summing-up. War is not so very much more dangerous than peace; one is almost as likely to be killed one way as the other. 'Every soldier's duty is the King's, but every subject's soul is his own', which if he keep clean, it does not very much matter whether he lives or dies. Death is not all that important — to Henry (who in the play was going to fight), to the lords, to the army, and, as a consequence, to the citizens of Harfleur. The Duke of Burgundy's oration in the last Act describes all the general advantages of peace, but it does not do more. Peace, as a general thing, is preferable to war, but life is pretty dangerous any way — pretty bloody, in every sense of the word — and a healthy male adult should be prepared for death at any moment. So what does it matter? It is not the modern view, but we are not Elizabethans, and our police are efficient.

Honour then — the capacity to challenge the world and to endure the result of challenge — is the state to be coveted.

> But if it be a sin to covet honour,
> I am the most offending soul alive.

Those lines come from the most famous of Henry's speeches. But there is another and much shorter and less famous speech which throws a stronger light on Henry. There had been a minor crisis — the conspiracy in the Second Act — before the great crisis of Agincourt. But as no one has the least interest in the Lord Scroop of Masham, and as no one can feel the King himself has had time to love him behind the scenes either in *Henry IV* or *Henry V*, the conspiracy fails to excite. We are left to listen to the King being merely vocal. When, however, the central crisis approached, Shakespeare had another way of being equivalent to it. This comes in the English camp by night before the battle, very soon after the greatest thing in the play, the sublime Fourth Chorus. In that Chorus a change had been presented as coming over the whole war. The venture had gone wrong, the challenge delivered to the world of the French had been accepted and that French world had trapped the English army and was on the point of destroying it. At the point of that pause the Fourth Chorus delivers its speech, describing the night, the gloom, and the danger. But its speech, if the words are literally followed, has two futures. The first is Agincourt; the second is the tragedies. There is not only a change in *Henry V*; there is a still darker change away from *Henry V*. The Muse of fire has been ascending her heaven — that is the poetry's own description of what it has been trying to do. But now it directly suggests that it is doing something quite different.

> Now entertain conjecture of a time
> When creeping murmur and the poring dark
> Fills the wide vessel of the universe.

The word 'universe' means, certainly, earth and heaven in that darkness before the battle. But there seems no reason why it should not also mean 'universe' in the accepted sense, the whole world and the whole heaven, including the brightest heaven of poetry with which we began. It is all this which is beginning to be filled with creeping murmur and the poring dark. Poetry and (so to speak) life are being occupied by this universal noise and night. It is not yet so fixed; it is but a guess and a wonder. 'Now entertain conjecture —' It is the prelude to all the plays that were to come.

From poetry thus conceiving of its own probable business, both locally at Agincourt and universally, and its future, two other enlargements follow. One concerns the English army; the other, the King.

The *Muse of Fire* is compelled to behold the army as 'so many horrid ghosts', and the description of the soldiers is that of men who are in the state she has described. It is an army but it is also humanity. To 'sit patiently and inly ruminate the morning's danger' is a situation familiar enough to us in peace as to them in war, if 'danger' also may be given a wider meaning than that of battle. Illness, unemployment, loneliness, these are the things that make sacrifices of 'the poor condemned English', that make them 'pining and pale'. It is among such a host of spectral images of mankind that the King moves, and the Chorus imagines him as their contrast and support : 'the royal captain of this ruined band'. It remains true, however, that the Chorus has to do this without having had, up to that point, much support from the play itself. Henry has been cheerful and efficient and warlike and friendly, but he has not suggested to us his capacity for being an almost supernatural 'little touch of Harry in the night'. The wider and the darker the night, the more that gleam shines. But why?

The cause follows. When the King appears he is speaking, more or less lightly, of the advantages which evil chances bring with them. It is not a particularly original remark, not a moment of 'great insight', and we need not perhaps suppose it is meant to be solemn or serious. It is in the next speech that the sudden difference between Henry and all the rest appears.

> 'Tis good for men to love their present pains
> Upon example; so the spirit is eas'd:
> And when the mind is quicken'd, out of doubt,
> The organs, though defunct and dead before,
> Break up their drowsy grave, and newly move
> With casted slough and fresh legerity.

This is the centre of Henry's capacity. He 'loves' his present pains, and his spirit is therefore eased. He has rather more than accepted darkness, danger, defeat, and death, and loves them. It is this which gives him a new quickening of the mind, new motions of the organs; it destroys sloth and the drowsy grave of usual life. It is this love and the resulting legerity of spirit which enable him to be what the Chorus describe, and what the rest of the Act accentuates.

> Upon his royal face there is no note
> How dread an army hath enrounded him;

how can there be when he loves being enrounded?

> But freshly looks and overbears attaint
> With cheerful semblance and sweet majesty.

It is precisely a description of what he has done within himself. Therefore every wretch 'plucks comfort from his looks', receiving the 'largess universal' from his liberal eye — from the eased spirit, the quickened mind, the moving organs, which are the effect of his love for present pains.

Perhaps this also was something of the explanation of the dead Falstaff; perhaps Henry was more like his old acquaintance than he altogether knew. Only the word 'love' can hardly be used of Falstaff in any sense; it was by no accident or haste that Shakespeare could not show him in more 'love' than the odd possibility of lechery excites. He enjoyed his dilemmas in the sense that he enjoyed being equal to them, but Henry enjoys them because he is careless of them.

There is a distinction, and it lies in the fact that the King's spirit is 'honour' whereas Falstaff's is the rejection of 'honour'. It also lies in the fact that Falstaff does die when he cannot conquer 'the King's unkindness'. If ever Falstaff's spirit was drawn reeking up to heaven, he would only enter it on his own terms, but Henry will enter it on Heaven's terms. It is Falstaff's greatness that we are delighted to feel heaven give way to him; Henry's that we are eased by his giving way to heaven. But the artistic difference is that there is no more to be done in the method of Falstaff — he is complete and final. He can be continually varied and repeated, but he cannot be developed. Henry is complete, but not final. For he, in whose honour there is no self-contradiction, could love his pains simply because there was nothing else to do except run away, and that the same honour forbade. The genius of Shakespeare proceeded, however, immediately to imagine an honour in which self-contradiction did passionately exist; it emerged as Brutus, and was set in front of a power which was more 'monstrous' than that of the French army; he called that monstrosity Caesar, and made another play out of those other conditions, in which the crisis is a more deeply interior thing, and the heaven of honour begins itself to be at odds.

Henry then has made of his crisis an exaltation of his experience; he has become gay. This gaiety — a 'modest' gaiety, to take another adjective from the Chorus — lasts all through the Act. It lightens and saves the speech on ceremony; more especially, it illuminates the speech to Westmoreland. In view of the King's capacity the stress there may well be on the adjective rather than the substantive: 'We few, we *happy* few'. His rejection of all those who have no stomach for the fight, his offer of crowns for convoy, is part of the same delight: so far as possible he will have no one there who does not love to be there. He makes jokes at the expense of the old men's 'tall stories' of the battle, and at the French demand for ransom. Be are clean away from the solemn hero-king, and therefore much more aware of the Harry of the Chorus, and of the thing he is — the 'touch of Harry in the night'. The very last line of that scene — 'how thou pleasest, God, dispose the day' — is not a prayer of resignation but a cry of complete carelessness. What does it matter what *happens*?

It is a legerity of spirit, the last legerity before the tragedies. Hamlet was to have a touch of it, but there is little else, in the greater figures, until, as from beyond a much greater distance, it is renewed by a phrase Kent uses of the Fool in *Lear*. Who, says a Gentleman on the moor, is with the King?

> None but the Fool, who labours to outjest
> His heart-struck injuries.

Henry's injuries are not heart-struck; he is no tragic figure. But he deserves more greatly than has perhaps always been allowed. The Muse, *entertaining conjecture* of a new and dreadful world, conjectured also a touch in the night, the thawing of fear, a royal captain of a ruined band, and conjectured the nature of the power of love and consequent lightness that thrills through the already poring dusk.

'Troilus and Cressida' and 'Hamlet'[1]

Troilus and Cressida has always been a problem. It has the signs of a great play, yet it hardly succeeds in being one; indeed it hardly succeeds in being a play at all. No other of Shakespeare's plays so misses a dramatic, a theatrical, conclusion; it ends indeed with the vague statement, by both armies and individuals, 'Well, we'll all fight again to-morrow'. Its love-concern is left as unconcluded, compared to every other Shakespearian love-affair, as its war, and we know that this was not because Shakespeare minded huddling up his characters in order to end a play. Hortensio and the widow at the beginning of his career, Camillo and Paulina at the end, are examples of this. He might not have been able to deal with Troilus — owing to the tradition — quite as easily, but that he should have desired no rounder ending is inconceivable.

Even the theme of Achilles is left unfinished. The policy of Ulysses, by which Achilles was to be brought from his tent into the field, produces no result: he has only succeeded in making Ajax as proud as Achilles, who himself — in spite of Ulysses' medicinal treatment — does not emerge until the death of Patroclus. So, as Thersites says, 'policy grows into an ill-opinion'.

These three themes of the play then are abandoned just as the fight between Ajax and Hector is abandoned. But the abandonment is not only on the side of action, but of intellect also.

Troilus and Cressida differs positively from the other plays in this — that there are here two full-dress debates which are not paralleled elsewhere. There are discussions elsewhere, some shorter, some longer; there are the King and his lords in *Love's Labour's Lost* who talk of what had better be done about their vows to study; and King Henry V's consultation of the Archbishop about his invasion of France, and so on. But none of these have, to anything like the same extent, the serious intellectual argument of the two *Troilus* debates. The first is the discussion between the Greek generals about the unfortunate position of the war. It is interesting because the first 54 lines are an example of Shakespeare's wonderful capacity for saying

1. *The English Poetic Mind* (1932).

nothing particular at great length — and saying it superbly. Agamemnon opens by saying:

1. Every earthly design falls short of what was hoped.
2. Checks occur in everything.
3. Every action fails to carry out the original intention.
4. These things are sent to try us.
5. They show us what men are made of.
6. We find out by these difficulties which men are really capable of perseverance.

This takes him 30 lines. Nestor then adds:

1. When things go smoothly everybody is happy.
2. But in dark hours we discover who has pluck and who has not.

This takes him 24 lines.

The second debate takes place between the princes of Troy on the Greek proposal (of which nobody up to then has heard a word) that, if the Trojans will give up Helen, the war shall be concluded, without any indemnities or annexations. There ensues then — a thing unique in Shakespeare — a two-hundred line discussion which passes from Helen to an abstract question: What exactly *is* value?

Hect. Brother, she is not worth what she doth cost The holding.

Tro. What is aught but as 'tis valued?

Hect. But value dwells not in particular will;

It holds his estimate and dignity
As well wherein 'tis precious of itself
As in the prizer. 'Tis mad idolatry
To make the service greater than the god.

Here, if anywhere, here, with really good arguments being exchanged, with a philosophic basis and a particular topical example to illuminate it, here we might expect the Shakespeare of whom we heard so much in our youth — the teacher, the philosopher, the sage — to solve for us one of our profoundest problems. How are we to value things? What principle of relativity ought to govern our actions? Shakespeare sets the two arguments, each with its full emotional vitality, against each other, and then causes the protagonist of one side to throw up his whole case. Hector has throughout been insisting that Helen ought to be given up; at the end of the scene we find, not only that he does not intend to act on his own belief, but that he never has intended to act upon it.

> Let Helen go . . .
> What merit's in that reason which denies
> The yielding of her up?
> If Helen then be wife to Sparta's king,
> As it is known she is, these moral laws
> Of nature and of nations speak aloud
> To have her back return'd: thus to persist
> In doing wrong extenuates not wrong,
> But makes it much more heavy. Hector's opinion
> Is thus, in way of truth: yet, ne'ertheless,
> My spritely brethren, I propend to you
> In resolution to keep Helen still;
> I have a roisting challenge sent amongst
> The dull and factious nobles of the Greeks
> Will strike amazement to their drowsy spirits.
> I was advertised their great general slept
> Whilst emulation in the army crept:
> This, I presume, will wake him.

And we are not meant to blame Hector for this; he is not presented as a blameworthy character. It might be argued that his own desire for personal glory is to be supposed to overcome his intellectual beliefs; but in that case, with a consciousness so developed as is Hector's, so vivid and complex a mind, we might reasonably expect to see something of an interior conflict. He shows no hesitation at all at his inconsistency. But as a result of this inconsistency of course the whole discussion stops — 'their unanimity is wonderful'. The intellectual arguments then are abandoned — as intellectual arguments — precisely as the action — as action — is abandoned. The whole play is full of this sense of things being left 'in the air'.

It is an old observation, again, that *Troilus* possesses an unusually Latinized vocabulary, sometimes used with an awkwardness which is unlike the normal Shakespeare and at times becomes almost funny. For the most striking examples—

> Checks and disasters
> Grow in the veins of actions highest rear'd,
> As knots, by the conflux of meeting sap,
> Infect the sound pine and divert his grain
> Tortive and errant from his course of growth.
> Why then, you princes,
> Do you with cheeks abash'd behold our works,
> And call them shames? Which are indeed nought else
> But the protractive trials of great Jove
> To find persistive constancy in men.
> 'Tis mad idolatry
> To make the service greater than the god;
> And the will dotes that is inclinable
> To what infectiously itself affects,
> Without some image of the affected merit.
> But I attest the gods, your full consent
> Gave wings to my propension and cut off
> All fears attending on so dire a project:
> For what, alas, can these my single arms?
> What propugnation is in one man's valour, . . .
> Sith yet there is a credence in my heart,
> An esperance so obstinately strong,
> That doth invert the attest of eyes and ears,
> As if those organs had deceptions functions,
> Created only to calumniate.

The voices of these characters labour with an unaccustomed trouble; their learned minds choose words with difficulty, instead of their high passion choosing their words for them. They have a speciously intellectual vocabulary, they toil at defining themselves in terms of the mind. Their subtleties are subtleties of argument; they lack the consummation of essential being.

Or almost lack it. For this play, full of abandoned action and arguments, yet contains one of the very greatest achieving lines in all Shakespeare, and one of the most splendid and complex speeches. It contains one of those moments where the poetry of human experience is as sublimely itself as ever before or after. Speech and line both occur in v. ii, after Troilus has become aware of Cressida's mutability. He is changed; and that change is not only in him, it is paralleled and expressed by a change in Shakespeare's own manner. Troilus, like Wordsworth, undergoes an entire subversion of his whole experience — he is given up to 'a conflict of sensations without name'.

To that conflict Shakespeare devoted a speech; but he expressed it also in a line. And that line is no longer an intellectual statement, however thrilling, or a beautiful reverie, however moving — it is a synthesis of experience, an achievement of a style, the style for which *Troilus and Cressida* had been looking.

The crisis which Troilus endured is one common to all men; it is in a sense the only interior crisis worth talking about. It is that in which every nerve of the body, every consciousness of the mind, shrieks that something cannot be. Only it is.

Cressida *cannot* be playing with Diomed. But she is. The Queen *cannot* have married Claudius. But she has. Desdemona *cannot* love Cassio. But she does. Daughters *cannot* hate their father and benefactor. But they do. The British Government *cannot* have declared war on the Revolution. But it has. The whole being of the victim denies the fact; the fact outrages his whole being. This is indeed change, and it was this change with which Shakespeare's genius was concerned.

> This she? no, this is Diomed's Cressida.
> If beauty have a soul, this is not she;
> If souls guide vows, if vows be sanctimony,
> If sanctimony be the gods' delight,
> If there be rule in unity itself,
> This is not she. O madness of discourse,
> That cause sets up with and against itself;
> Bi-fold authority! where reason can revolt
> Without perdition, and loss assume all reason
> Without revolt: this is, and is not, Cressid.
> Within my soul there doth conduce a fight
> Of this strange nature, that a thing inseparate
> Divides more wider than the sky and earth;
> And yet the spacious breadth of this division
> Admits no orifice for a point as subtle
> As Ariachne's broken woof to enter.
> Instance, O instance! strong as Pluto's gates;
> Cressid is mine, tied with the bonds of heaven:
> Instance, O instance! strong as heaven itself;
> The bonds of heaven are slipp'd, dissolv'd and loos'd;
> And with another knot, five-finger-tied,

> The fractions of her faith, orts of her love,
> The fragments, scraps, the bits, and greasy reliques
> Of her o'er-eaten faith, are bound to Diomed.

Troilus sways between two worlds. His reason, without ceasing to be reason, tells him that this appearance of Cressida is not true; yet his loss is reasonable and cannot protest because this is the nature of things. Entire union and absolute division are experienced at once : heaven and the bonds of heaven are at odds. All this is in his speech, but it is also in one line. There is a world where our mothers are unsoiled and Cressida is his; there is a world where our mothers are soiled and Cressida is given to Diomed. What connexion have those two worlds?

> Nothing at all, unless that this were she.

This is the 'inseparate thing' at a distance from which the earlier debates took place. Agamemnon and Nestor had made orations about the disappointments of life, the failure of 'the ample proposition that hope makes', and the need of courage and patience. Ulysses had answered by pointing out that degree and order were being lost, and had described what happens when degree is lost. It was all very wise, very noble, talk. But in Troilus the thing has happened : the plagues, portents, and mutinies have begun to 'divert and crack, rend and deracinate' his being. Order is wholly lost —

> Take but degree away, untune that string,
> And, hark! what discord follows.
> If there be rule in unity itself,
> This is not she. O madness of discourse,
> That cause sets up with and against itself.

The Grecian princes were in dismay and grief — 'what grief hath set the jaundice on your cheeks?' But Troilus, had Hector asked him a similar question, might have answered with Wordsworth

> Grief call it not — ['tis] anything but that,
> A conflict of sensations without name.

The conflict is recognized 'with glory not its own' in Troilus' single line.

It might be too much to say that the line is the first place in which that special kind of greatness occurs in Shakespeare; but it is, I think, true to say that never before in his work had such complexity of experience been fashioned into such a full and final line. It is his power entering into a new freedom.

But this freedom is of another kind from the general behaviour of his poetry in *Troilus*. The importance of *Troilus* is that we have Shakespeare's genius, as it were, compelling itself to look for a way of doing things, trying out one way and finding another. It has been said that he was, in parts of Troilus, trying to write as Chapman sometimes wrote. But *why* was he trying for this, if indeed he was? Because he was trying to press deeper and deeper into the complexities of experience, and because at first he tried to do it by a philosophical vocabulary, by intellectual summary, by argument. He came near to making 'long orations'; he passed — at a distance, but he passed — the place where

> opinions every day
> Grow into consequence, till round my mind
> They clung, as if they were its life, nay more,
> The very being of the immortal soul.
>
> [*Prelude,* xi. 219]

The dispute of value is a real and intense dispute, yet it is abruptly abandoned — not so much by Hector as by Shakespeare making use of Hector. It is not there that he must dwell, in the councils of the philosophers. This is not to be his poetry; a greater thing awaits him, a thing he has not yet fully attempted — change in the soul of man. His genius itself changed; it began to create lines so profound and intense that they cannot be analysed.

> Nothing at all, unless that this were she —

that he analysed himself. But that was the forerunner of other lines, unanalysable —

> She should have died hereafter.
> It is the cause, it is the cause, my soul.

On those lines there is perhaps no better comment than his own: they admit

> no orifice for a point as subtle
> As Ariachne's broken woof to enter.

If we take another 'problem' play we find a different but related effort.

Measure for Measure, as a play, is not a collapse as *Troilus* was, but neither is it a completeness as *Othello* was to be. It has a beginning, a middle, and an end: only they all belong to different ways of writing *Measure for Measure*. We can recognize in the middle the play of which we heard the beginning; and in the end both that and the play of which we heard the middle. The end is perhaps the least effective — it has less poetry in it than the other parts, but as it is the only end we have we must do our best with it. Isabella is a little badly treated by losing her proper place, but then Angelo loses an entire three-fifths of his play, so she did in fact have her revenge on him. So did Claudio, who, in the middle, occupies Angelo's place, and the topmost peak of poetry in the play.

Yet if one could give up that death-speech for anything, and still more the whole scene of confronting persons and values in which it occurs, it would be for a greater knowledge of Angelo. It is the cessation of all concern with him that makes the play so unsatisfactory. Why — with what poetry — did he determine to have Claudio executed? How — in what poetry — did he find himself when Mariana left him? It is true he has one speech (IV. iv) summing up both, but we could have done with much more. It was not to be, Shakespeare had moved away from the contrast between the untempted Isabella and the tempted Angelo to the contrast between the still-untempted Isabella and the tempted Claudio. It is this failure of temptation even to tempt her that makes the concluding threat of marriage from the Duke so unsatisfactory. What! she whose inviolable will desired strict rules in the convent and accepted the strict laws of Verona, and denied Angelo's fair promises and Claudio's anguish, she to fall to a couple of lines from the Duke? 'It cannot be; it is impossible.' Her entreaty for Angelo's life shows no lessening of her own imperious self-possession. Shakespeare might have persuaded us of a change in her no doubt; the fact remains that he did not. After the Claudio scene the poetry falls away into ordinary business, and indeed is often exchanged for prose. The mere operations of the play conclude crises originally proposed in poetry. It is for this reason that Mariana — attractive enough in herself — is, for the play, unconvincing. No one, I suppose, is ever quite certain that Angelo treated her as badly as she and the

Duke make out. For the intense conflict between Angelo's real austerity and real lust, the precise fact that it does need nothing less than 'a thing enskied and sainted' to cause his fall, removes him into a world where beliefs concerning him must be of that same poetic nature. They must conform to his poetic greatness, and this the statements concerning him hardly do.

I am a little inclined therefore to suggest that in *Measure for Measure* Shakespeare again half-tried a method which he abandoned. The three great scenes are not, certainly, arguments in the sense of the debates in *Troilus*. But they are certainly combats of values in a manner in which there is nothing in the following tragedies. The very fact that Isabella is *not* tempted leaves those combats undecided. She and Angelo part with their conflict unresolved, and it is more than a personal struggle — it is ethical. We do not merely think 'Will she give way?' We think 'Ought she to give way?' There was certainly no need for Shakespeare to decide; the important thing is that he never so clearly raised such a question again. One may think about Othello, Lear, Macbeth, 'O he's going to — do so and so'; even 'Will he — ?' But never 'He ought not to kill his wife', or what not.

Measure for Measure, then, remains poetically, like *Troilus*, an abandoned play. There may be every kind of noble lesson in it, but they have not been discovered by poetry. After it we are no more allowed to say 'What principle should govern man?'; we are to be permitted only to find out how much man can endure and still live. Othello *is* tempted and falls; and we follow him to the end.

As for *All's Well*, it seems to matter less than any. It is more of a play than *Troilus*, for it has an ending. But Shakespeare's genius does not seem to be engaged; Diana's gaiety at the end is a tiresome brightness, and even Helena depends for her praise rather on what other people say than on what she shows us. The Countess is a little too quick to contemplate her son's execution. In short, everything — poetry and characters and plot (even this!) — is a little below the Shakespearian par. But there is one great phrase in it, spoken by Parolles after his open disgrace —

> Simply the thing I am
> shall make me live.

That phrase looks forward to the future: it is the key to Shakespeare's latest poetry.

I return to *Hamlet*. There has been argument whether Hamlet does actually delay to kill Claudius and if so why. The ghost of Kyd and the ghost of Coleridge have been invoked to explain it. In fact, the only explanations of the delay (if it takes place) which I do not remember to have seen given are two : (1) that the Ghost of Hamlet's father knew his son's nature perfectly well, and intended Claudius to be, not directly killed but, worried out of his mind by having Hamlet's gloomy and threatening figure continually about him. A reproduction of the Ghost's own purgatory round Claudius would be, one would think, a much more satisfying revenge than mere straightforward death; and in support of this view we have Hamlet's dim realization of it in the prayer-scene. The Ghost, after all, must have known how Hamlet would be likely to behave, and it is possible that we have missed the point of the whole play by our failure to attribute sufficient intelligence to that paternal and intimate spectre.

If we abandon this explanation as too (what people call) flippant, there is a more serious possibility, and at is (2) that Shakespeare was not then capable of making Hamlet act, that the development of his genius ad reached precisely the point where it was intensely aware of man's distracted mind, of its own divided mind, and was not able to solve the problem. In short, that it is Shakespeare, and not Hamlet, who is seeking the springs of action, and he rather than the prince who therefore here delays.

He made this delay interesting and exciting. It was part of his greatness that he could, when he chose, make anything interesting and exciting. Whatever state his poetic mind was in, that was the state which he could present to us by thrilling words in the mouths of persuasive characters. But the fact that *Hamlet* is wonderful, and that Hamlet is attractive and repellent at once, does not alter the other fact that most poets are at most times trying to get at something a little beyond their reach, at 'something evermore about to be'. This, in a sense, was Shakespeare's state up to *Troilus* — up even to *Coriolanus*; he is in a continual condition of progress. 'The hiding-places of man's power' are not yet entirely open to him.

Whether — in the circumstances of the play — Hamlet does actually delay may admit of argument. But his continual self-accusations at least persuade most readers and spectators that he does. We are, of course, in a difficulty here; the play has been and is continually presented from Hamlet's point of view. If, for once, it could be shown us from the King's, it might make a difference. If, in that second scene, the dark and ominous figure poised beside the throne; if that first line breaking out in a suppressed savage hatred, making its dreadful half-jeer —'a little more than kin and less than kind'; if the continual danger of the enmity which a pretended dementia (Claudius sees through it) is meant to disguise; if that suppressed savagery and pretended dementia creating almost a real madness; if the bitter stabbing at Ophelia, his mother, and himself — if these things were stressed in their dreadfulness, we might be aware of more danger and less delay. This Hamlet would be quite as much Shakespeare's, if less traditionally theatrical. But I think such a production has not yet been given us, and we are therefore still under the effect of Hamlet's own statements about himself. And Hamlet's view is that he *is* continually delaying, unpacking his heart with words.

His own view, his own kind of consciousness, does not change at least until the last act. He is throughout in very much the state that Troilus was to find himself in after he had seen Cressida with Diomed : the world is executing an appalling outrage on his whole being. But he neither analyses his state of mind with such intense exactitude as Troilus was to do, nor can he discover within himself the initiative to action. He knows he has it, he sees it, he talks to himself about it. But seeing it is not the same thing as getting it to work. He can act as well as Troilus and in the same way when circumstances force him — Polonius, the death-warrant, the pirates, Laertes, the death-scene; just as Troilus makes use of the Trojan war to relieve his private feelings. But action from within, action of his own will, is beyond him. Yes, but Hamlet is, after all, a figure in a play. To say that he cannot discover within himself the initiative of action is to say that Shakespeare could not or would not discover it for him. Is it too much to say that Shakespeare would not because he could not? That he made *Hamlet* because he himself was trying to reach by his genius a poetic comprehension of the place where men act? I should be perfectly prepared even to accept the view that when Shakespeare began *Hamlet* he might have intended to make him kill the King much more adequately, that it was to be practical and not psychological difficulties which got in his way. We know — no the testimony of every popular novelist — that the characters of a book insist on acting 'on their own'; they will have their own way despite the author. This must make the writing of books very difficult, and the ending of novels almost impossible, since one would think no character would be willing to commit the happy dispatch. There is, nevertheless, a certain truth in this cheap chatter, and the truth is that a work may, in the working, become a very different thing from the original intention. It is certainly not beyond possibility that Shakespeare whose habit of arranging his plays seems often to have been casual enough, should have written *Hamlet* with a continual hope of 'something coming off — 'effort and expectation and desire', to put it Wordsworthianly : that Hamlet's character formed itself as his creator found himself continually disappointed in the effort to find the 'right convincing word'. It sounds an idiotic suggestion, but is it quite impossible that the 'To be or not to be' speech might arise from just this uncertainty? Of course it is Hamlet's and refers to Hamlet. But it is Shakespeare's; might it not unconsciously refer to Shakespeare? 'To be or not to be' — do we kill the King or don't we? It has been suggested that the speech in Hamlet's mouth does refer not to suicide but to killing the King. It is at any rate just possible that Shakespeare began the speech in this sense, and as he worked at it found it more and more impossible to find out the very words in which Hamlet should reach determination, more and more necessary to substitute for a discovery of action a discovery of inaction. It is just possible that this speech is the turning-point of the play.[2]

There had been an uncertain touch in shaping Brutus's own personal certainty; there was now a certain touch in shaping Hamlet's uncertainty. The whole combination of style and subject had slightly shifted. And what this shifting unity demanded, what the poetry that was at once its cause and its

2. Though the scene where Claudius is praying is almost exactly Shakespeare saying, 'I can't think what words the fellow would do it with. So he can't do it.'

result had to find first, was a more intense knowledge of the outraged heart of man, was (in fact) Troilus.

But it may be that Shakespeare deliberately determined to present the Coleridgian Hamlet. But still he must *then* have determined — his genius for poetry must have determined — that for a reason. I submit that the reason brings us back to the same place: he chose to work at a man who did not act (or said he didn't) rather than at a man who did. I submit that he possibly chose that subject because he felt safer with it, more competent to discover it. And (lastly) I submit that this means that his genius preferred to deal with a man looking for initiative rather than possessing initiative because it had not yet the 'liberty and power' to discover killing in poetry.

There is a perfectly definite progression in the presentation of the spiritual act of killing in the plays. In the old happy days when the villain came on at the beginning, and in a burst of magnificent stuff announced that he was 'determined to prove a villain', the thing was easy. Richard III, having need of a murderer, calls to the nearest page and asks if he knows any one whom gold 'will tempt unto a close exploit of death'. The page fortunately does, immediately calls him in, and the whole matter is settled with the utmost celerity and convenience. By *King John* matters had altered a little, and Shakespeare had got as far as to subdue the proposal to the two phrases dropped in Hubert's ear, 'Death' . . . 'a grave'. The assassination of Caesar is partly taken out of the realm of individual motives and made a high matter of state. Even Cassius is moved by public as well as private feelings, and Brutus, of course, acts on the noblest possible principles throughout, with his usual complete sympathy with, and entire disregard of, other people. But, after Hamlet, killing is a very different matter. It is forced on Othello as a result of his own completely changed consciousness; it is raised in Macbeth to become an act of the soul. The mysterious 'Third Murderer' who appears from nowhere, with no preparation, whose utterances only make the killing of Banquo more certain and easy, is the climax of murder in Shakespeare : he is murder itself. He has been taken for Macbeth or merely another ruffian, but the poetic strength of *Macbeth* makes him more than that. He seems to be kindred to the Witches and more than the Witches, to come from another world merely to make damnation sure.

Macbeth himself is rather like Hamlet, a private individual to whom the possibility of killing is presented. As a poetic problem the question of right or wrong does not enter; that the Ghost is 'good' and the Witches 'evil' makes no difference to the difficulty of showing forth the setting in motion of the human will. It is at least partly achieved in the later play by the presentation of it as an act already done — 'All hail, Macbeth! that shalt be king hereafter.' But nobody — not Horatio, not the Ghost, not Shakespeare — helps Hamlet in that way : he is left to find his own impulse of action.

Action, after all, is a very difficult thing. The normal acts of our lives are either habitual or compulsory. Either we act as we are used to act or circumstances compel us to some unaccustomed act. The extreme of our choice is to do or to refrain, but the deed is usually a mere variation on our ordinary deeds. After our first youth hardly anything is strange. Take forgery, take arson — the mere acts of writing, of lighting a fire are habitual; it is our knowledge of the result and of civil law that makes the variation. They injure others to our gain; it is an idea to which we are perfectly accustomed and perfectly agreeable. But the finality of killing, the strangeness of the act of killing, impose on us the need for a deeper impulse, an impulse which normally demands intensely vivid circumstances before it can be set in motion, and an intense profit to ourselves from the deed. Of the forgery of the death-warrant for Rosencrantz and Guildenstern we might all be capable. But the necessity laid on Hamlet is even heavier; it is to find out a way to act where his own profit is not concerned — it is literally to act disinterestedly, from free will.

Such a discovery — the presentation of such a discovery, of such a method of action, perhaps it is not in the power of man to make. But that the genius of Shakespeare was searching, if not as deeply as that (which may be only within the knowledge of sanctity), at least all but as deeply, appears certain. It was trying to find out — and in poetry to find out is to express, because expression is its only way of finding out — the springs of human action, which are the springs of change. Hamlet, more than most of Shakespeare's characters up to then, is shown us as being aware of a changed world; but we are not shown the change in his own awareness. It has happened before the play begins and it is not recalled. Ophelia remembers some other Hamlet, but perhaps Ophelia is not the most trustworthy witness. In any case, the event of the actual change is not presented to us; for that we have to wait for *Troilus*.

It is arguable that a certain acquiescence is to be felt in the last act; it is on the last act that a great deal of our 'sympathetic' Hamlet depends. But he has rather entered the shadow of death than emerged from the shadow of life. His last private utterance — the last words to Horatio, except for the great 'Absent thee from felicity' — is a curious one for Hamlet : 'The readiness is all.' But that readiness is for what he shall endure, not for what he shall do. It makes more shapely the end of Brutus; it is a preparation for the harvest of Lear. It is the maturing fruit:

> O! that a man might know
> The end of this day's business ere it come;
> But it sufficeth that the day will end,
> And then the end is known. Come, ho! away!

. . . If it be now, 'tis not to come; if it be not to come, it will be now; if it be not now yet it will come : the readiness is all. . . . Let be.

> Men must endure
> Their going hence, even as their coming hither:
> Ripeness is all. Come on.

What has to end, of course, is the play. It is to the play's conclusion that Shakespeare is addressing himself; it is that which forces from him an utterance consonant with the nature of whatever character speaks, but consonant also with his genius at that time. I cannot feel that it is entirely by accident that that genius in *Julius Caesar*[3] ended with a desire for, and an expectation of, a certitude dimly seen in the Ghost of Caesar; that directly afterwards in *Hamlet* — before the tragedies — it

3. It is a fantasy — and the Ghost of Banquo comes later to spoil it — but I have wondered whether the Ghost of Caesar and the Ghost of Hamlet's father are a visionary presentation of the visionary power (in Wordsworth's phrase) which was then pressing on him, apparitions of the 'something evermore about to be'.

ended with readiness; and after *Troilus* and *Othello* ended *Lear* with ripeness. Indeed it had reached ripeness then.

Nevertheless, in *Hamlet* the poetic genius was beginning again, like a 'fool of nature',

> to shake [its] disposition
> With thoughts beyond the reaches of our souls;

it also had

> something in [its] soul
> O'er which [its] melancholy sits on brood.

The hint of that is in the King's meditation — 'there the action lies In his true nature'. Until it found out the true nature of action, poetry had still to absent itself from its felicity. In the words of the play that was soon to follow, it might have said to itself

> Not poppy nor mandragora,
> Nor all the drowsy syrups of the world
> Shall ever medicine thee to that sweet sleep
> Which thou ow'dst yesterday.

8

Shakespeare and The Stoicism of Seneca[1]

T.S. Eliot

The last few years have witnessed a number of recrudescence's of Shakespeare. There is the fatigued Shakespeare, a retired Anglo-Indian, presented by Mr. Lytton Strachey; there is the messianic Shakespeare, bringing a new philosophy and a new system of yoga, presented by Mr. Middleton Murry; and there is the ferocious Shakespeare, a furious Samson, presented by Mr. Wyndham Lewis in his interesting book, *The Lion and the Fox*. On the whole we may all agree that these manifestations are beneficial. In any case so important as that of Shakespeare, it is good that we should from time to time change our minds. The last conventional Shakespeare is banished from the scene, and a variety of unconventional Shakespeares takes his place. About any one so great as Shakespeare it is probable that we can never be right; and if we can never be right, it is better that we should from time to time change our way of being wrong. Whether Truth ultimately prevails is doubtful and has never been proved; but it is certain that nothing is more effective in driving out error than a new error. Whether Mr. Strachey, or Mr. Murry, or Mr. Lewis, is any nearer to the truth of Shakespeare than Rymer, or Morgann, or Webster, or Johnson, is uncertain; they are all certainly more sympathetic in this year 1927 than Coleridge, or Swinburne, or Dowden. If they do not give us the real Shakespeare — if there is one — they at least give us

1. Shakespeare Association Lecture (1927), reprinted in *Elizabethan Essays* (1934).

several up-to-date Shakespeares. If the only way to prove that Shakespeare did not feel and think exactly as people felt and thought in 1815, or in 1860, or in 1880, is to show that he felt and thought as we felt and thought in 1927, then we must accept gratefully that alternative.

But these recent interpreters of Shakespeare suggest a number of reflections on literary criticism and its limits, on general aesthetics, and on the limitations of the human understanding.

There are, of course, a number of other current interpretations of Shakespeare: that is, of the *conscious opinions* of Shakespeare: interpretations of category, so to speak : which make him either a Tory journalist or a Liberal journalist, or a Socialist journalist (though Mr. Shaw has done something to warn off his co-religionists from claiming Shakespeare, or from finding anything uplifting in his work); we have also a Protestant Shakespeare, and a sceptical Shakespeare, and some case may be made out for an Anglo-Catholic, or even a Papist Shakespeare. My own frivolous opinion is that Shakespeare may have held in private life very different views from what we extract from his extremely varied published works; that there is no clue in his writings to the way in which he would have voted in the last or would vote in the next election; and that we are completely in the dark as to his attitude about prayer-book revision. I admit that my own experience, as a minor poet, may have jaundiced my Outlook; that I am used to having cosmic significances, which I never suspected, extracted from my work (such as it is) by enthusiastic persons at a distance; and to being informed that something which I meant seriously is *vers de societe'*; and to having my personal biography reconstructed from passages which I got out of books, or which I invented out of nothing because they sounded well; and to having my biography invariably ignored in what I *did* write from personal experience; so that in consequence I am inclined to believe that people are mistaken about Shakespeare just in proportion to the relative superiority of Shakespeare to myself.

One more personal 'note': I believe that I have as high an estimate of the greatness of Shakespeare as poet and dramatist as anyone living; I certainly believe that there is nothing greater.

And I would say that my only qualification for venturing to talk about him is? that I am *not* under the delusion that Shakespeare in the least resembles myself, either as I am or as I should like to imagine myself. It seems to me that one of the chief reasons for questioning Mr. Strachey's Shakespeare, and Mr. Murry's, and Mr. Lewis's, is the remarkable resemblance which they bear to Mr. Strachey, and Mr. Murry, and Mr. Lewis, respectively. I have not a very clear idea of what Shakespeare was like. But I do not conceive him as very like either Mr. Strachey, or Mr. Murry, or Mr. Wyndham Lewis, or myself.

We have had Shakespeare explained by a variety of influences. He is explained by Montaigne, and by Machiavelli. I imagine that Mr. Strachey would explain Shakespeare by Montaigne, though this would also be Mr. Strachey's Montaigne (for all of Mr. Strachey's favourite figures have a strong Strachey physiognomy) and not Mr. Robertson's. I think that Mr. Lewis, in the intensely interesting book mentioned, has done a real service in calling attention to the importance of Machiavelli in Elizabethan England? though this Machiavelli be only the Machiavelli of the *Contre-Machiavel,* and not in the least the real Machiavelli, a person whom Elizabethan England was as incapable of understanding as Georgian England, or any England, is. I think, however, that Mr. Lewis has gone quite wrong if he thinks (I am not sure what he thinks) that Shakespeare, and Elizabethan England in general, 'was influenced' by the thought of Machiavelli. I think that Shakespeare, and other dramatists, used the popular Machiavellian idea, for stage purposes; but this idea was no more like Machiavelli, who was an Italian and a Roman Christian, than Mr. Shaw's idea of Nietzsche — whatever that is — is like the real Nietzsche.

I propose a Shakespeare under the influence of the stoicism of Seneca. But I do not believe that Shakespeare was under the influence of Seneca. I propose it largely because I believe that after the Montaigne Shakespeare (not that Montaigne had any philosophy whatever) and after the Machiavelli Shakespeare, a stoical or Senecan Shakespeare is almost certain to be produced. I wish merely to disinfect the Senecan Shakespeare before he appears. My ambitions would be realized if I could prevent him, in so doing, from appearing at all.

I want to be quite definite in my notion of the possible influence of Seneca on Shakespeare. I think it is quite likely that Shakespeare read some of Seneca's tragedies at school. I think it quite unlikely that Shakespeare knew anything of that extraordinarily dill and uninteresting body of Seneca's prose, which was translated by Lodge and printed in 1612. So far as Shakespeare was influenced by Seneca, it was by his memories of school conning and through the influence of the Senecan tragedy of the day, through Kyd and Peele, but chiefly Kyd. That Shakespeare deliberately took a 'view of life' from Seneca there seems to be no evidence whatever.

Nevertheless, there is, in some of the great tragedies of Shakespeare, a new attitude. It is not the attitude of Seneca, but is derived from Seneca; it is slightly different from anything that can be found in French tragedy, in Corneille or in Racine; it is modern, and it culminates, if there is ever any culmination, in the attitude of Nietzsche. I cannot say that it is Shakespeare's 'philosophy'. Yet many people have lived by it; though it may only have been Shakespeare's instinctive recognition of something of theatrical utility. It is the attitude of self-dramatization assumed by some of Shakespeare's heroes at moments of tragic intensity. It is not peculiar to Shakespeare; it is conspicuous in Chapman : Bussy, Clermont, and Biron all die in this way. Marston — one of the most interesting and least explored of all the Elizabethans — used it; and Marston and Chapman were particularly Senecan. But Shakespeare, of course, does it very much better than any of the others, and makes it somehow more integral with the human nature of his characters. It is less verbal, more real. I have always felt that I have never read a more terrible exposure of human weakness — of universal human weakness — than the last great speech of Othello. (I am ignorant whether any one else has ever adopted this view, and it may appear subjective and fantistic in the extreme.) It is usually taken on its face value, as expressing the greatness in defeat of a noble but erring nature.

> Soft you, a word or two before you go.
> I have done the state some service, and they know't.
> No more of that. I pray you, in your letters,
> When you shall these unlucky deeds relate,
> Speak of me as I am; nothing extenuate,

Nor set down aught in malice: then you must speak
Of one that loved not wisely but too well;
Of one not easily jealous, but, being wrought,
Perplex'd in the extreme; of one whose hand,
Like the base Indian, threw a pearl away
Richer than all his tribe; of one whose subdued eyes,
Albeit unused to the melting mood,
Drop tears as fast as the Arabian trees
Their medicinal gum. Set you down this;
And say, besides, that in Aleppo once,
Where a malignant and a turban'd Turk
Beat a Venetian and traduced the state,
I took by the throat the circumcized dog,
And smote him, thus.

What Othello seems to me to be doing in making this speech is *cheering himself up*. He is endeavouring to escape reality, he has ceased to think about Desdemona, and is thinking about himself. Humility is the most difficult of all virtues to achieve; nothing dies harder than the desire to think well of oneself. Othello succeeds in turning himself into a pathetic figure, by adopting an *aesthetic* rather than a moral attitude, dramatising himself against his environment. He takes in the spectator, but the human motive is primarily to take in himself. I do not believe that any writer has ever exposed this *bovarysme*, the human will to see things as they are not, more clearly than Shakespeare.

If you compare the deaths of several of Shakespeare's heroes — I do not say *all*, for there are very few generalisations that can be applied to the whole of Shakespeare's work — but notably Othello, Coriolanus, and Antony — with the deaths of heroes of dramatists such as Marston and Chapman, consciously under Senecan influence, you will find a strong similarity — except only that Shakespeare does it both more poetically and more lifelike.

You may say that Shakespeare is merely illustrating, consciously or unconsciously, human nature, not Seneca. But I am not so much concerned with the influence of Seneca on Shakespeare as with Shakespeare's illustration of Senecan and stoical principles. Much of Chapman's Senecanism has lately been shown by Professor Schoell to be directly borrowed from

Erasmus and other sources. I am concerned with the fact that Seneca is the *literary* representative of Roman stoicism, and that Roman stoicism is an important ingredient in Elizabethan drama. It was natural that in a time like that of Elizabeth stoicism should appear. The original stoicism, and especially the Roman stoicism, was, of course, a philosophy suited to slaves : hence its absorption into early Christianity.

> A man to join himself with the Universe
> In his main sway, and make in all things fit —

A man does not join himself with the Universe so long as he has anything else to join himself with; men who could take part in the life of a thriving Greek city-state had something better to join themselves to; and Christians have had something better. Stoicism is the refuge for the individual in an indifferent or hostile world too big for him; it is the permanent substratum of a number of versions of cheering oneself up. Nietzsche is the most conspicuous modem instance of cheering oneself up. The stoical attitude is the reverse of Christian humility.

In Elizabethan England we have conditions apparently utterly different from those of imperial Rome. But it was a period of dissolution and chaos; and in such a period any emotional attitude which seems to give a man something firm, even if it be only the attitude of 'I am myself alone', is eagerly taken up. I hardly need — and it is beyond my present scope — to point out how readily, in a period like the Elizabethan, the Senecan attitude of Pride, the Montaigne attitude of Scepticism, and the Machiavelli attitude[2] of Cynicism, arrived at a kind of fusion in the Elizabethan individualism.

This individualism, this vice of Pride, was, of course, exploited largely because of its dramatic possibilities. But other drama had before existed without depending on this human failing. You do not find it in *Polyeucte*, or in *Phèdre* either. But even Hamlet, who has made a pretty considerable mess of things, and occasioned the death of at least three innocent people, and two more insignificant ones, dies fairly well pleased with himself —

2. I do not mean the attitude of Machiavelli, which is not cynical. I mean the attitude of Englishmen who had heard of Machiavelli.

> Horatio, I am dead;
> Thou liv'st; report me and my cause aright
> To the unsatisfied . . . .
> O good Horatio, what a wounded name,
> Things standing thus unknown, shall live behind me!

Antony says, 'I am Antony still', and the Duchess, 'I am Duchess of Malfy still'; would either of them have said that unless Medea had said *Medea superes*?

I do not wish to appear to maintain that the Elizabethan hero and the Senecan hero are identical. The influence of Seneca is much more apparent in the Elizabethan drama than it is in the plays of Seneca. The influence of any man is a different thing from himself. The Elizabethan hero is much more stoical and Senecan, in this way, than the Senecan hero. For Seneca was following the Greek tradition, which was not stoical; he developed familiar themes and imitated great models; so that the vast difference between his emotional attitude and that of the Greeks is rather latent in his work, and more apparent in the work of the Renaissance. And the Elizabethan hero, the hero of Shakespeare, was not invariable even in Elizabethan England. A notable exception is Faustus. Marlowe — not excepting Shakespeare or Chapman, the most *thoughtful* and philosophic mind, though immature, among the Elizabethan dramatists — could conceive the proud hero, as Tamburlaine, but also the hero who has reached that point of horror at which even pride is abandoned. In a recent book on Marlowe, Miss Ellis-Fermor has put very well this peculiarity of Faustus, from another point of view than mine, but in words from which I take support:

> Marlowe follows Faustus further across the borderline between consciousness and dissolution than do any of his contemporaries. With Shakespeare, with Webster death is a sudden severing of life; their men die, conscious to the last of some part at least of their surroundings, influenced, even upheld, by that consciousness and preserving the personality and characteristics they have possessed through life. . . . In Marlowe's Faustus alone all this is set aside. He penetrates deeply into the experience of a mind isolated from the past, absorbed in the realization of its own destruction.

But Marlowe, the most thoughtful, the most blasphemous (and therefore, probably, the most Christian) of his contemporaries, is always an exception. Shakespeare is exceptional primarily by his immense superiority.

Of all of Shakespeare's plays, *King Lear* is often taken as the most Senecan in spirit. Cunliffe finds it to be imbued with a Senecan fatalism. Here, again, we must distinguish between a man and his influence. The differences between the fatalism of Greek tragedy, and the fatalism of Seneca's tragedies, and the fatalism of the Elizabethans, proceed by delicate shades; there is a continuity, and there is also a violent contrast, when we look at them from far off. In Seneca, the Greek ethics is visible underneath the Roman stoicism. In the Elizabethans, the Roman stoicism is visible beneath the Renaissance anarchism. In *King Lear* there are several significant phrases, such as those which caught the attention of Professor Cunliffe, and there is a tone of Senecan fatalism: *fatis agimur.* But there is much less and much more. And this is the point at which I must part company with Mr. Wyndham Lewis. Mr. Lewis proposes a Shakespeare who is a *positive* nihilist, an intellectual force *willing* destruction. I cannot see in Shakespeare either a deliberate scepticism, as of Montaigne, or a deliberate cynicism, as of Machiavelli, or a deliberate resignation, as of Seneca. I can see that he *used* all of these things, for dramatic ends: you get perhaps more Montaigne in *Hamlet,* and more Machiavelli in *Othello*, and more Seneca in *Lear*. But I cannot agree with the following paragraph:

With the exception of Chapman, Shakespeare is the only thinker we meet with among the Elizabethan dramatists. By this is meant, of course, that his work contained, apart from poetry, phantasy, rhetoric or observation of manners, a body of matter representing explicit processes of the intellect which would have furnished a moral philosopher like Montaigne with the natural material for his essays. But the quality of this thinking — as it can be surprised springing naturally in the midst of the consummate movements of his art — is, as must be the case with such a man, of startling force sometimes. And if it is not systematic, at least a recognizable physiognomy is there.

It is this general notion of 'thinking' that I would challenge. One has the difficulty of having to use the same words for different things. We say, in a vague way, that Shakespeare, or Dante, or Lucretius, is a poet who thinks, and that Swinburne is a poet who does not think, even that Tennyson is a poet who does not think. But what we really mean is not a difference in quality of thought, but a difference in quality of emotion. The poet who 'thinks' is merely the poet who can express the emotional equivalent of thought. But he is not necessarily interested in the thought itself. We talk as if thought was precise and emotion was vague. In reality there is precise emotion and there is vague emotion. To express precise emotion requires as great intellectual power as to express precise thought. But by 'thinking' I mean something very different from anything that I find in Shakespeare. Mr. Lewis, and other champions of Shakespeare as a great philosopher, have a great deal to say about Shakespeare's power of thought, but they fail to show that he thought to any purpose; that he had any coherent view of life, or that he recommended any procedure to follow. 'We possess a great deal of evidence', says Mr. Lewis, 'as to what Shakespeare thought of military glory and martial events.' Do we? Or rather, did Shakespeare think anything at all? He was occupied with turning human actions into poetry.

I would suggest that none of the plays of Shakespeare has a 'meaning', although it would be equally false to say that a play of Shakespeare is meaningless. All great poetry gives the illusion of a view of life. When we enter into the world of Homer, or Sophocles, or Virgil, or Dante, or Shakespeare we incline to believe that we are apprehending something that can be expressed intellectually; for every precise emotion tends towards intellectual formulation.

We are apt to be deluded by the example of Dante. Here, we think, is a poem which represents an exact intellectual system; Dante has a 'philosophy', therefore every poet as great as Dante has a philosophy too. Dante had behind him the system of St. Thomas, to which his poem corresponds point to point. Therefore Shakespeare had behind him Seneca, or Montaigne, or Machiavelli; and if his work does not correspond point to point with any or a composition of these, then it must be that he did a little quiet thinking on his own, and was better than any of these people at their own job. I can see no reason for believing that either Dante or Shakespeare did any thinking on his own. The people who think that Shakespeare thought, are always people who are not engaged in writing poetry, but who are engaged in thinking, and we all like to think that great men were like ourselves. The difference between Shakespeare and Dante is that Dante had one coherent system of thought behind him; but that was just his luck, and from the point of view of poetry is an irrelevant accident. It happened that at Dante's time thought was orderly and strong and beautiful, and that it was concentrated in one man of the greatest genius; Dante's poetry receives a boost which in a sense it does not merit, from the fact that the thought behind it is the thought of a man as great and lovely as Dante himself: St. Thomas. The thought behind Shakespeare is of men far inferior to Shakespeare himself : hence the alternative errors, first, that as Shakespeare was as great a poet as Dante, he must have supplied, out of his own thinking, the difference in quality between a St. Thomas and a Montaigne or a Machiavelli or a Seneca, or second, that Shakespeare is inferior to Dante. In truth neither Shakespeare nor Dante did any real thinking — that was not their job; and the relative value of the thought current at their time, the material enforced upon each to use as the vehicle of his feeling, is of no importance. It does not make Dante a greater poet, or mean that we can learn more from Dante than from Shakespeare. We can certainly learn more from Aquinas than from Seneca, but that is quite a different matter. When Dante says *la sua voluntade e nostra pace* it is great poetry, and there is a great philosophy behind it. When Shakespeare says

> As flies to wanton boys, are we to the gods;
> They kill us for their sport,

it is *equally* great poetry, though the philosophy behind it is not great. But the essential is that each expresses, in perfect language, some permanent human impulse. Emotionally, the latter is just as strong, just as true, and just as informative — just as useful and beneficial in the sense in which poetry is useful and beneficial, as the former.

What every poet starts from is his own emotions. And when we get down to these, there is not much to choose between Shakespeare and Dante. Dante's railings, his personal spleen — sometimes thinly disguised under Old Testamental prophetic denunciations — his nostalgia, his bitter regrets for past happiness — or for what seems happiness when it is past — and his brave attempts to fabricate something permanent and holy out of his personal animal feelings — as in the *Vita Nuova* — can all be matched out of Shakespeare. Shakespeare, too, was occupied with the struggle — which alone constitutes life for a poet — to transmute his personal and private agonies into something rich and strange, something universal and impersonal. The rage of Dante against Florence, or Pistoia, or what not, the deep surge of Shakespeare's general cynicism and disillusionment, are merely gigantic attempts to metamorphose private failures and disappointments. The great poet, in writing himself, writes his time.[3] Thus Dante, hardly knowing it, became the voice of the thirteenth century; Shakespeare, hardly knowing it, became the representative of the end of the sixteenth century, of a turning-point in history. But you can hardly say that Dante believed, or did not believe, the Thomist philosophy; you can hardly say that Shakespeare believed, or did not believe, the mixed and muddled scepticism of the Renaissance. If Shakespeare had written according to a better philosophy, he would have written worse poetry; it was his business to express the greatest emotional intensity of his time, based on whatever his time happened to think. Poetry is not a substitute for philosophy or theology or religion, as Mr. Lewis and Mr. Murry sometimes seem to think; it has its own function. But as this function is not intellectual but emotional, it cannot be defined adequately in intellectual terms. We can say that it provides 'consolation': strange consolation, which is provided equally by writers so different as Dante and Shakespeare.

What I have said could be expressed more exactly, but at much greater length, in philosophical language: it would enter into the department of philosophy which might be called the Theory of Belief (which is not psychology but philosophy, or

3. Remy de Gourmont said much the same thing, in speaking of Flaubert.

phenomenology proper) — the department in which Meinong and Husserl have made some pioneer investigation; the different meanings which belief has in different minds according to the activity for which they are oriented. I doubt whether belief proper enters into the activity of a great poet, *qua* poet. That is, Dante, *qua* poet, did not believe or disbelieve the Thomist cosmology or theory of the soul: he merely made use of it, or a fusion took place between his initial emotional impulses and a theory, for the purpose of making poetry. The poet makes poetry, the metaphysician makes metaphysics, the bee makes honey, the spider secretes a filament; you can hardly say that any of these agents believes: he merely does.

The problem of belief is very complicated and probably quite insoluble. We must make allowance for differences in the emotional quality of believing not only between persons of different occupation, such as the philosopher and the poet, but between different periods of time. The end of the sixteenth century is an epoch when it is particularly difficult to associate poetry with systems of thought or reasoned views of life. In making some very commonplace investigations of the 'thought' of Donne, I found it quite impossible to come to the conclusion that Donne believed anything. It seemed as if, at that time, the world was filled with broken fragments of systems, and that a man like Donne merely picked up, like a magpie, various shining fragments of ideas as they struck his eye, and stuck them about here and there in his verse. Miss Ramsey, in her learned and exhaustive study of Donne's sources, came to the conclusion that he was a 'mediaeval thinker'; I could not find either any 'mediaevalism' or any thinking, but only a vast jumble of incoherent erudition on which he drew for purely poetic effects. The recent work of Professor Schoell on the sources of Chapman seems to show Chapman engaged in the same task; and suggests that the 'profundity' and 'obscurity' of Chapman's dark thinking are largely due to his lifting long passages from the works of writers like Ficino and incorporating them in his poems completely out of their context.

I do not for a moment suggest that the method of Shakespeare was anything like this. Shakespeare was a much finer instrument for transformations than any of his contemporaries, finer perhaps even than Dante. He also needed less contact in order to be able to absorb all that he required. The element of Seneca is the most completely absorbed and transmogrified, because it was already the most diffused throughout Shakespeare's world. The element of Machiavelli is probably the most indirect, the element of Montaigne the most immediate. It has been said that Shakespeare lacks unity; it might, I think, be said equally well that it is Shakespeare chiefly that *is* the unity, that unifies so far as they could be unified all the tendencies of a time that certainly lacked unity. Unity, in Shakespeare, but not universality; no one can be universal: Shakespeare would not have found much in common with his contemporary St. Theresa. What influence the work of Seneca and Machiavelli and Montaigne seems to me to exert in common on that time, and most conspicuously through Shakespeare, is an influence toward a kind of self-consciousness that is new; the self-consciousness and self-dramatization of the Shakespearian hero, of whom Hamlet is only one. It seems to mark a stage, even if not a very agreeable one, in human history, or progress, or deterioration, or change. Roman stoicism was in its own time a development in self-consciousness; taken up into Christianity, it broke loose again in the dissolution of the Renaissance. Nietzsche, as I suggested, is a late variant: his attitude is a kind of stoicism upside-down: for there is not much difference between identifying oneself with the Universe and identifying the Universe with oneself. The influence of Seneca on Elizabethan drama has been exhaustively studied in its formal aspect, and in the borrowing and adaptation of phrases and situations; the penetration of Senecan sensibility would be much more difficult to trace.

9

Metaphor[1]

J. Middleton Murry

Discussions of metaphor — there are not many of them — often strike us at first as superficial. Not until we have ourselves made the attempt to get farther do we begin to realize that the investigation of metaphor is curiously like the investigation of any of the primary data of consciousness: it cannot be pursued very far without our being led to the borderline of sanity. Metaphor is as ultimate as speech itself, and speech as ultimate as thought. If we try to penetrate them beyond a certain point, we find ourselves questioning the very faculty and instrument with which we are trying to penetrate them. The earth trembles and yawns beneath the explorer's feet. *Medio tutissimus ibis;* but the middle way is hard to find.

Suppose we take a familiar metaphor, as that the fiery spirit of Emily Brontë burned up her body. It cannot fairly be called *cliché;* it is rather a familiar and necessary idiom. Necessary, because we find that there is no way of saying what we want to say about Emily Brontë save by this metaphor or one of its variations. This obvious necessity of the metaphor, this absence of genuine alternatives, seems to make it clear that so soon as one person perceived in another and sought to describe such a quality as Emily Brontë's, a kindred metaphor was forced upon him. We may even say that the quality could not have been perceived without the metaphor. The imagination that the soul inhabits the body as fine inhabits the material which it burns must surely go back to the moment when the existence of the

1. *Countries of the Mind*, Second Series (1931).

soul was first surmised; for only by such an image could the nature of the soul's existence be at all apprehended. And we may leave it undecided, or as impossible of decision, whether the creation of the metaphor was the result of a search for a description of the previously felt existence of the soul, or the existence of the soul was suggested by the manner of the flame's existence.

For, whichever it may have been, and perhaps the processes were equally prevalent, metaphor appears as the instinctive and necessary act of the mind exploring reality and ordering experience. It is the means by which the less familiar is assimilated to the more familiar, the unknown to the known: it 'gives to airy nothing a local habitation and a name', so that it ceases to be airy nothing. To attempt a fundamental examination of metaphor would be nothing less than an investigation of the genesis of thought itself — a dangerous enterprise. Therefore we instinctively seek to circumscribe our own inquiries by leaving out of account as far as may be the countless host of dead or dormant metaphors of which the most part of language is composed, and concentrating upon the living ones. We take for granted the past exploration of reality of which dead and dormant metaphors are the record, and try to focus our minds on that present, hazardous, incomplete, and thrilling exploration of reality which is represented by metaphors which still retain their vitality.

Such are the metaphors of what we call creative literature. These remain alive because they are the records of an exploration of reality by men who stood head and shoulders above their fellows, who discerned resemblances between the unknown and the known which the generality could not accept nor common speech assimilate. Their metaphors are felt still to be the vehicle of some immediate revelation to those who attend to them. As Aristotle said, 'But the greatest thing of all by far is to be a master of metaphor. It is the one thing that cannot be learned from others; and it is also a sign of original genius, since a good metaphor implies the intuitive perception of the similarity in dissimilars.' The statement, made so long ago, seems final still.

But before we hazard a small attempt to advance from it towards Coleridge's discussion of imagery, we need to inquire, for the sake of clarity, whether there is any but a formal difference between metaphor and simile and image. 'Far out, as though idly, listlessly, gulls were flying. Now they settled on the waves, now they beat up into the rainy air, *and shone against the pale sky like the lights within a pearl*' The last words would be called indifferently an image or a simile. Change them to 'shining lights in the pale pearl of sky', it becomes — not by any means to its advantage, for a reason we may discover — a metaphor. But the act of creative perception remains the same. And it seems impossible to regard metaphors and similes as different in any essential property: metaphor is compressed simile. The word 'image', however, which has come to usurp a prominent place in these discussions, is more recalcitrant. It not only narrows the content of the word 'simile', but tends to force unduly into the foreground the part played by the visual image. In the beautiful simile quoted above the visual image is preponderant; in Baudelaire's agonizing one:

> Ces affreuses nuits

Qui compriment le cœur comme un papier qu'on froisse the visual image has no part at all. Again, it is obvious foolishness to persuade oneself that any visual image underlies the magnificent metaphors —

> Thou still unravish'd bride of quietness:
> Thou foster-child of Silence and slow Time.

Yet though the suggestion of the word 'image' is dangerous, the word is necessary. For metaphor and simile belong to formal classification. The word 'image', precisely because it is used to cover both metaphor and simile, can be used to point towards their fundamental identity; and if we resolutely exclude from our minds the suggestion that the image is solely or even predominantly visual, and allow the word to share in the heightened and comprehensive significance with which its derivative 'imagination' has perforce been endowed — if we conceive the 'image' not as primary and independent, but as the most singular and potent instrument of the faculty of imagination — it is a more valuable word than those which it subsumes: metaphor and simile. To them clings something worse than false suggestion, a logical taint, an aura of irrelevancy.

The image may be visual, may be auditory, may refer back to any primary physical experience — as those hoary metaphors which describe the process of thought itself as a grasping or apprehension — or it may be wholly psychological, the reference of one emotional or intellectual experience to another, as

> Then felt I like some watcher of the skies
> When a new planet swims into his ken . . .

The essential is simply that there should be that intuitive perception of similarity between dissimilar of which Aristotle speaks. What we primarily demand is that the similarity should be a true similarity, and that it should have lain hitherto unperceived, or but rarely perceived by us, so that it comes to us with an effect of revelation: something hitherto unknown is suddenly made known. To that extent the image is truly creative; it marks an advance, for the writer who perceives and the reader who receives it, in the conquest of some reality.

We also in our inquiry may take a step forward. That we demand more of imagery than this may be seen in our instinctive refusal of the image of a modern prose-writer, who speaks of the 'churches, like shapes of grey paper, breasting the stream of the Strand'. There are two images, and they war with each other. If the churches really breasted the stream of the Strand, they were not at that moment like shapes of grey paper. Possibly both perceptions are valid in isolation; in association they nullify one another. Yet how often does Shakespeare seem to commit the same offence.

> It is great
> To do that thing that ends all other deeds:
> Which shackles accident, and bolts up change;
> Which sleeps, and never palates more the dug,
> The beggar's nurse and Caesar's.

Yet the offence is only apparent. The images do not in fact disturb each other, whereas the modern writer's images do. This is partly because in the modern writer's imagery the stress lies wholly upon the visual: if we do not see what we are required to see, the sentence fails of its effect; and partly because of the characteristic swiftness of Shakespeare's language. We have not, and we are not intended to have, time to unfold his metaphors;

and, moreover, the boldest and most abrupt transition among them is in its effect the smoothest. For the rhythm leaves no doubt that it is not 'the dug' but Death that is 'the beggar's nurse and Caesar's'. Death which in the previous line was the child sleeping against the heart, becomes the bosom that receives mankind. We may say it is the mere verbal suggestion that links the metaphors. Yet, though it is true that verbal 'self-suggestion' is potent in high poetry ('Forlorn! the very word is like a knell . . .'), it seems truer in this case to say that the one metaphor grows immediately out of the other. It is as though the vague 'thing', from which the images take their rise, swiftly groped after shapes before our mind's eye, and finally achieved a full realization — 'the beggar's nurse and Caesar's'.

This is the work of the greatest of all masters of metaphor, and it would be preposterous to try others' achievement by its standard. The self-creative progress of Shakespeare's imagery is a thing apart. But by comparing small things with great we may see that the internal harmony which the modern writer fails to secure is a necessary quality of true imagery. Shakespeare's methods of securing it are indeed startling; he takes what seem to be impossible risks, and wins with ease. His success, when we examine it, is not really so surprising, for the extent to which images are discordant depends upon the extent to which we unfold them, and that is wholly within the great poet's control, for it in turn depends primarily upon the rhythm and tempo of his writing. And this, more than any other, is the reason why the successful use of metaphor is infinitely bolder in poetry than in prose. The poet's means of control — that is to say, the possibilities of tempo and rhythm in poetry — are infinitely richer and more flexible than in prose. He has our sensibilities, our powers of realization and comparison, far more completely under his thumb than the prose-writer. So that we may hazard a generalization and say that the creative simile is by nature more appropriate to prose than the creative metaphor. Prose gives us time to bear upon the comparison, which if it be exact and revealing, will stand the strain of our attention, and is better frankly exposed to the inquiry it must receive. And, again, the function of imagery in poetry differs perceptibly from the function of imagery in prose. In poetry metaphor is chiefly a means to excite in us a vague and heightened awareness of qualities we can best call spiritual. Exactness and precision are seldom sought, and, if they are, are seldom valuable; and often, where an apparent exactness exists, as in the Homeric simile, it is an incidental exactness and does not reinforce the point of specific analogy. Set two equally famous heroic portraits by great poets against each other.

> His legs bestrid the ocean; his rear'd arm
> Crested the world: his voice was propertied
> As all the tuned spheres, and that to friends;
> But when he meant to quail and shake the orb,
> He was as rattling thunder. For his bounty,
> There was no winter in 't; an autumn 'twas
> That grew the more by reaping: his delights
> Were dolphin-like; they show'd his back above
> The element they liv'd in: in his livery
> Walk'd crowns and crownets; realms and islands were
> As plates dropp'd from his pocket . . .

> He above the rest
> In shape and gesture proudly eminent
> Stood like a Tower; his form had not yet lost
> All her original brightness, nor appear'd
> Less than archangel ruin'd, and th' excess
> Of glory obscur'd, as when the sun new risen
> Looks through the horizontal misty air
> Shorn of his beams; or from behind the moon
> In dim eclipse disastrous twilight sheds
> On half the nations; and with fear of change
> Perplexes monarchs.

The Miltonic tempo, as ever, is far slower than Shakespeare's; therefore we bear more heavily upon his comparisons, and in sufficient measure they stand the strain; but the whole effect is not precise, but rather vague, vast, and foreboding. So also, in its totally different kind, the picture of Antony that is impressed upon our minds is of something (rather than someone) immense, generous, genial, a careless and over-flowing force of nature — a dynamic phenomenon as peculiar to Shakespeare's view of the universe as the static figure of Satan to Milton's. Exactness of this kind there is in both; but it comes not from the exactness of the particular comparisons, it is a total effect of many comparisons, as it were a painting of one great and indefinable quality by many strokes of minor yet allied analogies. To evoke such elemental spirits is seldom the purpose of prose, nor of the imagery proper to it. It also seizes, in so far as it is creative, indefinable qualities, but they are more specific and more local.

Soon after daybreak we were steaming down the arrowy Rhone, at the rate of twenty miles an hour, in a very dirty vessel full of merchandise, and with only three or four other passengers for our companions: among whom the most remarkable was a silly old, meek-faced, garlic-eating, immeasurably polite Chevalier, with a dirty scrap of red ribbon at his buttonhole, *as if he had tied it there to remind him of something.*

It is perfect, it gives us the man — an individual and comic inhabitant of earth. Perhaps as an example it suggests that the prose use of simile must be more prosaic than we mean to imply. We have quoted solely to point an essential difference between the imagery of prose and poetry. The imagery of poetry is in the main complex and suggestive; the imagery of prose single and explicit.

But the three examples serve also to illustrate what is the highest function of imagery — namely, to define indefinable spiritual qualities. All metaphor and simile can be described as the analogy by which the human mind explores the universe of quality and charts the non-measurable world. Of these indefinite qualities some are capable of direct sensuous apprehension, while others can be grasped only by a faculty which, though obviously akin to sensuous apprehension, yet differs from it. Sensuous perception is of the qualities of the visible, audible, tangible world; of the spiritual qualities of the more recondite world of human personality and its creations there is intuition. Both faculties are necessary to the great poet, but there have been many who, though richly gifted with sensuous perception, have been deficient or altogether lacking in spiritual intuition. To the great poet his constant accumulation of vivid sense-perceptions supplies the most potent means by which he articulates his spiritual intuitions, for recognitions of spiritual quality can be most forcefully and swiftly conveyed through analogous recognitions of sensuous quality. One has only to imagine how much, and how much in vain, another writer might toil to render the quality of Antony that is given once for all in the words, grammatically confused though they are:

> . . . his delights
> Were dolphin-like; they show'd his back above
> The element they lived in . . .

or to consider the pregnant subtlety of these two kindred images:

> This common body,
> Like to a vagabond flag upon the stream,
> Goes to and back, lackeying the varying tide,
> To rot itself with motion . . . .
> Her tongue will not obev her heart, nor can
> Her heart inform her tongue — the swan's down- feather
> That stands upon the swell at full of tide
> And neither way inclines . . .

to realize the enormous resources for describing the subtlest nuances of emotion and character which a vivid percipience of the sensuous world can give.

But the greatest mastery of imagery does not lie in the use, however beautiful and revealing, of isolated images, but in the harmonious total impression produced by a succession of subtly related images. In such cases the images appear to grow out of one another and to be fulfilling an independent life of their own. Yet this apparent autonomy is as strictly subordinated to a final impression as the steps of a logical argument are to their conclusion. Such triumphs of imagery are to be conceived as a swift and continuous act of exploration of the world of imagination — though an obvious metaphor is in that phrase. A magnificent example of this peculiar movement of mind on a scale so large that it can be carefully examined is Keats's *Ode to a Nightingale*. The strange combination of imaginative autonomy and profound total harmony in that poem is characteristic of the movement of creative imagery in its highest forms. We can perhaps get a clear glimpse of the nature of this contradictory process of creative imagery — the maximum of independence combined with the most complete and pervasive subordination — in one of the rare moments when we can honestly claim to look over Shakespeare's shoulder. The famous picture of Cleopatra on Cydnus comes substantially from North's Plutarch, of which the following sentence is the original of Shakespeare's first seven lines:

She disdained to set forward otherwise, but to take her barge in the river of Cydnus, the poope whereof was of gold, the sails of purple, and the owers of silver, which kept stroke in rowing after the sound of flutes, how boys, cythem, violls, and such other instruments as they played upon the barge . . . .

It is often said that Shakespeare followed North as closely as he could, with the minimum of original effort. It is not true. North's sentence would fall quite easily into good blank verse, but it would be nothing like —

The barge she sat in, like a burnish'd throne,
Burn'd on the water: the poop was beaten gold;
Purple the sails, *and so perfumed that*
The winds were love-sick with them; *the oars were silver,*
Which to the tune of flutes kept stroke, *and made*
The water which they beat to follow faster,
As amorous of their strokes . . . .

The phrases in italics are Shakespeare's additions: afterwards he keeps more closely to North, until he comes to the climax. North has it:

Others also ran out of the city to see her coming in. So that in the end, there rann such multitudes of people one after another, that *Antonius* was left post alone in the market-place, in his Imperiall seate to give audience.

Which is transformed into:

The city cast
Her people out upon her, and Antony,
Enthron'd in the market-place, did sit alone,
Whistling to the air; which, but for vacancy,
Had gone to gaze on Cleopatra too
And made a gap in nature.

The additions are worth attention. North's somewhat amorphous prose is given a beginning and an end. The additions are all, in spite of formal differences, essentially similes and metaphors; and, after the first, which gathers the vision into one whole which it puts imperishably before the mind's eye, the second and third develop the theme which is clinched in climax by the fourth. In them the successive elements — the winds, the water, the air — are represented all as succumbing to the enchantment of love which breathes from the great Queen and her burning barge; and by this varied return on a single motive North's inconsequential panorama is given an organic unity. It is quite impossible to conceive Shakespeare as dovetailing old and new together. Before his mind's eye as he read North had risen a picture half visible, half spiritual, in short, truly imaginative — the manifestation of Egypt, before whom the elements made obeisance. All of North that was congruous with this enchanted vision he incorporated with a flowing pen into his new creation. And the added imagery, about which he probably took no second thought, grew naturally into harmony with itself and with the whole.

To this strange but strangely natural process Coleridge was referring in his often-quoted and sometimes violently interpreted words:

> Images, however beautiful, though faithfully copied from nature, and as accurately represented in words, do not of themselves characterize the poet. They become proofs of original genius only in so far as they are modified by a predominant passion, or by associated thoughts and images awakened by that passion; or when they have the effect of reducing multitude to unity, or succession to an instant; or lastly when a human and intellectual life is transferred to them from the poet's own spirit.

Instances, and better instances than Coleridge himself gives, of all the qualities which he demands of truly creative imagery are obviously to be found in the picture of Cleopatra. 'Multitude is reduced to unity' by the first of the added images; and in the other three a human and intellectual life is transferred to the images (Coleridge should perhaps have said, to the objects of the images) from the poet's own spirit. This last desideratum had been put forward long before by Aristotle in his discussion of 'vividness' in the *Rhetoric*. Vividness, he there says, depands upon metaphor and on 'setting things before the eyes'; but 'setting things before the eyes' turns out itself to be a metaphor, and not, as one might imagine, a demand for the *visual* image. 'This is my definition', says Aristotle.

Those words set a thing before the eyes which describe it in an active state. . . . Or we may use the device often employed by Homer of giving life to lifeless things by means of metaphor. In all such cases he wins applause by describing an active state, as in the line

'Back to the plain rolled the shameless stone'.

Whether the process is described thus dryly as by Aristotle, or more transcendentally by Coleridge, as the working of the poetic spirit 'which shoots its being through earth, sea, and air', the fact is indubitable. It seems to be an imperious need of the creative spirit of the poet to impart life to the apparently lifeless. This may appear a 'device' in the cold light of analysis; but nothing is more certain than that when it is used as a device it is intolerable. No conscious contrivance produced. 'Thou still unravish'd bride of quietness', or 'Joy, whose hand is ever at his lips, Bidding adieu'. Such things as these — and how many of the most magnificently natural achievements of poetry belong to this kind — are, beyond all doubt, the effect of some 'silent working of the spirit'. By the intensity of the poet's contemplation the lifeless thing lives indeed.

Probably the world of true imagination of which these miracles are the common substance is for ever inviolable by intellectual analysis. Even to apprehend its subject-matter the intellect must suffer a sea-change, so that it is no longer itself and cannot perform its proper function. Restore its power to the intellect, again, and that which it seeks to understand has ceased to exist as what it really is. This world of imagination is a universe wherein quality leaps to cohere with quality across the abysms of classification that divide and category the universe of intellectual apprehension. Its true citizens are few and far between; they are the masters of metaphor, and the authentic messages they bring from that near yet distant country perplex our brains and comfort our souls with the half-assurance that the things that are may be otherwise than as we know them.

Towards this exalted region, as to the sole reality, Coleridge was ever groping; and what he meant by the 'predominant passion' which modifies the images of original genius is the power by which genius comprehends its chosen region of this world of qualitative interpenetration. The passion is a passionate contemplation of the unity which pervades the chosen region: a creative passion to correspond with an organic unity. Whether the unity proceeds from the passion, or the passion from the unity, it would be profitless to inquire. They are knit together, as knower and known, in one act of creative comprehension. But if we are shy of the notion of Coleridge which seems to give the poetic spirit an actually plastic power over the material world, we have only to reflect that the predominant passion of the poet's mind is but the counterpart of a predominant quality of the region of the universe which he contemplates. His passion roused by the quality is reflected back upon the quality, and gives it redoubled power; so that it begins to dominate all other qualities and properties, to suffuse them with itself till it becomes as it were the living and governing soul of that which the poet contemplates. By means of his passion the actual realizes its own idea.

However much we struggle, we cannot avoid transcendentalism, for we are seeking to approximate to a universe of quality with analogy for its most essential language through a universe of quantity with a language of identities. Sooner or later, and sooner rather than later, a transcendentalism (which is only the name for a prodigious metaphor) is inevitable. But the process may be brought a little closer to the light of common day if we take once more that region of the qualitative universe which Shakespeare embodied in Cleopatra. She was, we may say, the incarnation of love: the mighty, elemental power which, in Shakespeare's experience, was love, was made corporeal in her. She is possessed by it; from her it radiates and compels obeisance from the elements. But she is not merely a contemplated but a self-uttering thing; and this power that informs her body informs her soul also. All her thoughts are shaped by it. Without her love she will die, she must die; but when she imagines death, she imagines it as a consummation of love, as the thing

> Which sleeps, and never palates more the dug,
> The beggar's nurse and Caesar's. . . .

She dies, and her dying she imagines as a reliving of her triumph on Cydnus. 'I am again for Cydnus, to meet Mark Antony!' And it is a more wonderful triumph. 'Yare, yare, good Iras.' The flower-soft hands that yarely framed the office frame one last office more; and at the aspic's touch the Queen is wholly dedicate to the love she is and serves. The winds, the water, the air obeyed on Cydnus; now the most fickle element of all obeys — her own secret self, from which well up the images of love in death, and death in love:

> The stroke of death is as a lover's pinch
> That hurts and is desired . . .
>   Peace, peace!
> Dost thou not see my baby at my breast
> That sucks the nurse asleep?

In the intensity of Shakespeare's imagination the great property takes utter and complete possession of that it dwells in. By the alchemy of Cleopatra's images death is transmuted into a sleep of love. But her thoughts are Shakespeare's thoughts, her predominant passion his. Therefore it is not strange that Caesar, who in the waking world knows nothing of her dying words, should echo them, and prolong her triumph beyond her death.

>   She looks like sleep,
> As she would catch another Antony
> In her strong toil of grace.

But Caesar did not know what Shakespeare knew, that it was the self-same Antony whom she had taken.

10

Romanticism in Shakespearian Comedy[1]

H.B. Charlton

It is a commonplace of criticism to label Shakespeare's comedies romantic comedies. What else should one call comedies which are set in Illyria or in forests of Arden, and through which Violas and Orsinos, Rosalinds and Orlandos fleet the time to such music as is the food of love? And what is a fantasia like *The Midsummer Night's Dream* but the very ecstasy of romanticism? So the epithet goes unquestioned. It not only seems to fit the quality of Shakespeare's comedies; it catches in a word the prevailing atmosphere of Elizabethan literature at large. And for what concerns comedy in particular, it has an additional recommendation. Being named 'romantic comedies', Shakespeare's can be easily and conveniently distinguished from the counterblasts with which, in the name of the classical comedians, Ben Jonson retaliated on them. Why not, therefore, let well alone, and continue to talk of Shakespeare's romantic comedies, especially as 'romantic' is so variable and vague in its connotation that it can be used to mean almost anything which anybody may take Shakespeare's comedies to be.

Moreover, there can hardly be any doubt that Shakespeare's audience clamorously demanded that their comedies should include certain features which in any sense of the word must be called romantic, features which enter comedy for the first time in Shakespeare's day, features which more than any others

1. A lecture reprinted from *The Bulletin of the John Rylands Library*, vol. 14, No. 2, July 1930.

bear the stamp of the imaginative and emotional fashion of his generation.

His *Comedy of Errors* provides an excellent clue to the taste of his times. He took the main tale of it from Latin comedy, from Plautus. But he made strange additions. His Plautine material is in the boisterous, gross, realistic pattern of Latin comedy: a virago of a wife, a thick-skinned husband, and a common courtesan deal with each other in the coarser way of earthy trafficking. But into this Hogarthian group Shakespeare slips one or two figures who belong to another world: an old man weighed down by the grief of many years' fruitless search for the wife and son tom from him by shipwreck, and a gentle-hearted girl whose lips speak in the sweet new style singers and sonneteers were consecrating to lovers and to love-making.

Such incongruously intrusive figures can only have gained their entry by being the sort of people Shakespeare's public wanted. They surround a Dutch interior with a tale of love and of adventure; and what is a romance but a tale of love and adventure, of prouesse and courtesie? That is the justification for calling the Elizabethan age a romantic age. Shakespeare and his fellows were romantic in the strict sense that they clamoured for fuller draughts of that spirit of romanticism which the Middle Ages had first discovered and revealed in their tales of chivalry and knight-errantry. To them, a lover and his lass were the most engrossing of God's creatures: their comedies, as Jonson contemptuously said, had to be of a duke in love with a countess, the countess to be in love with the duke's son, and the son to love the lady's waiting-maid, with other such cross-wooing. For wooing was the most exciting of man's emotional experiences; and tuned to that key he eagerly responded to those other phases of existence wherein the stress of exceptional circumstances aroused stranger stirrings of the passionate life. The plot of the *Comedy of Errors* is Roman, classical, realistic; but old Ægeon and fair Luciana are the offspring of an un-Roman, unclassical, and unrealistic sentiment: they are the outcome of romance. Of the two, Luciana is the more significant.

Romantic comedy is pre-eminently the comedy of love. It is its specific occupation with wooing which distinguishes it most markedly from classical or Roman comedy. And although between a fully grown romantic comedy such as *As You Like It*, and a Roman comedy such as the *Menœchmi* of Plautus, there may appear to be the widest difference in matter and in spirit, the one has in fact grown out of the other by a gradual modification of the current view of the way of a man with a maid. Classical dramatists dealt freely with amorous intrigues between young men and girls; but solicitation is a social institution, whereas wooing is a mystical experience. The Romans treated such situations as mere incidents in the casual sowing of wild oats, which was by no means a bad training for a young fellow about to enter the world at large. Their real concern was with the older men who had already taken rank in that world. When modern comedy started in Italy at the beginning of the sixteenth century, its founders eagerly imitated classical models. But in the intervening sixteen hundred years, man and his universe had moved. He had been initiated into notions of chivalry. Italian audiences in 1500 were descended from knights who had given their lives to courtesy and to high endeavour. Dante had transmuted womankind for them. He had opened their eyes to the image of woman whose coming is as from heaven to reveal a miracle, and at the sound of whose voice the heart is filled with all of sweetness and humility:

> E par che sia una cosa venuta
> Di cielo in terra a miracol mostrare . . . .
> Ogni dolcezza, ogni pensiero umile
> Nasce nel core a chi parlar la sente.

Merely to see her is to add to one's spiritual stature a new susceptibility, an *intelligenza nuova*. By the simple glance of her eye mankind is lifted to a finer civilisation: 'empiendo il core a ciascun di virtute.' Perhaps such a transcendent 'intellect of love' was too ideal for the sense of the bulk of men. But Petrarch had made the miracle manifest on earth. He had clothed the new soul of woman in the human beauty of woman's body:

> ogni virtute
> Ogni bellezza, ogni real costume
> Giunti in un corpo a mirabil tempre —

and had made her earthly existence more intimate by turning from the idea she symbolized in heaven to lament the heaviness of life when the transfiguring angel of it departs, leaving her lover a desolate and solitary voyager on the dreary waves of time.

With these new sensations pulsing in their blood, Italy's audiences in the sixteenth century were much more thrilled by youth than by age, and youth in love was its most alluring theme. Its comic writers might set themselves to imitate Roman drama as closely as possible; but without knowing it, they could not escape dallying with the young folks of the play far more than Roman precedent warranted. At the very outset of the new comedy, for his *Calandria*, Bibbiena borrows largely from the self-same play of Plautus from which Shakespeare was to borrow for his *Comedy of Errors*. But Bibbiena, taking his twins from Plautus, transforms one of them into a woman, as the later Shakespeare was to do for his *Twelfth Night*. And in Ariosto's comedies, the young gradually supersede the old, until the old man, who stood in the middle limelight of Roman comedy, is pushed into the wings of the stage to make room for the youthful lovers whose Roman prototypes were but accessory figures. The plot of his *Cassaria* is a typically classical plot, except that the old man has at the beginning embarked on a journey which keeps him out of the play until almost the end of it. There is still, of course, as there must be in any play for an audience of Boccaccio's countrymen, much of the bawdy side of love: but the object of exhibiting it is, nominally at all events, to expose it to the flick of satire, whilst in Roman comedy it enters more or less as a natural escapade of the admirable young spark. Moreover, Ariosto's last comedy, the *Scolastica*, not only ties its interest down to the love of its youths for its maidens; it even gives to that love something of the quality of romantic devotion. Without intention, and as yet without much change in outward form, classical comedy is moving gradually to romantic comedy, and is taking to itself a situation and a temper which in due course will transform the type to the sort which characterises romantic comedy. The transition is not so clearly discernible in the work of the English comic dramatists of the sixteenth century. For one thing, classical comedy never fastened itself so securely onto our stage as it did in Italy: and when our Elizabethan comedy was being forged, our romantic temper was urgent and largely conscious of itself. Yet something of the transitional process may be seen in the plays of John Lyly: and its main stages stand out clear as signposts in the two plots which together make *The Taming of a Shrew*. But in the main, Elizabethan romantic comedy did not emerge through a process of natural evolution: it was the product of an obligation imposed ruthlessly on the dramatists by their own age. They were required to beat out a play which should be comic and romantic at once; and at first they scarcely realized that the task involved almost insuperable difficulties. It seemed a simple matter merely to lift the romances bodily on to the comic stage: the whole history of Elizabethan comedy is a tale of the reluctance of comedy to compromise itself with romance. Not realizing his difficulties, Shakespeare sat down light-heartedly to write a romantic comedy, *The Two Gentlemen of Verona*. Before he had finished, he had encountered and had blundered through unexpected obstacles.

To realize what they were and to appreciate the reluctance of romantic material to be naturalized on the comic stage will involve us in a closer examination of romantic taste and of its primary cause, the romances of the Middle Ages. Romantic taste will not tolerate any sort of love-story. Medieval romances are love-stories, and something besides. Not only are they stories of a particular kind of love; they also incorporate a larger tradition which moulds the quality of every element in their material. The range of their incidents, the temper of their sentiments, the pattern of their heroes, the atmosphere of their scenery, and the trend of their ideas, each and all contribute to the homogeneity of the tradition. And in the making of the tradition, life and literature had played complementary parts. The romances reflect the ideal of knighthood by their imaginative idealisation of the experience of knights.

What chivalry is in morals and feudalism in politics, so are the romances in literature. They are the artistic counterpart of the moral and political society which produced them. Socially, one thinks of the Middle Ages as a feudal edifice. Feudalism built itself on an ascending scale of suzerainties. Its elaborate distinctions of precedence created colleges of heralds and a code of social etiquette, as well as a Round Table compromise. But politically and socially speaking, such a system was fragile as a castle of cards, capable of destruction by mere exposure to the winds of heaven, unless cemented by the strongest of moral and sentimental ties. And the only moral tie which could hold the fabric erect was the sense of loyalty. So, out of mere political necessity in the first place, loyalty is the virtue above all other virtues in the medieval knight's equipment; to be false to a plighted oath is first in the catalogue of a recreant's sins. As in the life of the body politic, so in the communion of the Catholic Church. The representative of God on earth called for absolute obedience, and religion consecrated loyalty. Life's highest ideal was unswerving devotion to an all-exacting service, the quest of a holy grail. Inevitably these public ideals were closely reflected in those phases of man's life which come most intimately to his hearth. His private and domestic existence was governed by a code of conduct in the same range of values. Like his worship of God and his faith to his suzerain was the love of his lady. It called for a dedicated life. And as it was the article of his faith which lay closest to his bosom, his love of woman tended to loom more largely in his consciousness than did the less peculiar elements of his creed. Love became the corner-stone of the whole fabric of chivalry. The *chansons de geste* passed into the romances of a Chretien de Troyes: and in them, the love of woman was the cause and not the consequence of devotion to God and to king.

> Qui fist Lancelot et Artus
> En armes si aventureux,
> Tristan, Percheval et Pontus,
> Sinon qu'ilz furent amoureux?

But, theoretically, it was love more like Dante's for Beatrice than Petrarch's for Laura. The pattern knight was he whose days were solemnly devoted to unselfish service for his church, his country, or his love. He was vowed to absolute renunciation of all merely personal desire in the pursuit of his hazardous quest. The superhuman exaltation of the ideal transfigured every circumstance connected with it. The love of woman was a state of mystic adoration removed entirely from the attractions of the flesh. The worshipper was a Sir Galahad, a maiden knight to whom is given such hope he knows not fear, whose strength is as the strength of ten because his heart is pure. A love like this has become a ritual, and expresses itself in social behaviour with an elaborate etiquette of courtesy in word and deed. Medieval romance depicts an ideal world of which each element is occasioned by the ideal of chivalry. It is a world of prouesse and courtesie. Its heroes are without fear and without reproach. They are initiated in courtly forms of service in the lady's bower, until with manhood they lay their heart before the lady of their choice, and from thenceforward their lives are dedicated to proofs of their worthiness by facing unprecedented trials and overcoming incredible obstacles in the uttermost parts of the earth. That is why the medieval love-story is perforce a story of adventure. Its wooing follows elaborately prescribed formalities, and its quests penetrate strange remote regions where deeds of unexampled valour are called forth by the attacks of terrifying monsters more horrible than the eye of man has seen.

Turn, for instance, to the tale of Owein and Lunet. 'Having', says Cynon, 'conquered in all deeds of valour those who were in the same country as myself, I equipped me and travelled through the uttermost parts of the earth and its wildernesses'. Amongst his adventures, he is told that he will meet 'a large black man on the top of a tumulus, who is in no way smaller than two of the men of this world'. When, in fact, he meets the man, even expectation is outdone: 'I had been told he was huge; much larger was he than that; and his iron staff which it had been said to me was a burden for two men, it was clear to me was a burden for four warriors' — Falstaff s romancing about men in Lincoln green scarcely outdoes the original romances themselves. Of course there was variety in the haps of knight-errantry. Not always was it a black man who crossed one's path. Owein, at one point of his journey, finds himself in the presence of maidens sewing brocaded silk in golden chairs, and more marvellous by far was their fairness and beauty than what Owein had been told. At such a revelation, every true man 'must bum with love until every part of him is filled'. One is reminded of the solemn injunction laid on Peredur: 'Should you see a fair woman, woo her, even if she desires you not; she will make you, for that reason, a better man and a more flourishing leader'. These are examples from the *Mabinogion*, that is, from the body of romance before it had been fully romanticised. But for that very reason they display even more clearly the elements which are indigenous to romance. In the full elaboration to which they were to grow, everything — incident, figure, atmosphere, and sentiment — shapes itself to play its part naturally in the whole substance. Comprehensively, these elements provide a universe in which the code of chivalry as a moral and as a social ideal can exemplify itself most significantly. No doubt in the historic origins of romance, the material adventures provide the main if not the entire interest: the *chansons de geste* precede the romances. But the prevailing current of ideals infused itself slowly through the corporal matter, until the whole of it became the visible incorporation of the spirit and the temper of the medieval world. And at the moment of its highest attainment, the soul of it was indubitably its characteristic sense of the meaning of woman and of love.

In its first intention, Elizabethan romantic comedy was an attempt to adapt the world of romance and all its implications to the service of comedy. *The Two Gentlemen of Verona* shows that intention at its crudest. In the story of it there are all the main marks of the medieval tradition as that tradition had been modified, elaborated, and extended by the idealism of Petrarch and by the speculations of the Platonists. It is yet the same tradition in its essence, corroborated rather than altered by the modifying factors; as, for instance, at the hands of Ficino, Platonism brought a medico-metaphysical theory to explain the love-laden gleam of a beautiful eye. Shakespeare's play embodies a literary manner and a moral code; its actions are conducted according to a conventional etiquette and are determined by a particular creed; and every feature of it, in matter and in sentiment, is traceable to the romantic attitude of man to woman. It presents as its setting a world constituted in such fashion that the obligations and the sanctions of its doctrines could best be realized. The course of the whole play is determined by the values such doctrine attaches to the love of man and woman.

A note struck early in the play recalls one of the few passionate love-stories of classical legend — 'how young Leander crossed the

Hellespont' — and at another moment, Ariadne is remembered 'passioning for Theseus' perjury'. But the real colour of the tale is given unmistakably by the presence amongst its characters of Sir Eglamour. By his name is he known and whence he springs. He points straight back to the source of the religious cult of love: 'servant and friend' of Sylvia, he is ready at call to rush to any service to which she may command him. His own lady and his true love died, and on her grave he vowed pure chastity, dedicating himself to the assistance of lovers in affliction, recking nothing what danger should betide him in the venture. His home is in the land of medieval romance; and his brethren are those consecrated warriors who will undertake all danger, though it stands next to death, for one calm look of Love's approval. He comes to life again in a play where knightly vows are spoken, where errantry is the normal mode of service, where the exercise of tilt and tournament is the traditional recreation, where lovers name themselves habitually the servants of their ladies, where such service may impose as a duty the helping of one's lady to a rival, and where the terms of infamy to which the utmost slander can give voice are 'perjured, false, disloyal'. And that is the world in which Shakespeare makes his Two Gentlemen live.

> Throughout the play, 'Love's a mighty lord',
> There is no woe to his correction
> Nor to his service no such joy on earth.

This is the state of the lover as the old *Romaunt of the Rose* had depicted it:

> The sore of love is marvelous,
> For now is the lover joyous,
> Now can he pleyne, now can he grone,
> Now can he syngen, now maken mone;
> To day he pleyneth for hevynesse,
> To morowe he pleyeth for jolynesse.
> The lyf of love is full contrarie,
> Which stounde-mele can ofte varie.

Heavy penance is visited on unbelievers

> for contemning Love,
> Whose high imperious thoughts will punish him
> With bitter fasts, with penitential groans,
> With nightly tears and daily heart-sore sighs.

Sleep is chased from such a rebel's now enthralled eyes, to make them watchers of his own heart's sorrow. From true votaries, nothing less than absolute devotion is required. They must hold no discourse except it be of love. Absent from their lady, they must let no single hour o'erslip without its ceremonial sigh for her sake. The more such languishing fidelity appears to be spurned, the more must it grow and fawn upon its recalcitrant object. Apart from Jove, nothing in life has the least significance:

> banished from her,
> Is self from self, a deadly banishment.
> What light is light, if Sylvia be not seen?
> What joy is joy, if Sylvia be not by?
> Except I be by Sylvia in the night,
> There is no music in the nightingale.
> Unless I look on Sylvia in the day,
> There is no day for me to look upon.
> She is my essence, and I leave to be,
> If I am not by her fair influence
> Fostered, illumined, cherished, kept alive.

Such is the consecrated desolation of the romantic lover: the medieval sense of a world emptied of its content persists through romantic poetry and is the undertone of the Renaissance sonneteers' woe. Bembo puts it not unlike Valentine in the play:

> Tu m'hai lasciato senza sole i giomi,
> Le notte senza stelle, e grave e earo
> Tutto questo, ond'io parlo, ond'io respiro:
> La terra scossa, e'l ciel turbato e negro;
> Et pien di mille oltraggi e mille scomi
> Me sembra ogni parte, quant'io miro.
> Valor e cortesia si dipartiro
> Nel tuo partire; e'l mondo infermo giacque;
> Et virtu spense i suoi chiari lumi;
> Et le fontane a i fiumi
> Nega la vena antica e l'usate acque:
> Et gli augelletti abandonaro il canto,
> Et l'herbe e i fior lasciar nude le piaggie,
> Ne più di fronde il bosco si consperse.

But the lover has ample recompense for his sorrow. Setting the world at nought, he gains a heaven in its stead:

> she is mine own,
> And I as rich in having such a jewel
> As twenty seas if all their sand were pearl,
> The water nectar, and the rocks pure gold.

Inevitably, a creed of such ardent devotion has its appropriate liturgy. Stuffed with protestation, and full of new-found oaths, the lover utters his fears in willful sonnets, whose composed rhymes are fully fraught with serviceable vows:

> . . . and on the altar of her beauty
> You sacrifice your tears, your sighs, your heart:
> Write till your ink be dry, and with your tears
> Moist it again, and frame some feeling line
> That may discover such integrity:
> For Orpheus' lute was strung with poets' sinews,
> Whose golden touch could soften steel and stones,
> Make tigers tame, and huge leviathans
> Forsake unsounded deeps to dance on sands.
> After your dire-lamenting elegies,
> Visit by night your lady's chamber window
> With some sweet concert, to their instruments
> Tune a deploring dump: the night's dead silence
> Will well become such sweet-complaining grievance.
> This, or else nothing, will inherit her.

With oceans of tears, and twenty thousand soul-confirming oaths, the lover excites himself to a fervid bacchanalian orgy, and in his braggardism proclaims his lady 'sovereign to all the creatures on the earth', threatening destruction to all who will not at once subscribe, and extermination to any who but dare to breathe upon her. In the intervals of these ecstatic outbursts, the lover stands before the picture of his love, sighing and weeping, wreathing his arms like a malcontent, until at length he walks off alone like one that hath the pestilence.

When cruel circumstance separates him from his lady, etiquette prescribes the proper behaviour and the right demeanour. He resorts to the congenial solitude of woods or wildernesses. In the earlier days of the cult, his manner on these occasions was more violent than ceremonious. Tristan, as

Malory tells us, exiled and separated from his love, goes mad for grief; he would unlace his armour and go into the wilderness, where he 'brast down the trees and bowes, and other-whyle, when he found the harp that the lady sent him, then would he harped and played thereupon and weep together'. But in the course of time the manners of solitaries became more polite. Chaucer (or the author of the *Romaunt of the Rose)* advises the lover to cultivate a proper solitude:

> For ofte, whan thou bithenkist thee
> Of thy lovyng, where so thou be,
> Fro folk thou must departe in hie,
> That noon perceyve thi maladie.
> But hyde thyne harme thou must alone,
> And go forthe sole, and make thy mone.

It is only one more stage to the final artistic decorum of the habit. The lover in the French romance *Flamenca* 'in the dark of night goes of custom to listen to the nightingale in the wood'. Just, in fact, as does Valentine: in the intervals between inspecting the arms or allocating the booty of his bandit-band, he takes his laments for Sylvia into the woods for orchestral effects from the nightingales:

> These shadowy, desert, unfrequented woods
> I better brook than flourishing peopled towns:
> Here can I sit alone, unseen of any,
> And to the nightingale's complaining notes
> Tune my distresses and record my woes.

Such is the way of lovers in romances, and in *The Two Gentlemen of Verona*. Their state of spiritual ecstasy is revealed by the progressive etherialisation of their sustenance. A collection of the menus of romantic feasts is more than a gastronomic document. In the beginnings of romance, eating and drinking was a major occupation. Owein ate and drank 'whilst it was late in the time of the nones'; and once he was bidden to a feast which took three months to consume and had taken three years to prepare. But later, the initiates have so far purged their mortal grossness, that eating and loving begin to appear incompatible. Again the *Romaunt of the Rose* brings the evidence:

> Such comyng and such goyng
> Such hevynesse and such wakyng

Makith lovers, withouten wene,
Under her clothes pale and lene.
For love leveth colour ne cleemesse,
Who loveth trewe hath no fatnesse;
Thou shalt wel by thy-silf ysee
That thou must nedis assaied be;
For men that shape hem other weye
Falsly her ladyes to bitraye,
It is no wonder though they be fatt,
With false othes her loves they gatt.
For oft I see suche losengours
Fatter than abbatis or priours.

On occasion, the true lover, like Jehan in *Jehan and Blonde*, is like to fade away, and can only eat when his lady serves the dishes to him with her own delicate hands. Our Valentine had been a good trencherman before he became a romantic lover; in those days, when he fasted, it was presently after dinner. But once he becomes a votary not even ambrosia nor nectar is good enough for his ethereal table: 'now can I break my fast, dine, sup, and sleep upon the very naked name of love.' How he thrives on this diet will become a primary article of the literary and dramatic criticism of *The Two Gentlemen of Verona*.

So much for the spirit of romance in the play. Now for the world in which it is set — since, taking its religion thence, it must also take the romantic world in which such religion may reveal itself. Not men living dully sluggardized at home, but those bred and tutored in the wider world, seeking preferment out, trying their fortunes in war or discovering islands far away — these are they who have scope to put such religion to the proof. So in *The Two Gentlemen of Verona*, the scene is laid in Italy, the country which to Shakespeare's fellows was the hallowed land of romance. But it is an Italy of romance, not of physiographic authenticity. It has inland waterways unknown to geographers; the journey from Verona to Mantua is a sea-voyage; it is indeed a scenario in which all the material trappings of romance may be assembled. Mountain and forest are indispensable, mountains which are brigand-haunted, and forests in the gloom of which are abbeys from whose postern gates friars creep into the encircling woods, so rapt in penitential mood that lurking lions, prowling hungrily for food, are utterly forgotten. In such a locality, the tale of true love may run its uneven course. The poetically gifted lover meets such obstacles as a rival at whom he hurls his cartel, and a perverse father whose plans for his daughter are based on such irrelevant considerations as the rivals' bank-balances. The father's castle has its upper tower far from the ground, and built so shelving that to climb it is at apparent hazard of one's life. And here is the angelic daughter's chamber wherein she is nightly lodged, within doors securely locked, so that rescue can only be by a corded ladder to her chamber window. Then unexpected difficulties will be expected to intrude: the best-laid plot to carry her away is foiled by the machinations of a villain out of the least suspected quarter. Banishment naturally follows, and at length, with the flight of the heroine and the pursuit of her by the entire court, all will work out well by a series of surprising coincidences, to which rivals, brigands, friars, and lions are all somehow contributory. In this way, romantic love makes its romantic universe; and this in fact is the setting and the story of *The Two Gentlemen of Verona*.

This, both in matter and in spirit, is the tradition which the Elizabethan dramatists desired to lift bodily on to their comic stage. But something somehow went wrong. The spirit of medieval romance seemed to shrivel in the presence of comedy. Something similar had in fact happened in the real world outside the theatre. The last hero of romance had lived gloriously and had died quite out of his part. Jacques de Lalaing, le bon chevalier, the mirror of knighthood who adorned the Burgundian court in the middle of the fifteenth century, had become the pattern of chivalry for all Europe. To his contemporaries 'fair was he as Paris, pious as Aeneas, wise as Ulysses, and passionate as Hector': and his exploits in tournament and in knight-errantry had carried his fame through many lands. He died an early death in 1453. But he did not die of a lover's broken heart; nor was he slain in tourney by a foeman worthy of his steel and of his thirty-two emblazoned pennants. He was shot down by a cannonball in an expedition against the merchants and shopkeepers of Ghent. The gross, ponderable facts of a very material world swept the symbol of an outworn ideal from off the face of the earth. So in *The Two Gentlemen*, a sheer clod of earth, Launce by name, will, quite unwittingly, expose the unsubstantiality of the romantic hero with whom the play throws him into contact. But we are anticipating. The consequences of Shakespeare's attempt to dramatize romance must be watched in closer detail.

There is little wonder that the Elizabethan dramatists saw the dramatic possibilities of such material, and did not at first perceive its dramatic disadvantages. They felt the dramatic thrill of following these lovers and setting the world at nought. Nor is it very difficult to set the geographical world at nought, at least to the extent of making inland seas in Italy or liberating living lions in its woods. Yet sometimes the distortions of the physical universe necessarily ventured by the romanticist entail violent wrenches of our common consciousness. The dukes of Shakespeare's Italy, for instance, apparently have magic power over the flight of time; for whilst a banished man is speaking but ten lines, the proclamation of his banishment is ratified, promulgated, and has become publicly known throughout the duchy, and sentinels have already been posted along the frontiers to prevent a surreptitious return of the exile to the land which he has not yet had time to pack his suit-case for leaving. It is a land, too, where optical illusions, or perhaps optical delusions, are the normal way of vision. A man seeking a pageboy interviews an applicant for the post; he is just enough of a business man to know that some sort of reason must be advanced for taking on a servant who can show neither character nor reference from previous employers, and so Proteus, engaging the disguised Julia, says that the engagement is specifically on the recommendation of the applicant's face; but he does not recognize, as he gazes into this face, that it was the one he was smothering with kisses a few weeks before when its owner, in her proper dress, was his betrothed. Yet these are really only minor impediments, requiring but a little and a by no means reluctant suspension of our disbelief. They are altogether insignificant compared with the reservations involved when romance displays its peculiar propensity for setting the world of man at nought. To satisfy its own obligations, it perforce demanded super-men; at all events, the heroes it puts forward as its votaries in the play are something either more or less than men.

Romantically speaking, Valentine is the hero, and not alone in the technical sense. In classical comedy the hero is simply the protagonist, the central figure who is the biggest butt of the comic satire. But here the protagonist is the upholder of the faith on which the play is built, the man with whom the audience is called upon to rejoice admiringly, and not the fellow at whom it is derisively to laugh. He is to play the hero in every sense of the word. Yet in the event, the prevailing spirit of romance endows him with sentiments and provides him with occupations which inevitably frustrate the heroic intention. The story renders him a fool. Convention may sanctify his sudden conversion from the mocker to the votary of love, and may even excuse or palliate his fractious braggardism when he insults Proteus with ill-mannered comparisons between Silvia and Julia. But his helplessness and his impenetrable stupidity amount to more than the traditional blindness of a lover. Even the clown Speed can see through Silvia's trick, when she makes Valentine write a letter to himself. But Valentine plays out the excellent motion as an exceeding puppet, unenlightened by the faintest gleam of common insight. And despite his vaunt that he knows Proteus as well as he knows himself, he is blind to villainies so palpable that Launce, the other clown of the piece, though he be but a fool, has the wits to recognize them for what they plainly are. The incidents are dramatically very significant, for both Launce and Speed come into the play for no reason whatever but to be unmistakable dolts. One begins to feel that it will be extremely difficult to make a hero of a man who is proved to be duller of wit than the patent idiots of the piece. Even when Valentine might have shone by resource in action, he relapses into conventional laments, and throws himself helplessly into the arms of Proteus for advice and consolation. Heroic opportunity stands begging round him when he encounters the brigands. But besides demonstrating that he can tell a lie — witness his tale of cock and bull about having killed a man — the situation only serves to discredit him still more: for the words of his lie, his crocodile tears for the fictitious man he claims to have slain, and his groundless boast that he slew him manfully in fight without false vantage or base treachery, are in fact nothing but an attempt to make moral capital by means of forgery and perjury. They have not even the recommendation of the Major-General's tears for the orphan boy. When at length Valentine is duly installed as captain of the brigands, his chief occupation is to vary highway robbery with sentimental descants on the beauty of nature in her 'shadowy, desert, unfrequented woods':

> Here can I sit alone, unseen of any —

and we already know his favourite hobby on these saunterings —

> And to the nightingale's complaining notes
> Tune my distresses and recording woes.

He is own brother to Gilbert's coster, who, when he isn't jumping on his mother, loves to lie a basking in the sun, and to the cut-throat, who, when not occupied in crimes, loves to hear the little brook a gurgling and listen to the merry village chimes. But Valentine's utmost reach of ineptitude comes with what, again romantically speaking, is meant to be the heroic climax of the play. When he has just learnt the full tale of the villainy of Proteus, the code permits him neither resentment nor passion. Like a cashier addressing a charwoman who has pilfered a penny stamp, he sums up his rebuke — 'I am sorry I must never trust thee more'. And worse follows immediately. With but five lines of formal apology from the villain, Valentine professes himself so completely satisfied that he enthusiastically resigns his darling Silvia to the traitor. Even Valentine must have seen that the gesture was a little odd, because he quotes the legal sanction. It is the code, a primary article in the romantic faith — 'that my love may appear plain and free'. But it makes a man a nincompoop. Nor does it help much that after his preposterous episode, Valentine is allowed to spit a little fire in an encounter with another rival, Thurio. He has already proved himself so true a son of romance that he can never again be mistaken for a creature of human nature.

Proteus is less hampered by romantic obligation; because the plot requires him to have just sufficient of salutary villainy to make him throw over their commandments for his own ends. Yet the villain of romance suffers almost as much from the pressure of romanticism as does the hero. The noble fellows whom he, as villain, is called upon to deceive are such gullible mortals that little positive skill is necessary. Proteus can fool Thurio and Valentine and the Duke without exerting himself. But on the one occasion when he might have shown his wits, he only reveals his lack of them. Making love to Silvia, he meets her protest against his disloyalty to Julia by inventing the easy excuse that Julia is dead. Silvia replies that, even so, he should be ashamed to wrong Valentine. It is, of course, a tight corner: but the best Proteus can do is to say 'I likewise hear that Valentine is dead'. He might at least have displayed a little more ingenuity in invention; he fails in precisely such a situation as would have permitted the clown of classical comedy to triumph. Moreover, the main plot requires Proteus to be guilty of incredible duplicity, and of the most facile rapidity in changing morals and mistresses. But he need scarcely have made the change explicit in words so ineptly casual and banal as his remark: '*Methinks* my zeal to Valentine is cold'. The phrase is accidentally in keeping with the unintended complacence he displays when, wooing the lady who will have none of him, he begins by informing her that 'he has made her happy' by his coming. The trait becomes intolerably ludicrous when, all his sins forgiven him and Julia restored to his arms, all he can utter in confession is his own fatuous self-conceit:

> O heaven, were man
> But constant, he were perfect.

It is, of course, a fine sentiment; but the audience, having seen Valentine, simply will not believe it.

Even the brigands of romance will scarcely stand the test of the stage. They enter with metaphorical daggers in mouths bristling with black mustachios and with desperate oaths. Callous and bloodthirsty ruffians, spoiling for a fight, their chief regret is that fate is sending only one defenceless traveller to be rifled instead of ten. But when the destined victim turns out to be two, courage perhaps abates a little: at all events, the travellers are warned to keep their distance, and throw over the booty or otherwise to assume a sitting posture, whilst the rifling is safely done by the desperadoes themselves. Perhaps this, and not his customary ineptitude in speech, is what makes Valentine address the villains as 'My friends'. But, of course, his assumption is, for the trade of brigandage, economically unsound. And so, with apologies for correcting him, Valentine is informed that he is not playing the game — 'that's not so, sir; we are your enemies'. But the outlaws are connoisseurs of masculine beauty, and Valentine's fine figure secures him an opportunity for a hearing: one cannot but note that this is the first time that any of his romantic attributes has made for his advantage, and that he misuses it scandalously for his lying brag. Hearing the fiction, however, the bandits feel at once that here is a fellow spirit, given like themselves to 'so small a fault' as homicide. Straightway they implore him to show them his diploma in the modern languages, promising him the kingship of the band if it is of good honours' standard. Becoming convivial, they reveal their amiable dispositions in snatches of their life-history. One has amused himself with attempts at abduction. Another, when the whim takes him, 'in his mood', has the merry trick of stabbing gentlemen unto the heart; and his gaiety makes us forget that a mood in Shakespeare's English was not quite the casual fancy it now is. Another acclaims these and other 'such like petty crimes' as congenial peccadilloes in his own repertory. By this time the brigands have become so hilarious with their reminiscences that they are no longer minded to scrutinise Valentine's academic credentials. They will take him for a linguist merely 'on his own report', and, mainly because he 'is beautified with goodly shape', they offer him the leadership, pathetically promising to love him as their commander and their king. Clearly such a thoroughly unbrigandlike procedure as this election has almost put them out of their parts. They must be allowed to recover in a traditional tableau. Daggers are whipped out, threats become fierce, and Valentine, with steel points at his throat, is given the choice of being a king or a corpse. Perhaps his fear is responsible for the odd proviso that 'silly women' shall be exempt from the depradations of the gang over which he is to rule; but it is of course too much to expect of better men than Valentine to require them to anticipate a variation in the meaning of a word. Neither before nor after *The Two Gentlemen of Verona* has dramatic literature known a band of outlaws like to these — except once: there are the Pirates of Penzance: but then Gilbert meant his to be funny.

One begins to suspect that everything which is hallowed by the tradition of romance is made thereby of no avail for the purposes of drama. But there are Julia and Launce to reckon with;

and these are figures universally accounted the most substantial beings in the play. So indeed they are. But they owe it entirely to the fact that they are under no obligation whatever to the code of romance. The behaviour of Valentine is entirely conditioned by the doctrine of romantic love. But the code allowed to woman no duty but to excite by her beauty the devoted worship of her knight. If England instead of France had performed the final codification of chivalry, its women might have had other and less lady-like propensities, such, for instance, as King Horn's Rimenhild displayed. But when a French romance elaborates its portrait of womanhood it gives her patience rather than character: women with the forcefulness of a distinct personality might have turned the energies of their knights away from consecrated paths of knighthood, as Chretien's Enide turned her Erec:

> Mes tant l'ama Erec d'amors
> Que d'armes mes ne li chaloit,
> Ne a tomoiemant n'aloit
> N'avoit mes soing de tomoiier.

Wherefore Chretien's romance tells of Erec's regeneration through the discipline by which he reduces his Enide to absolute submission. At the end she has attained complete self-suppression—

> Ne je tant hardie ne sui
> Que je os regarder vers lui —

and, to the modern eye, has become the perfect pattern of an exquisitely charming non-entity.

When Shakespeare takes over a tradition whose women are like these, so long as he preserves the beauty of their faces, he can endow them with whatever character he may please. His Julia is a creation, not a convention. As she is a woman, acting on a woman's instinct — 'I have no other but a woman's reason, I think him so because I think him so' — she is depicted in moods, whimsies, and vagaries which are in fact the stuff of dramatic characterisation. Like the heroine of romance, she will cover her first love-letter with kisses, and press the precious manuscript to her heart. But like the spirited independent young lady of the world, she will not expose herself to the chuckles of her maid by exhibiting the common symptoms of her affections. Hence the pretended contempt and the struggle to keep up appearances, even at considerable risk to the sacred document. But for what seriously concerns her love, Julia is too levelheaded to overreach herself. As far as maybe she will avoid the disapproval of opinion: but where there is no remedy, she will defy a scandalised world and undertake her pilgrimage of love. She knows the hazards of the road and the many weary steps it will involve. But she also knows her own capacities, and has duly taken note of all material things she will stand in need of. And although Proteus is a poor thing on whom to lavish so much love, Julia knows that love is indeed a blinded god; and in her capable hands even a Proteus may be moulded to something worth the having.

Launce is another who insists on remaining in the memory. He has no real right within the play, except that gentlemen must have servants and Elizabethan audiences must have clowns. But coming in thus by a back-door he earns an unexpected importance in the play. Seen side by side with Speed, his origin is clear. Whilst Speed belongs to the purely theatrical family of the Dromios, with their punning and logic-chopping asininities, Launce harks back to the native Costard. And as Costard shows his relationship to Bottom by his skill in village theatricals, so Launce reveals by his wooing his family connexion with Touchstone and Touchstone's Audrey, who was a poor thing, but his own. All the kind of the Launces are thus palpably a mighty stock. Their worth, compared with that of the Speeds and the Dromios, is admirably indicated by Launce's consummate use of Speed's curiosity and of his better schooling. Launce gets his letter deciphered; he gets also an opportunity to display his own superior breeding and to secure condign punishment for the ill-mannered Speed: 'now will he be swinged for reading my letter; an unmannerly slave, that will thrust himself into secrets! I'll after, to rejoice in the boy's correction'.

Launce is happiest with his dog. Clownage can go no farther than the pantomimic representation, with staff and shoe and dog, of the parting from his home-folks. Laughter is hilarious at Launce's bitter grief that his ungrateful cur declined to shed a tear. That Launce should expect it is, of course, the element of preposterous incongruity which makes him a clown. But when he puts his complaint squarely, that his 'dog has no more pity in him than a dog', the thrust pierces more than it was meant to. Romance itself has expected no less largely of Valentine, of Proteus, and of the rest. It has demanded that man shall be more than man, and has laid upon him requisitions passing the ability of man to fulfill. At the bidding of romance Valentine and Proteus have become what they are in the play, and the one thing they are not is men like other men. A further incident in which Launce is concerned takes on a similarly unexpected significance. He has made as great a sacrifice as did Valentine himself: he has given up his own cur in place of the one which Proteus entrusted to him to take to Silvia. But the effect hardly suggests that self-sacrifice is worldly-wise. And so once more it seems to bring into question the worldly worth of the code which sanctifies such deeds. Unintentionally, Launce has become the means by which the incompatibilities and the unrealities of romantic postulates are laid bare. And Launce is palpably the stuff of comedy: awakening our comic sense, he inevitably sharpens our appreciation of the particular range of incongruities which are the province of comedy — the incongruity between what a thing really is and what it is taken to be.

Romance, and not comedy, has called the tune of *The Two Gentlemen of Verona* and governed the direction of the action of the play. That is why its creatures bear so little resemblance to men of flesh and blood. Lacking this, they are scarcely dramatic figures at all; for every form of drama would appear to seek at least so much of human nature in its characters. But perhaps the characters of the Two Gentlemen are comic in a sense which at first had never entered the mind of their maker. Valentine bids for the sympathy, but not for the laughter, of the audience: the ideals by which he lives are assumed to have the world's approbation. But in execution they involve him in most ridiculous plight. He turns the world from its compassionate approval to a mood of sceptical questioning. The hero of romantic comedy appears no better than its clowns. And so topsy-turvy is the world of romance that apparently the one obvious way to be reputed in it for a fool is to show at least a faint sign of discretion and of common sense. Thurio, for instance, was cast for the dotard of the play, and of course he is not without egregious folly. But what was meant in the end to annihilate him with contempt turns out quite otherwise. Threatened by Valentine's sword he resigns all claim to Silvia, on the ground that he holds him but a fool that will endanger his body for a girl that loves him not. The audience is invited to call Thurio a fool for thus showing himself to be the one person in the play with a modicum of worldly wisdom, a respect for the limitations of human nature, and recognition of the conditions under which it may survive. Clearly, Shakespeare's first attempt to make romantic comedy had only succeeded so far that it had unexpectedly and inadvertently made romance comic. The real problem was still to be faced.

11
Shakespeare's Topical Significances[1]

G.B. Harrison

1. Wing John

There is such constant contention among Shakespearian critics between those who 'see things' and those who do not that anyone who ventures on an exposition of contemporary allusions in the plays takes great risks. Critics, too fastidious for the dusty labours of scholarship, will dismiss him as a pedant; scholars who regard caution as the greatest of virtues will call him 'rash', 'speculative', 'unsound', or even 'ingenious'. Yet Shakespeare was interested in his fellow creatures; he can scarcely have avoided all comment upon the events of his time; and, indeed, so soon as one sees the plays against the background of their own times it becomes clear at once that they were full of special meaning to their original audiences. When the story gave him a chance of creating a situation or a speech full of significance to his audience, Shakespeare seldom neglected it; but because his sense of dramatic fitness was so acute the speech remains apt long after the significance has been lost. Direct topical allusions are not very common in Shakespeare, but topical significances abound.

At all times those plays are most popular which have some special meaning for their first audiences. Such was Mr. Drinkwater's *Abraham Lincoln*, written and first produced in the summer and autumn of 1918. The dialogue in *Abraham Lincoln*

1. *The Times Literary Supplement*, November 13 and 20, 1930.

was entirely relevant to its theme; there were no obvious glances at Haig or Foch, no gags about Blighty, nor phrases borrowed from the trenches; and yet no play written during the War was more topical in its significances:

> Isn't it possible for you to Stop this war? In the name of a suffering country, I ask that . . . .
>
> But it must be endured. The cause was a right one two years ago. It is unchanged . . . .
>
> But the best of us have an instinct to resist aggression if it won't listen to persuasion . . . .
>
> This appeal to force is the misdeed of an imperfect world . . . .
>
> Goliath couldn't be spared. He's doing contracts for the government, you know. Goliath couldn't possibly go . . . .
>
> These gentle people are mistaken, but they are mistaken cleanly, and in a great name. It is you that dishonour the cause for which we stand — it is you that make it a mean and little thing . . . .
>
> Yes; but don't ask me for reprisals.

Such speeches as these had a peculiar incandescence twelve years ago which has now almost faded away; the immediate success of *Abraham Lincoln* was largely due to its special significance in 1918.

Shakespeare also lived through a great war, and for those who will make the effort to hear he has recorded, perhaps unconsciously, its phases and its moods. At least seven of his plays (apart from the *Henry VI* series) are definitely 'war plays' — *King John*, the two parts of *Henry IV, Henry V*, *Troilus and Cressida*, *Coriolanus*, *All's Well*; there is war in the background of *Richard II*, *Much Ado*, *Hamlet*, *Macbeth*, *Antony and Cleopatra*. Of these the most obviously significant is the worst — *King John*, which I take to have been written between June and September, 1596.

In the autumn of 1595 and until the late summer of 1596 a feeling of deep anxiety was very generally prevalent amongst Englishmen. By August, 1595, it had been realized that a new and greater Spanish Armada was preparing. Drake and Hawkins sailed on their last voyage at the end of the month; but their departure at such a time was felt to be a dangerous mistake in policy. Moreover many, and especially scholarly persons, were genuinely alarmed because on September 6, 1595, the Queen entered upon her ninth or grand climacteric — that is, her sixty-third year, when the mystic numbers nine and seven were united. Her eighth climacteric — the year '88 — had been a time of threatened disaster, and the prophets had been busy that year; but the ninth was astrologically far more alarming.

This uneasiness is expressed in a book which was put forth about this time at Cambridge by William Coveil, Fellow of Queens' College. It was called *Polimanteia; or the means, lawful and unlawful, to judge of the fall of a Commonwealth, against the frivolous and foolish conjectures of this age*. It discusses oracles, divinations, and such subjects, endeavouring to limit the range and reliability of supernatural methods of foreknowledge. Among other opinions which Covell confutes is a dangerous tenet of Bodin, 'who saith, that if we mark the great and notable changes of states and kingdoms, we shall find the most part to have been in September, in which month God gave the beginning to all the world'. (Sig. f2.) In the book the essay on divination is followed by exhortations in the person of England to her three daughters, Cambridge, Oxford, and the Inns of Court, and to all her inhabitants, beseeching them to remain loyal at this anxious time. In one place (Sig. v2^{v}) England laments that she is torn in pieces by her own inhabitants; Coveil comments in the margin, 'England cannot perish but by Englishmen'.

Nor were relations between England and France at all happy as Henry IV became more dissatisfied with the lack of direct help which the Queen would afford him. In October M. de Lomenie was sent over to lay his needs before the Queen and the Council; and he presented the King's letters with such stout speeches that the Queen, who disliked plain speaking, was alarmed and angry.

Early in November the perpetual bogy of the succession suddenly reappeared. A copy of Doleman's book, *A Conference about the next Succession to the Crown of England*, with its dedication to the Earl of Essex, came into the Queen's hands. She demanded an explanation and for a short while Essex was under a cloud. A few days later emergency measures were put in hand to deal with a threat of invasion; and from London and Southampton and fifteen home and south coast counties a force of over sixty thousand men was prepared.

By the end of the year the situation in France was worse. M. de Lomenie brought back no satisfactory answer from London, and the general opinion was that the alliance was rapidly dissolving. Early in January Sir Henry Unton was sent over to the French King to mend matters, if possible; but at his first public audience he was received coldly and scornfully and told that, as nothing would prevail with the Queen, the King must provide for his own safety as best he could. The general alarm at home increased. In January one C. G., another Cambridge man, published a book called *A Watchword for War* to confute various fearful alarms that were being circulated — that the enemy was great; that may be he will have the aid of the Indians, or the Pope; and perhaps of some that had greater cause to gratify us than be against us. C. G. had no fear of the papists, for, said he, when they should see the Spaniard they would join against them. Nor need they fear civil troubles so long as the common saying remained true — 'If we be true within ourselves, we need not care or fear the enemy'. To the like effect Thomas Nun, in *A Comfort against the Spaniard*, wrote:

> Is it true that the Spaniards will come this spring? And is it not true that we are ready to receive them? Hath this land at any time had either better provision or more soldiers? Braver captains to lead them, or sounder divines to encourage them?

By the end of January, 1596, it was believed that Henry was about to desert his allies and make a separate peace with the enemy; the gossip in his camp was that the Cardinal Archduke of Austria, who was then at Namur, had received instructions from the King of Spain to negotiate. In March Unton died having accomplished nothing. Meanwhile at home a great fleet (as great as in '88) was being mobilized and fitted out.

At the beginning of April news came that the Cardinal had suddenly invested Calais, which could only hold out for a few days. On the 5th Mr. John Norden, the topographer, entered *A Christian familiar comfort and encouragement unto all English subjects*, urging his readers not to be alarmed at the Spanish threats. He warned especially the inferior magistrates to beware of sudden and indiscreet hurly burlies, for it was a policy of the enemy to draw on tumults by sudden reports, dangerous bruits, and open hoobubs. The Queen hesitated to send relief to Calais; but after some ignoble bargaining orders were given on the afternoon of Good Friday (April 9) that 6,000 men should march at once for Dover, where Essex and the Lord Admiral were waiting to lead over a relief force; and such expedition was used by the Lord Mayor that most of them were ready by 8 o'clock at night.

A few days earlier the Bishop of St. Davids, preaching before the Queen and Court, most unhappily chose as his text, 'O teach us to number our days that we may incline our hearts unto wisdom', whereto he attached a sermon on mystical numbers, and the grand climacteric, devising some suitable prayers for the Queen, as one who had now reached that age when 'the senses begin to fail, the strength to diminish, yea all the powers of the body daily to decay'. The prayer included these words:

> O Lord, I am now entered a good way into the climacterical year of mine age, which mine enemies wish and hope to be fatal unto me. But Thou, Lord, which by Thy prophet Jeremy command the House of Israel not to learn the way of the heathen, nor be afraid of the signs of heaven, and who by Thy Almighty hand and outstretched arm, maddest the year of greatest expectation, even '88, marvellous by the overthrow of Thine and mine enemies, now, for Thy Gospel's sake, which hath long had sanctuary in this land, make likewise '96 as prosperous unto me and my loyal subjects.

The Queen was not grateful and told him bluntly that he should have kept his arithmetic to himself.

On 10th April it was reported that Calais could hold out no longer, and the levies were therefore dismissed. But at 10 o'clock on Easter Sunday they were again demanded. The people at this moment were making their Easter Communion; the constables were therefore sent round to the parish churches to close the doors till the necessary men had again been pressed. The levies were marched off to Dover. Two days later the sound of the cannon could be heard all day in London: on the 16th, when the men had been embarked and were ready to sail, news came that Calais had fallen. Some very ugly stories of French treachery were soon in circulation. Stow says that 400 old soldiers, sent by the States, succeeded in breaking through the Spaniards and reaching the citadel. But the garrison refused to admit them and they were all slain, the French declaring that they would rather have the Spaniards in Calais than the English or their other friends, for 'if the Spaniards win it, yet there is good hope by mediation of the Church to regain it; but if the English repossess it they will never restore it'.

Such alarms naturally gave rise to a number of rumours and panics. In Sussex dark things were reported of the recusants. At the time of the Calais anxiety they raised a rumour that the Spaniards had landed in three places in Sussex and were burning Pevensey, which caused 'woeful outcries of the people' and not a little hindered the dispatch of troops from Rye. On April 29, one Smith, one of the men pressed for the Calais service, was sentenced in the Star Chamber for spreading a rumour that when the Lord Admiral's ship was searched by the Earl of Essex the powder barrels were found to contain ashes and sand. About this time, too, the survivors of Drake's fleet were coming into Plymouth with the full story of their failure and of the deaths of Drake and Hawkins. In June, Sir John Smythe, a very doughty old soldier, addressed traitorous and dangerous words to the train bands at Colchester and was hurriedly thrust in the Tower. Sir John's misdemeanours were caused rather by personal dislike of Lord Burleigh and over draughts of white wine and sack on a midsummer morning; but they added to the general anxiety. At last, after one false start, the great fleet sailed on June 3. It was, I believe, about a month later that Shakespeare's *King John* was first produced.[2]

If these events are taken as the contemporary background of the play, certain passages will assume a new significance; such as Austria's remark

2. If the description of the lost Arthur is based on Shakespeare's own loss of Hamlet (August, 1596), then the play should be dated some weeks later.

I will no more return
Till Angiers, and the right thou hast in France
Together with that pale, that white-fac'd shore,
Whose foot spurns back the ocean's roaring tides
And coops from other lands her islanders,
Even till that England, hedg'd in with the main,
That water-walled bulwark, still secure
And confident from foreign purposes,
Even till that utmost corner of the west
Salute thee for her king.

(II. i. 20-9.)

There is a passing reference to the swarms of young gallants who had just sailed for Cadiz in

And all the unsettled humours of the land,
Rash, inconsiderate, fiery voluntaries,
With ladies' faces and fierce dragons' spleens,
Have sold their fortunes at their native homes,
Bearing their birthrights proudly on their backs,
To make a hazard of new fortunes here.
In brief, a braver choice of dauntless spirits
Than now the English bottoms have waft o'er
Did never float upon the swelling tide,
To do offence and scathe in Christendom.

(II. i. 66-75.)

Nor was the Bastard's speech on 'Commodity' without its special meaning:

This same bias, this Commodity,
This bawd, this broker, this all-changing word,
Clapp'd on the outward eye of fickle France,
Hath drawn him from his own determin'd aid,
From a resolv'd and honourable war,
To a most base and vile-concluded peace . . .
Since kings break faith upon Commodity,
Gain, be my lord, for I will worship thee!

(II. i. 580-6, 597-8.)

In the play another Cardinal would separate France from England; and John defies him as a true-blue Protestant should:

What earthly name to interrogatories
Can task the free breath of a sacred king?
Thou canst not, cardinal, devise a name

So slight, unworthy and ridiculous,
To charge me to an answer, as the pope.
Tell him this tale; and from the mouth of England
Add thus much more: that no Italian priest
Shall tithe or toll in our dominions;
But as we under heaven are supreme head,
So under him that great supremacy,
Where we do reign, we will alone uphold,
Without the assistance of a mortal hand:
So tell the pope; all reverence set apart
To him, and his usurp'd authority.
(III. i. 147-60.)

The whole passage which follows is but a slight transposition of the situation of Henry IV of France.

'Hoobubs' and 'hurly-burlies' trouble John's London, and Shakespeare sketches them from his own immediate observations:

Old men and beldams in the streets
Do prophesy upon it dangerously:
Young Arthur's death is common in their mouths;
And when they talk of him, they shake their heads
And whisper one another in the ear;
And he that speaks doth gripe the hearer's wrist
Whilst he that hears makes fearful action,
With wrinkled brows, with nods, with rolling eyes.
I saw a smith stand with his hammer, thus,
The whilst his iron did on the anvil cool,
With open mouth swallowing a tailor's news;
Who, with his shears and measure in his hand,
Standing on slippers — which his nimble haste
Had falsely thrust upon contrary feet —
Told of a many thousand warlike French,
That were embattled and rank'd in Kent.
Another lean unwash'd artificer
Cuts off his tale and talks of Arthur's death.
(IV. ii. 185-202.)

Uneasily stirring in every one's mind was the terrible dread of what might, what surely would, happen when anarchy should be let loose at the Queen's death. The author of the 'Conference about the next Succession' declared that the issue would not be decided without a war; and the Bastard's words over dead Arthur were grim, but unfulfilled, prophecy:

How easy dost thou take all England up!
From forth this morsel of dead royalty,
The life, the right and truth of all this realm
Is fled to heaven; and England now is left
To tug and scamble and to part by the teeth
The unow'd interest of proud swelling state.
Now for the bare-pick'd bone of majesty
Doth dogged war bristle his angry crest,
And snarleth in the gentle eyes of peace:
Now powers from home and discontents at home
Meet in one line; and vast confusion waits —
As doth a raven on a sick-fallen beast —
The imminent decay of wrested pomp.
(IV. iii. 142-54.)

And in the last words of the play Shakespeare gathers all these feelings together in his most significant patriotic outburst:

This England never did, nor never shall,
Lie at the proud foot of a conqueror,
But when it first did help to wound itself.
Now these her princes are come home again,
Come the three corners of the world in arms,
And we shall shock them. Nought shall make us rue,
If England to itself do rest but true.
(V. viii. 112 to end.).

No one would claim *King John* as one of Shakespeare's successes, but these passages show that the play had at least some very personal meanings for the audiences of 1596.

2. She Earl of Essex

The anxious situation of the early summer of 1596 changed quite suddenly. In the middle of July the first news of the great victory at Cadiz reached London. On August 8 a service of thanks giving was held in London. By the end of the month a new alliance had been arranged with the French king whereby both sides promised not to make peace separately, and on August 29 the Queen solemnly swore to observe it. A week later the Queen passed out of her grand climacteric, and once more the prophets of disaster were obliged to 'mock their own presage'.

But the Cadiz voyage brought its troubles. The Queen was dissatisfied with the profits of the expedition, and in September there was a regrettable scene in Court. Essex had claimed the ransoms of his prisoners for himself when the Queen demanded them. The Queen appealed to old Lord Burleigh; but when he suggested that Essex should be heard she lost her temper with the old man, called him a miscreant and a coward, and accused him of regarding the Earl for fear or favour more than herself. Essex was equally angry, for he had suspected that Burleigh was crossing him. For the last eight years Essex had been becoming steadily more conspicuous. As a young man of twenty-five he had shown himself a gallant and romantic warrior, and if he was rash and irresponsible as a general, doubtless in time he would mature; but as he grew older the less attractive side of his character had revealed itself, and acute observers could already see that he was heading for disaster.

Essex remained at Court for the next six months. He was growing continually more difficult. In March he quarreled openly with Sir Robert Cecil, but by Ralegh's mediation they were reconciled for the time. In June he was put in sole command of thc Fleet which was being prepared for a fresh attack on Spain, with Lord Thomas Howard and Sir Walter Ralegh under him. In July they sailed, but Essex's luck was now out. The Fleet was twice turned back by tempests; and it was not until the middle of August that the expedition got away, by which time many of the young gallants had slipped off home.

On August 27 Shakespeare's *Tragedy of King Richard II* was entered for publication; it was published during the year and two further editions came out in 1598. Clearly *Richard II* had a significance for the original audiences which has now faded. The Deposition scene was omitted from these quartos, presumably because it was thought to have a bearing on the times; three and a half years later the Essex conspirators paid the players to produce it as a piece of revolutionary propaganda; in August, 1601, Queen Elizabeth rounded on Lambarde, Keeper of the Records of the Tower, who was showing off his treasures, with 'I am Richard the Second, know ye not that'?[3]

---

3. The various references to Richard II are collected in an article by Miss E.M. Albright in *P.M.L.A.* xlii. 3, entitled 'Shakespeare's *Richard II* and the Essex Conspiracy'.

The connexion between Richard II and Queen Elizabeth is not at all obvious to modem readers; but there is in the play a short passage, describing Bolingbroke's 'popular courses' as he went off to banishment, which could scarcely have been overlooked by contemporaries:

> Ourself and Bushy, Bagot here and Green
> Observ'd his courtship to the common people,
> How he did seem to dive into their hearts
> With humble and familiar courtesy,
> What reverence he did throw away on slaves,
> Wooing poor craftsmen with the craft of smiles
> And patient under bearing of his fortune,
> As 'twere to banish their affects with him.

This speech seems to be written in a freer metre than most of the rest of the play, as if it had been added later. Yet it is difficult to see how Essex's followers could have derived much inspiration from the play. The familiar cycle of the Henry VI plays showed what disasters followed upon the deposition of Richard, and twice in the play the fearful results of disloyalty were prophesied.

Essex was still away with the Fleet when the Queen decided to honour the Lord Admiral, Lord Charles Howard, who was created Earl of Nottingham on October 23 as a reward for his great services in '88 and recently at Cadiz. He thus took precedence over Essex. The Fleet came back from the 'Islands Voyage' in November. The expedition had not been a success; and the testimony of those present showed that several fine chances had been thrown away by the vanity and incompetence of Essex, who at one time had almost court-martialled and executed Ralegh for robbing him of the glory of taking Fayal. When he returned to Court his actions were very freely criticised, Essex regarded the promotion of the Lord Admiral (who incidentally was thirty years older than himself) as a direct affront, and, as usual, he took to his bed. It was now regrettably obvious that the romantic pursuit of honour which was so charming in a young man of twenty-five was degenerating into a petulant vanity and a jealousy of other men's honours. Essex vainly tried to have the new Earl's patent altered, wished to challenge both him and his sons to a duel, and absented himself from Court and Parliament. His conduct was causing so much comment that men came almost to be divided into parties pro- or anti-Essex. Shortly afterwards — in December — he was wooed back to good humours by the Queen, who made him Earl Marshal, thereby restoring him to precedence over the Admiral.

On February 26, 1598, Shakespeare's *Henry IV,* Part I, was entered for publication; presumably it had been produced some weeks at least earlier, when the fat knight had first appeared as Oldcastle. The play is full of allusions and significances, as indeed are both the second part and *Henry V.* The parodies of Alleyn and the rival company at the Rose in the person of their faithful admirer Ancient Pistol and in the playlet of *The Prince Rebuked* (with Falstaff as tragic King in the Tamburlaine strain) have been noted elsewhere. Of wider significance are such phrases as:

> O, sir, your presence is too bold and peremptory,
> And majesty might never yet endure
> The moody frontier of a servant brow.
> You have good leave to leave us; when we need
> Your use and counsel we shall send for you.

The dispute between Henry IV and Hotspur over the prisoners may not have reminded the audience of the similar dispute between Essex and Queen Elizabeth a year before, but I fancy that the 'certain lord, neat and trimly dress'd', was once recognisable. Hotspur's conception of honour, especially in the last phrase, was very similar to that of Essex:

> By heaven methinks it were an easy leap
> To pluck bright honour from the pale-fac'd moon,
> Or dive into the bottom of the deep,
> Where fathom-line could never touch the ground,
> And pluck up drowned honour by the locks;
> So he that doth redeem her thence might wear
> Without corrival all her dignities.

De Maisse, who was in London in November, 1597, noted of Essex, 'Il est tout son conseil luy mesmes. . . . Il est desireux de gloire' — a remarkable thing in an Englishman! Nor would Shakespeare leave us unconscious of Hotspur's faults:

> In faith, my lord, you are too willful-blame;
> And since your coming hither have done enough
> To put him quite beside his patience.

> You must needs learn, lord, to amend this fault:
> Though sometimes it show greatness, courage, blood—
> And that's the dearest grace it renders you—
> Yet oftentimes it doth present harsh rage,
> Defect of manners, want of government,
> Pride, haughtiness, opinion, and disdain:
> The least of which haunting a nobleman
> Loseth men's hearts and leaves behind a stain
> Upon the beauty of all parts besides,
> Beguiling them of commendation.

A year before, Bacon had said very much the same to Essex.

Moreover, Shakespeare is a little cynical about this romantic humour; he parodies it in Falstaff s brief catechism on Honour; at the battle of Shrewsbury he degrades it in: 'Sir Walter Blunt: there's honour for you! here's no vanity'. . . 'I like not such grinning honour as Sir Walter hath: give me life; which if I can save, so; if not, honour comes unlooked for, and there's an end'. The pathos of Percy's end is deliberately turned into ridicule when the sham-dead Falstaff rises and stabs the hero, and afterwards tumbles the body down and claims his blood money. Shakespeare's sympathy seems to be definitely turning away from glory, and in the survival of Falstaff is shown his version of 'The death of a Hero'.

However, a *caveat* is here needed against the assumption that 'Hotspur is Essex' or that Shakespeare meant him so to be taken. Shakespeare finds opportunities in the character of Hotspur for significant speeches and takes them, but he is writing a play and not an allegory of the times.

The difference in tone between 1 and 2 *Henry IV* and *King John* is worth noting, because it reflects the general mood as the war continued. In '95 and '96, when Englishmen thought themselves to be fighting backs to the wall, noble and heroic speeches came natural, for the English people were for the moment keen. Indeed for these few months it is noticeable that the Privy Council actually dispatched a number of letters of commendation for public duties zealously performed. But the mood was not lasting. Military scandals, at home over recruiting and impressments, in the field in France, and especially in Ireland, made a poor setting for glistening heroic personages. 'Honour pricks me on; yea, but how if honour prick me off when I come on'? Whether Shakespeare invented this little jest, or whether it is one of the phrases produced in a war — like 'If you knows of a better'ole, go to it' — it appears in a letter of Toby Matthew written on September 20, 1598:

In Ireland the Lord Ormond is hurt and since the great overthrow four hundred more throats cut. Sir Francis Vere is coming towards the Low Countries, and Sir Alexander Ratcliffe and Sir Robert Drury with him. Honour pricks them on, and the world thinks that honour will quickly prick them off again.

This cynical mood is prevalent in the second part of the play, which I guess to have been written in Lent, 1598 (for no better reason than that there are two jokes about Lent diet). Falstaff's choice of his recruits is a piece of simple unheroic realism — cases in real life can be exactly paralleled; there is no longer any glamour about this war. Moreover, Shakespeare is now beginning to drop the exaltation of 'this other Eden, demiparadise', and to sink to 'it was always a trick of our English nation, if they have a good thing, to make it too common'.

Meanwhile the Essex faction was increasing its noise. His followers were hot the kind to inspire confidence in more intelligent observers, and they were now making no secret of their intention that one day the army would set Essex on the throne. In mere self-preservation, apart from any more patriotic motive, it was vital for the Cecils and the anti-Essex party to undermine his followers by policy. From picturesque biographies the feeling is created that all proper-minded persons were on the side of Essex and against the scheming Cecil: but Shakespeare, if the passages in the plays written at this time have any significance, was definitely against the party of heroics. He stresses more than once the responsibilities of kingship, as in Henry IV's bitter cry for sleep, with its concluding sentence:

Then, happy low, lie down!
Uneasy lies the head that wears a crown.

The thought is repeated by the Prince in:

Why doth the crown lie there upon his pillow,
Being so troublesome a bedfellow?

> O polish'd perturbation! golden care!
> That keep'st the ports of slumber open wide
> To many a watchful night! Sleep with it now!
> Yet not so sound, and half so deeply sweet
> As he whose brow with homely biggin bound
> Snores out the watch of night. O majesty!
> When thou dost pinch thy bearer, thou dost sit
> Like a rich armour worn in heat of day,
> That scalds with safety.

Henry V, if the Chorus to Act V was part of the original play, was written in the spring of 1599. The mood has changed once more back to the patriotism of 'Rule Britannia'; it was the mood of that spring when the departure of Essex for Ireland was made a great patriotic occasion by the citizens of London. Again Shakespeare shows his sympathy with the Queen in the finest of his speeches on kingship:

> Upon the king! let us our lives, our souls,
> Our debts, our careful wives,
> Our children, and our sins lay on the king!
> We must bear all. O hard condition.
> Twin-born with greatness, subject to the breath
> Of every fool, whose sense no more can feel
> But his own wringing. What infinite heart's ease
> Must kings neglect that private men enjoy!

Nowhere is there a keener appreciation of the difficulties, the responsibility and the loneliness of kingship. The man who wrote this passage in 1598 or 1599 was scarcely in sympathy with the Essex faction, nor is there much more than formal compliment in the reference to Essex in the Chorus to Act V.

On April 1, 1598, George Chapman's translation of *Seven Books of the Iliades of Homer, Prince of Poets*, had been entered for publication; and presumably it came out in the early summer. This was the first of Chapman's Homeric translations to appear, and was subsequently rewritten. The story covered by these books concerns the origin of the wrath of Achilles and the attempts to win him back to his rightful place in the Greek host. It has been shown (in the edition in the Arden Shakespeare, for instance) that this translation was the original source of the political passages in Shakespeare's *Troilus and Cressida*, a play which seems to consist of two strata at least, the earlier containing the original medieval Troilus story, the later concerned with the sulking of Achilles. Moreover, the play was written for private performance; it was 'never staled with the stage, never clapper clawed with the palms of the vulgar'. If (as I suspect) it was written soon after Chapman's translation appeared it was the most daring piece of topical significance that Shakespeare ever wrote.

On June 30 or July 1 Essex committed his act of 'great contempt', which only Camden has recorded in detail, when he turned his back on the Queen, received a box on the ear, threatened her with his sword, and stalked away from the palace. It was not until the middle of September that the Queen and the Earl were reconciled. In the middle of August came news of the great disaster at Blackwater, near Armagh, where some 2,000 English soldiers and fifteen captains had been killed by Tyrone. Essex was summoned to take his place in the Council to advise on Irish affairs, and did indeed attend once, on the 22nd; but he refused to take any further part and continued to nurse his wrongs in retirement. In the meantime various tactful friends were urging him to withdraw from his impossible position. The whole affair caused an immense sensation, which is but feebly echoed in a few letters that have survived.

A very similar situation is discussed in *Troilus and Cressida*, Act I, Sc. iii. Few contemporaries of Shakespeare in 1598 could have heard Ulysses's great speech on Degree without thinking of certain modern instances, especially when it continued:

> The great Achilles, whom opinion crowns
> The sinew and the forehand of our host,
> Having his ear full of his airy fame,
> Grows dainty of his worth, and in his tent
> Lies mocking our designs.

Achilles, like Essex, suffered from politic sicknesses:

> 'We saw him', says Ulysses, 'at the opening of his tent: He is not sick'.
>
> 'Yes', answers Ajax, 'lion-sick, sick of proud heart: you may call it melancholy if you will favour the man; but, by my head, 'tis pride: but why, why? let him show us a cause'.

And Ulysses in his speech to Achilles is but repeating what all his friends kept on saying to Essex:

Time hath, my lord, a wallet at his back,
Wherein he puts alms for oblivion,
A great-siz'd monster of ingratitude's:
Those scraps are good deeds past; which are devour'd
As fast as they are made, forgot as soon
As done: perseverance, dear my lord,
Keeps honour bright: to have done, is to hang
Quite out of fashion, like a rusty mail
In monumental mockery. Take the instant way . . .

These parallels between Achilles and Essex may at first sound a little fantastical; but then Shakespeare read the story of Achilles in Chapman's translation of *Seven Books of the Iliades*, wherein he found this dedication: 'To the most honoured now living instance of the Achilleian virtues eternized by divine Homer, the Earl of Essex, Earl Marshal, & C'. Reading further in the epistle dedicatory, he lighted upon this apostrophe to Essex:

Most true Achilles (whom by sacred prophecy, Homer did but prefigure in his admirable object) and in whose unmatched virtues shine the dignities of the soul and the whole excellence of royal humanity, let not the peasant-common polities of the world, that count all things servile and simple, that pamper not their own sensualities, burying quick in their filthy sepulchres of the earth the whole bodies and souls of men, stir your divine temper from perseverance in godlike pursuit of Eternity.

And, as Achilles had Homer to eternize him, so 'help then renowned Achilles to prefer and defend your grave and blameless Prophet of Phoebus from the doting and vicious fury of the two Atrides — Arrogancy and Detraction'. Unfortunately for the price of glory, both war-men had another quality in common: they sulked. The reasonable inference is that *Troilus and Cressida,* in its present form, was performed privately before an anti-Essex audience, either in the summer of 1598, or else about two years later when Essex and his followers were brewing treason.[4]

4. Since this essay was first written, these and other parallels have been worked out at length in the author's *Shakespeare at Work*, 1591-1603.

12

Shakespeare as Man of the Theatre[1]

J. Isaacs

It is a modern fashion, and the dictates of fashion must be obeyed, to speak of the art of the theatre and of men of the theatre. A new attitude has made us pay homage to Mr. Granville-Barker and Mr. Gordon Craig in England, to Professor Max Reinhardt in Germany, to Jacques Copeau, Firmin Gemier, and Pitoeff in France, to Stanislavsky, Tairov, and Meierhold in Russia. All these men have a sense of the theatre, all have been actors, all are producers. It is the object of this paper to examine Shakespeare's sense of the stage and of the theatre, his understanding of the nature and evolution of theatre-craft, to expose the problems he faced and solved, to see how far the modern conception of a 'producer' may be found valid in helping to understand Shakespeare as 'a man of the theatre'.

We are helped in our inquiry if we can prove the existence of an art of the theatre and an international interest in theatre-craft in and before Shakespeare's lifetime. The best of all citations is from Kyd's *Spanish Tragedy.*

Hieronymo says:

> The Italian Tragedians were so sharpe of wit,
> That in one hours meditation
> They would perform anything in action.

---

1. *Shakespeare and the Theatre,* by Members of the Shakespeare Association (1927).

Lorenzo replies:

And well it may, for I have seene the like
In Paris, amongst the French Tragedians.

There was an art, purely of the theatre, not concerned with any formal stage, made up largely of that 'eloquence of the body' admitted even by its enemies. Italy, with its *Commedia dell'Arte*, its comedy of types and vivid gesture and improvization, taught France where the stiff reconstructed theatre of the Renaissance impinged on the elaborate staging of the Mystery and Passion plays. In France in 1571, Lord Buckhurst, part author of *Gorboduc*, saw 'a comedie of Italians that for the good mirth and handling thereof deserved singular commendation'. This same troupe of the Gelosi laid the foundations of French theatrical art, and a little later even Moliere was not ashamed to learn his art from Scaramouche.

In England the 'producer' has never been a prominent figure. The very name does not go back more than thirty years, the years in which his function, over and above that of stage-manager, has become naturalised. As sole director of the conscious artistic unity of a performance he is, as a result of the theatrical degradation of the late seventeenth, the eighteenth, and early nineteenth centuries, often regarded as a modern invention. Yet we have actually a portrait of a continental producer in a miniature painted by Jean Fouquet in 1461. He wears a long clerical robe and cape, a tiara-like hat on his head, holds a prompt-book in his left hand, and with a baton in his right directs a beautifully organised medley of late medieval religious performers. We have the greater faith in the accuracy of this representation since Fouquet is known to have assisted in preparing a theatrical welcome for the entry of Louis XI into Tours in 1461. A little later we hear of Jean Bouchet, whose success as producer of a Passion play at Poitiers in 1508 caused his services to be demanded all over France and Belgium. When even vast sums did not tempt him to go in person, he sent his prompt-books and advice, chiefly about costume, and sweetness and softness of voice, and clarity of articulation. In England, until later, costume that 'was good enough for an English bishop was good enough for Ananias and Caiaphas'; but in France it was decreed that 'Pharisees must not be dressed like Pilate'. In France competent producers were haled in from distant cities, in England the producer was often the Mayor and Corporation. Later, in 1547, we have the famous contract for the Passion Play at Valenciennes, the document that gives us the classical picture of the multiple staging system. Therein we hear of stage discipline, of the supreme authority of the producer, to whom no complaints are to be made, particularly at rehearsals, and of a ban against the haunting of taverns during the days of performance.

Our knowledge of medieval staging has, until recently, been built up by laborious reconstruction of tiny facts and vast conjectures. To Professor Gustave Cohen of the Sorbonne, we owe the discovery of the most valuable document in the history of the early European theatre. It was published in 1925, and is no less than the producer's complete prompt-book for the great Passion Play at Mons in 1501. We have, in its modern form, nearly a thousand columns of close print describing the actual presentation of a religious cycle at the summit of its magnificence. We have the full constitution of the play, the names of the players, their professions, their parts, their entrances and exits, their positions, their actions, their first and last lines, a description of the scenery, of the musical accompaniment, of the machinery and stage effects even to the provision of a Deluge for Noah and a moving star for the Nativity. The producers, whose official title was 'Superintendents of the Performance' or 'Conductors of the Secrets', were two brothers, Guillaume and Jehan de la Chière.

In this medieval theatrical system the manner of playing appears to have been as rigidly laid down as that of a player in an orchestra, and the resemblance of this huge prompt-book to an orchestral score is perhaps the best proof of the autocratic power of the producer. The Renaissance with its ambivalence of submission to classical authority and indulgence in wild and passionate individuality gave a new world of activity to the actor. In the dialogues of Leone da Sommi of the mid-sixteenth century, in the scenarios of the *Commedia dell'Arte,* we see the actor compelled to that team-work that is inseparable from true theatrical activity, yet permitted liberty so far as his body will adapt itself to the mood of the play. When this liberty swells into licence, we have Shakespeare warning his clowns not to speak more than is set down for them.

We shall never know the full details of this gestatory period, but we may hope to recover something of the Elizabethan practice by probing a little further into the European situation of the drama. The theatre of Germany was definitely and admittedly born of the English theatre, and in the documents of its early progress we have material that has not been fully utilized for theatrical history. In the last fifteen years of the sixteenth century English companies wandered to Germany and Holland and played condensed versions of popular English plays. Their success was prodigious, they were soon forced to act in German, and from the *Englische Komödianten*, as they were called, grew the German theatre. The best contemporary account is by Fynes Moryson who was at Frankfort in September, 1592:

Germany hath some few wandering comedians, more deserving pitty than prayse, for the serious parts are dully penned, and worse acted, and the mirth they make is ridiculous, and nothing less than witty (as I formerly have showed). So as I remember that when some of our cast despised stage players came out of England into Germany and played at Franckford in the tyme of the Mart, having neither a complete number of actors, nor any good apparel, nor any ornament of the Stage, yet the Germans, not understanding a worde they sayde, both men and women, flocked wonderfully to see their gesture and Action, rather than hear them, speaking English which they understood not; and pronouncing pieces and patches of English plays which my selfe and some English men their present could not hear without great wearysomenes. Yea myself coming from Franckford in the Company of some cheese merchants Dutch and Flemish, heard them often bragge of the good market they had made, only condoling that they had not the leisure to heare the English players.

Again, in the Netherlands, he says:

For Commedians, they little practise that arte, and are the poorest Actours that can be imagined, as myself did see when the Citty of Gertrudenberg being taken by them from the Spaniards, they made bonfires and publicly at Leyden represented that action in a play, so rudely as the poore artizans of England would have both penned and acted it much better. So as at the same tyme when some cast players of England came into those partes, the people not understanding what they sayd, only for there action followed them with wonderful concourse, yea many young virgins fell in love with some of the players, and followed them from citty to citty, till the magistrates were forced to forbid them to play anymore.

This gives a valuable contrast between England, which already had a developed art of the theatre, and the northern continent. It is not merely patriotic pride because the statements are supported with naive emphasis from German sources. Balthasar Paumgartner writes to his wife from the same Frankfort Fair visited by Moryson:

> Here are some English actors whose plays I have seen. They have such splendid good music, and are perfect in their dancing and jumping, whose equal I have never yet seen. There are ten or twelve of them, all richly and magnificently clothed.

Our most valuable evidence for the nature of these players' art comes from the work of Jakob Ayrer who wrote 140 plays in 15 years, half of them fortunately lost, but important because he was not original enough to depart widely from the models he used. Sackville's troupe of players performed in Nuremburg from 26 April to 23 May 1596, and immediately after their departure Ayrer began his second Roman Drama, containing the figure of John Posset the English clown based on Sackville's favourite role of Johan Bouset. The preface to his *Opus Theatricum* speaks of 'everything arranged according to life and so drawn up that everything can be acted and performed in person after the new English manner and style'. The Germans were impressed by the English naturalistic style of acting and the complete absorption of each actor in his part. Their imitations afford valuable evidence for the reconstruction of Shakespeare's practice.

In this European situation, Shakespeare grew up and lived. It is not too much to say that there is hardly a detail in the evolution of the theatre of his time with which he is not familiar.

He came in time to be a pioneer, to feel that the theatre was still in its crudity, and therefore mocks while learning from the older systems of staging and theatrical presentation. Most of his comment on the older forms of drama is condemnatory, but it is difficult to mock without acquaintance. He laughs, in *Henry V*, IV. iv, at

This roaring devil i' the old play, that everyone may pare his nails with a wooden dagger.

In *Lear*, I. ii, he gibes at earlier mechanical construction:

And pat he comes like the catastrophe of the old comedy.

In *Love's Labour's Lost*, the conventional ending is blown upon:

> Our wooing doth not end like an old play,
> Jack hath not Jill.

Justice Shallow, who was no Roscius, is permitted to remember his mummings,

I remember at Mile-end-Greene, when I lay at *Clements* Inn, I was then Sir *Dagonet* in *Arthurs* Show.

He knew of, and may have seen the miracles, and calls upon them when he talks of the theatre and out-Heroding of Herod. The creaking solemnity of Cambises vein is used to mark the pompousness of Polonius or the mock seriousness of Feste. Seneca to him is heavy, dumb show and amateur pageantry are suspect, and the pious moralities give him occasion for parody. It is difficult to prove parody, but much of Launce's speech about his shoes in *Two Gentlemen of Verona*, some of Falstaff's comment on his honour, and all of Launcelot Gobbo's speech in *Merchant of Venice*, II. ii, can be traced back to the debating systems of this old form.

Certainly, my conscience will serve me to run from this Jew my Maister: the fiend is at mine elbow, and tempts me, saying to me, Gobbo, Launcelot Gobbo, good Launcelot, or good Gobbo, or good Launcelot Gobbo, use your legs, take the start, run awaie: my conscience saies no; take heede honest Launcelot, take heed honest Gobbo, or as afore-said honest Launcelot Gobbo, doe not runne, scorne running with thy heeles; well, the most coragious fiend bids me pack, *via* saies the fiend, away saies the fiend, for the heavens rouse up a brave minde saies the fiend, and run; well, my conscience hanging about the necke of my heart, saies verie wisely to me: my honest friend Launcelot, being an honest mans sonne, or rather an honest womans sonne, for indeede my Father did something smack, something grow too; he had a kinde of taste; wel, my conscience saies Launcelot bouge not, boiige saies the fiend, bouge not saies my conscience, conscience say I you counsaile well, fiend say I you counsaile well, to be rul'd by my conscience I should stay with the Jew my Maister, who (God blesse the marke) is a kinde of divell; and to run away from the Jew I should be ruled by the fiend, who saving your reverence is the divell himselfe: certainely the Jew is the verie divell incarnation, and in my conscience, my conscience is a kinde of hard conscience, to offer to counsaile me to stay with the Jew; the fiend gives the more friendly counsaile: I will runne fiend, my heeles are at your commandement, I will runne.

It seems, moreover, no accident that in the plays used or alleged to have been touched up by Shakespeare, we have a museum of thc evolution of theatre-craft, a museum that should be utilized to peer into Shakespeare's workshop.

What are the problems of a man of the theatre? First it may be suggested that the actual staging and stage carpentry are somewhat from our purpose. His real business is the disposition of characters, the spacing, the grouping, the business of ensemble, the maintenance of continuity and variety, the achievement of various systems of illusion; whether boys as women, day as night, two men as the armies of France, two human throats as a vast tempest, the maintenance of melody and harmony, the establishment of unity and poetry and even philosophy amid the trivialities of artificial thunder and glued-on beards. Shakespeare took the shape of his theatre for granted and frankly accepted and utilized its limitations. In *Pericles*, Act II, the prologue says:

> In your imagination hold
> This stage the ship, upon whose deck
> The sea-tost Pericles appears to speak.

In *Henry V* the chorus say:

> And so our Scene must to the Battaile flye,
> Where, O for pitty, we shall much disgrace,

With foure or five most vile and ragged foyles,
(Right ill dispos'd, in brawle ridiculous)
The Name of Agincourt.

Where then does he clearly show his sense of the theatre, of the movement of human bodies sculpturally on a stage viewed almost from all angles? In *Hamlet*, Act I, Scene V, where the ghost in the cellarage drags Hamlet and his friends about the stage. In *Macbeth*, Act V, Scene iii, where he never forgets for a moment that Macbeth is putting on his armour.

Macbeth. *Give me mine armour.*
How does your patient, doctor?
. . . .
Throw physic to the dogs; I'll none of it.
Come, put mine armour on; give me my staff.
Seyton, send out. Doctor, the thanes fly from me.
Come, sir, dispatch. If thou couldst, doctor, cast
The water of my land, find her disease,
And purge it to a sound and pristine health,
I would applaud thee to the very echo,
That should applaud again — *Pull't off, I say,—*
What rhubarb, cyme, or what purgative drug,
Would scour these English hence? Hear'st thou of them?
Doctor. Ay, my good lord; your royal preparation
Makes us hear something.
Macbeth. *Bring it after me.*
I will not be afraid of death and bane
Till Bimam forest come to Dunsinane,

where the gestures help the psychological conduct of the drama. Clearest of all is it seen in *Antony and Cleopatra*, Act IV, Scenes iii and iv, where the soldiers come on guard — 'good night — good night' — strange music of hoboyes under the stage — the night becomes conscious and its passing is marked, and then in the reluctant dawn Cleopatra helps Antony on with his armour, for Antony will stay no longer abed, and later the captain comes to say the mom is ready — and so time moves in the enchantment of Shakespeare's illusion.

He has restrictions all the time — he works with well-marked conventions: two colours symbolize two armies; space is gained when kings and armies march about the stage in procession —

one of the chief of Elizabethan stage conventions. In *Henry V*, before Agincourt, the shabby coats of England contrast with the bright armour of the French — the Romans and Egyptians are differentiated with subtle art in *Antony and Cleopatra*, the British and the Romans in *Cymbeline*. Trumpets make a battle. Time passes in divers ways. The stage must be emptied, and therefore bold formal processions end the tragedies, *Lear* with a dead march, *Hamlet* with Fortinbras bearing off the bodies and then a peal of ordnance shot off. This practical necessity of clearing the stage was so present that when in the German imitations it is necessary to leave a dragon to be found by one of the players — the stage direction says specifically

> This worm must not be removed.

Such general indications almost convince us that the Elizabethans would have understood our notion of a 'producer'. Fortunately we have definite evidence on the matter. John Aubrey, in writing of Shakespeare, points a contrast: 'Now B. Johnson was never a good actor but an excellent instructor', and the Induction to *Cynthia's Revels*, 1600, has:

> I would speak with your author, where is he?

Not this way, I assure you, Sir, we are not so officiously befriended by him, as to have his presence in the tiring-house, to prompt us aloud, stamp at the book-holder, swear for our properties, curse the poor fireman, rail the music out of tune, and sweat for every venial trespass we commit;

and in *Bartholomew Fair* a little later (1614):

I am looking, lest the Poet heare me . . . hee has kick'd me three, or foure times about the Tyring-house for but offering to putt in, with my experience;

but most important is evidence from a German writer Johannes Rhenanus in prefacing a play adapted from the English '*Lingua*' in 1613:

So far as actors are concerned they, as I noticed in England, are daily instructed, as it were in a school so that even the most eminent actors have to allow themselves to be instructed by the Dramatists, which arrangement gives life and ornament to a well-written play, so that it is no wonder that the English players

(I speak of the skilled ones) surpass and have the advantage of others.

This seems to be a direct allusion to rehearsals, to which Rhenanus was perhaps admitted. In any case, in Quince we have Shakespeare's satirical portrait of a producer at work.

We may now endeavour to reconstruct what took place on the stage, how Shakespearian players acted. We can be certain the Elizabethan acting was bolder than now, that speech was much quicker, that gesture was wilder, that bodily movements were more actorish. It is still possible to see the equivalent of Shakespeare's audience at the few remaining melodrama theatres of London, at Collins' Music Hall or the Elephant, where *Sweeney Todd — the Demon Barber of Fleet Street* and *Maria Marten or the Murder in the Red Barn* are still played. There can be found, perhaps not the Elizabethan stench of gralic — but one might easily.

be pasted
To the barmy jacket of a bere-brewer.

There, too, will be found those 'Squirrels that want must', who are warned by Shirley, 'Pray do not crack the benches'. There will be found an audience alive to every jest, quick to accept the fun of exaggeration, to distinguish between good and evil, to hiss at vice and applaud virtue. There the acting is perhaps our nearest to Shakespeare's acting. There illusion is complete. There the good wife of *The Knight of the Burning Pestle* makes her comment on the gladness and the sadness of the scenical happenings.

Jonson, in his *Staple of News,* used the term 'over-act'. The actor 'does over-act, and having got the habit of it, will be monstrous still in spite of counsel'. The stamping, robustious player existed

whose conceit
Lies in his hamstring, and doth think it rich
To hear the wooden dialogue and sound
'Twixt his stretched footings.

And we learn something of Alleyn's manner of playing Tamburlaine from T.M.'s *The Blacke Booke* (1604): 'the spindle-shanke Spyders . . . went stalking over his head, as if they had bene conning of *Tamburlaine*'. Women when distraught rushed in with 'their haire about their eares'. Brutus 'suddenly arose and walked about, musing and sighing, with his arms across'. Othello shouts O, O, O, and falls on the bed. Boyet says he is 'stabbed with laughter', and acts accordingly. Regan, in the old play of *King Lear*,

> Knits her borw, and bytes her lips
> And Stamps and makes a dump show of disdayne;

the affected Boyet darts his hand, and the very stairs kiss his feet, *i.e.,* even his walk is indicated. In *Titus,* the mutilated Lavinia tosses a book about and turns over pages with her stumps, and Titus himself asks,

> How can I grace my talk,
> Wanting a hand to give it action.

If this is the general condition of gesture, how then could the German writer speak of the charm and appropriateness of gesture and Shirley of 'graceful and unaffected action'? Delicacy in acting can be amply and wonderfully proved from Shakespeare. Restrained emotion is shown in *Coriolanus*, V. iii, where the folio stage direction reads, after Volumnia's speech of pleading,

> Holds her by the hand silent.

And in *Macbeth*, Act IV, Scene iii, the scene of exquisite management and restraint when Macduff is told of his wife's death, he pulls his hat over his face and is silent.

> *Malcolm.* Merciful Heaven:
> What man, ne're pull your hat upon your browes:
> Give sorrow words; the griefe that do's not speake,
> Whispers the o're-fraught heart, and bids it breake.

Perhaps it was the stage quality in these lines that Ford expanded to majestic proportions in his *Broken Heart.* In *Richard II* we have a gesture exquisitely poised and used magnificently as a structural symbol, in the march of the play's action. In Act III, Scene ii, comes Richard's sad speech on hearing of his defeat,

> Let's talk of graves, of worms and epitaphs.

He speaks of death,

> Within the hollow crown
> That rounds the mortal temples of a king

Keeps Death his court and there the antic sits,
Scoffing his state and grinning at his pomp,
. . . .
Comes at the last and with a little pin
Bores through his castle wall, and farewell King!
Cover you heads and mock not flesh and blood
With solemn reverence:

Clearly he has wrenched off his crown at 'farewell king', an omen of the abdication later; all present sweep off their headgear to avoid being covered in the presence of an uncovered king.

Those who begrudge the actor or the singer his concentrated fame, forget that his, even more than the tumbler's or dancer's, is a short-lived fame, vanishing with the echoes of his voice. The nineteenth century, with its slow deliberate intellectual distortions of famous speeches, almost ruined our understanding of the Shakespearian world of sound. It is clear that the Elizabethans spoke quickly and distinctly to achieve the two or three hours traffic of the stage. It must be remembered that much of it was open-air speaking. Overbury said of 'an excellent actor', perhaps of Burbage,

for his voice, 'tis not lower than the prompter nor louder than the foil or target.

In the *Spanish Tragedy* we have a hint in praise of the 'Oxford accent':

Hier. It was determined to have beene acted,
By gentlemen and schollers too;
Such as could tell what to speake.

Bal And now it shall be said, by Princes and Courtiers
Such as can tell how to speak.

We may recover at least a fragment of Shakespearian diction from Shakespeare's own joke about the producer who could not understand punctuation. In *A Midsummer Night's Dream*, v. i, Quince enters as Prologue, and the punctuation kept faithfully, through Quarto and Folio, points the joke.

Pro. If we offend, it is with our good will.
That you should thinke, we come not to offend,
But with good will. To shew our simple skill,
That is the true beginning of our end.

Consider then, we come but in despight.
We do not come, as minding to content you,
Our true intent is. All for your delight,
We are not heere. That you should here repent you,
The Actors are at hand; and by their show,
You shall know all, that you are like to know.

The comments that follow, exquisitely and almost foppishly punctuated, may serve as a contribution to the present-day quarrels about the dramatic use of stops in Shakespeare's works.

Theseus. This fellow doth not stand upon points.

Lysander. He hath rid his Prologue, like a rough Colt: he knowes not the stop. A good morall my Lord. It is not enough to speake, but to speake true.

Hippolyta. Indeed hee hath plaid on his Prologue, like a childe on a Recorder, a sound, but not in government.

Theseus. His speech was like a tangled chaine: nothing impaired, but all disordered. Who is next?

Although it is probable that the Elizabethan actor, especially in bold thunderous plays, spoke almost in an avalanche, there can be little doubt that the prologues and epilogues were regarded as special displays of elocution and, being written and punctuated to that end, still retain their magic, that reaches a summit in the epilogue to *As You Like It*. How far the soliloquy was an exercise in diction will never be known. It has a peculiar emphasis where it is an element in exposition or character-building, and derived vast theatrical relief owing to the special contact established when the actor advanced to 'the skirt of the stage', and spoke his lines into the individual ears of his audience.

Before we examine the more delicate function of the clown in the Shakespearian system, it would be well to glance at him in the raw state from which Shakespeare refind him. His chief fault lay in straying from the text, though Thomas Hughes, many years before, complained of similar behaviour in the Gentlemen of Gray's Inn, in their treatment of his *Misfortunes of Arthur*, 'here set downe as it past from under his handes and as it was presented excepting certaine wordes and lines, where some of the Actors either helped their memories by brief omission; or fitted their acting by some alteration'. Hamlet's complaint was clear enough, and I am tempted to see an allusion to an early form of his advice to the players in Robert Amim's statement in his *Quips upon Questions or A clownes conceite on occasion offered*. By Clunnyco de Curtanio Snuffe. 1600.

> True it is, he playes the Foole indeed;
> But in the Play he playes it as he must.

In any case this is the only confession I have been able to find in which a clown, in his own person, admits any restraint laid on him. The clown's tricks are many, from eating bread and butter through a curtain to playing with huge slippers or big boots. Kemp's slippers were as famous then as Little Tich's or Mr. Charles Chaplin's today, and Sackville, who used the same trick, was described by a German poet in 1597 as wearing shoes 'neither pincheth him a whit'. The German fools took over the English clown's drum and fife, they came on with armour back to front, and a German stage direction shows one of the rare concrete allusions to the necessity of getting a laugh.

John Pansser comes in wondrously clad, not clownishly but venerably and honourably, yet so that there is something to laugh at. He takes his hat off, bows to all four comers of the stage, clears his throat, wanders around a long time, and when that raises a laugh, he laughs too and waves his hands.

From the German imitations we have some valuable hints concerning details of stage behaviour and stage effects. In the *Spanish Tragedy* the direction for Hieronymo is, 'He bites out his tongue'. In Ayrer's adaptation, 'he produces a knife, cuts his tongue off, throws it away, and holds a blood-stained cloth to his mouth'. In the death scene, when Petrian shoots Niclaus, 'he has inwardly a small squirt full of red liquid. This he presses as if he were clutching his wound, squirts the liquid through a little hole on to his belly, like blood, and rolls round till he dies'. These details take us back to the English *Cambises*, where, 'Enter Crueltie and Murder with bloody hands', and when Smirdis is killed, Crueltie cries

> Even now I strike his body to wound:
> Beholde now his blood springs out on the ground,

and the stage direction reads, 'A little bladder of Vineger prickt'. In another play the storming of Jerusalem is minutely described for stage purposes and would repay careful examination, while rain is produced in this wise:

> The waterworks are so arranged that the water is poured into a hanging dish hidden above and the dish has a string behind it, so that when John conveniently pulls the string the water falls into a sieve, that is also covered over with leaves and falls on John and makes him somewhat wet.

It would be easy to carry this discussion of the material side of the Elizabethan stage much farther, to speak of costume and make-up, of ghosts and storms, thunder, atmospheric effects and extemporizing, of properties and loose heads, of 'noises off'. All these things, though important in helping us to get the 'feel' of the theatrical practice of Shakespeare's time, can be regarded as little more than the canvas and pigments with which the painter works, and in their highest form as the mere subject-matter that a Signorelli or a Cezanne forces to his own ends, whether of design or significance.

Let us bc bold and take Shakespeare's greatest play, *King Lear,* that by nineteenth-century distorting criticism has been bracketed with *Love's labour's Lost,* as unplayable. It contains more problems of the theatre than almost any other existing play. In Germany, at any rate, to play a good *King Lear* is the summit of an actor's career. The problems of production are of the highest complexity, arising out of Shakespeare's manipulation of his theatrical material. There is not, from beginning to end of the play, one single stage direction giving the scene, it has no 'local habitation and a name'. Such localization as there is comes from within the text. We are thrown back immediately to the actors whose groupings and movements and linked speeches must provide the theatrical unity over and above the dramatic unit of the plot and its intellectual problem. Modem dramatists, apart from sentimental entertainers, fear this homelessness and timelessness. Only a rare piece like Benavente's *Los Intereses Creados* dares to build a serious fantasy, 'Once upon a time, in a certain place'. And of all fantasies *King Lear* contains the most impossible when Edgar builds up a cliff with his voice, gives it shape and dimensions from above and below to cure Gloucester's despair. It is a fantasy that can exist only within the conditions of the actor's art, and is so written, with mathematical perspective that even the Italian decorated stage of the time could not better, and as for the voices, it would be well to study the changed rhythms. There is a bold difference between Edgar's speech before and after the fancied leap, there has already been a change from his 'Poor Tom' voice, and this is marked by Gloucester for theatrical, practical purposes, since the poetical description of the cliff would have had comical rather than magical value in a contorted accent, and there are quieter, more composed tones in Gloucester's second voice. I emphasise these important trivialities because it is not in pious philosophical generalities that Shakespeare's art of the theatre can be displayed.

Edgar is the most complex of all Shakespearian parts. No conscious conceited actor dare attempt it. We do not know who played it originally, but it is no unjustifiable assumption that it formed part of Shakespeare's researches into the dramatic function and theatrical capability of the clown or fool, and was performed by an actor who, if not a genius, possessed enough of that quality to harmonize the part's discordancies and make it credible on the stage. It is not too much to say that *King Lear* is an arabesque of fools or that in the evolution of the Shakespearian fool we have the most valuable field of inquiry for the examination of Shakespeare's structural development. It would be difficult to go beyond *King Lear* in complexity of fools. In Lear himself, who is mad, in his pendant professional fool who becomes more foolish in his terror, Gloucester, who is on the verge of suicidal mania, and in Edgar the artificial fool, we have all four grades of genuine, professional, partial, and factitious fool. It must not be forgotten that one of the chief of Shakespeare's favourite words is 'fool'. To trace Shakespeare's use in detail is difficult in our uncertainty of his chronology, but we may indicate some landmarks. In *Love's Labour's Lost*, a verbal play, Costard the clown is used for dictionary humour, and uses his body but little more than the others in the *Masque of the Nine Worthies*. In the *Comedy of Errors*, an exercise in dramatic archaeology, the sets of twins, over and above the verbal factor, which is almost a dramatic constant in all Shakespeare's fools, are used for humour from the hall of mirrors. In *Two Gentlemen of Verona*, Speed, after the Spanish manner, is a distorted echo and a crude chorus, but in Launce we have the beginning of the true Shakespearian clown, who, as he must have been in his original form, is closely allied to the music-hall comedian who, with his unaided personality, entertains the audience with his moods and gestures. Of this kind, and in close brotherhood with Launce and his shoes and dog, is Mr. Charles Chaplin, by many regarded as the greatest living actor of today. It is not unamusing to note an earlier experiment in the music-hall manner in the cross-talk between Moth and Armado in *Love's Labour's Lost*. In a recent performance of this play in modern costume it was found that the only plausible manner of presenting this scene was to bring the players close to the footlights and give them the position of display and contact possessed in Elizabethan times by the soliloquy or the explanatory openers of the play. *A Midsummer Night's Dream* is a fable with the motto, 'What fools these mortals be'. The dramatic problem is to link the never-ending succession of condescensions with the dramatic irony provided by the theatrical necessity of creating foolishness suited to the three spheres of existence. It is the comic arabesque of which *Lear* is the tragic counterpart. Falstaff is one half of a problem in dramatic psychology, of which the concluding portion is Hamlet, and does not affect the progress of the fool. In *As You Like It* and *Twelfth Night* we have the maturity of the Shakespearian clown. He is, no both plays, an independent figure yet linked inextricably with the essential substance of the play. In *As You Like It* Touchstone and Jacques are the two significant figures. Touchstone, a man of the court who has fled to the fields for happiness; Jacques, who is half-way to revolt against the world and wants to be a fool. Touchstone marries Audrey to close the door against all return to the follies of court life. That this interpretation has theatrical plausibility was proved in a Berlin performance in which Elizabeth Bergner and Fritz Kortner demonstrated the intellectual flexibility of a play that is usually smothered in leaves like the *Babes in the Wood*. In Act III, Scene iii, Jacques and Touchstone play not as lord and clown, but well-nigh as equals, and when Touchstone announces that he is to marry Audrey, a smile appears on Jacques' face, growing to a laugh and finally to uncontrolled merriment in which Touchstone joins, the two men of the court have their secret, and a flash of illumination fills the play with more than pastoral quality. Shakespeare is beginning to be serious. *Twelfth Night* is in many ways the most serious of all under a mask of lightness. Its problem is the enternal antagonism of Puritan and light-heart, the protagonists are Feste and Malvolio. In the end Feste wins and Malvolio loses, but in his victory Feste is sad. Feste is no boy as so often played; he must be of years to make the conflict with Malvolio more real, more respectful. The clown is here entangled in the main plot, which is the Malvolio plot. We may even go so far as to say that the masquerade plot of the Duke and Viola is a kind of extended scenery in which the tragi-comedy can take place. Music may be the food of love to begin with, but music is the substance of tragedy when Feste sings the dirge of his youth at the end. After this, so far as the fool is concerned there is decadence, if we can take decadence to be the excessive preoccupation of the artist with his technique.

Beyond Feste the fool cannot go with impunity, but in two plays Shakespeare makes an attempt to stretch him beyond his function. In *King Lear,* as we have seen, the distribution of this function over the chief figures of the play has produced a technical disaster that cannot be redeemed without the return of the original conditions of the stage and perhaps without another genius such as played the original Edgar. The other play, strange as it may seem to bring it within this particular discussion, is *Antony and Cleopatra*. There two of the clown's chief functions are divided, that of the buffoon is given to Antony on Pompey's galley, that of the chorus to Enobarbus. In this connexion it is a some historical interest to note a modern use of Shakespearian technique that has won the highest honours on the modern stage. The substance of Act III, Scene vi, in which Pompey at one side and Caesar, Antony, and Lepidus at the other, their armies symbolized by leaders and standards, engage in negotiations while Enobarbus the plain-spoken adds his thread, is, save for Enobarbus' interference one of the commonest of Elizabethan conventions for the close conflict of powers, whether in war or diplomacy. Mr. Bernard Shaw, in the discussion scene in the tent in *St. Joan*, has gone back, wittingly or unwittingly, to this device. The power of England in the person of the Earl of Warwick deals with the power of the Church in the person of the Bishop of Beauvais, and Enobarbus is still present as plain-spoken Stogumber. Perhaps this is Shakespeare's revenage for some of Mr. Shaw's stricutres on his theatrical capacity. This discussion has, I hope, hinted at the way in which the practical necessity of having bodily humour in his theatre was utilized by Shakespeare to produce the subtlest of dramatic essences.

Lest I be accused of neglecting Shakespeare's boards, let us see how Shakespeare himself treats them with sublime insolence. For him the stage has a magic adaptability; locality, except by accident, has no existence; space to him has no more logic than in a hashish dream. Thomas Platter, on a visit to England in 1599, saw *Julius Caesar* acted with about fifteen actors, and yet the dramatis personae amount to thirty-three, excluding citizens, senators, soldiers, and attendants. If a change of place is to be achieved by a journey, the players move about the stage in full view of the audience; sometimes a change of scene is made by a character going out by one door and coming in immediately by another; a general and his standard-bearer are sufficient to fill a stage with the symbol of an army; Romeo bids farewell to Juliet in a room overlooking the garden which on the entrance of her mother becomes, without logical question, another part of the house. With a few trumpet noises and two pairs of men in single combat the ends of a vast battlefield are telescoped within the dimensions of the stage. More wonderful still, and accepted without a blink, is the convention by which the stage may represent two places at once. We scoff at the cineme, yet the convention by which the blank screen may be any place without unity or succession of time is paralleled in one of the most magical pieces of Shakespearian illusion. In *Richard III*, Act V, Scene ii, to build up the contrasting moods of Richard and Richmond the night is made to pass. Richmond says:

> The weary sunne, hath made a golden set.

Catesby, a little later, says:

> It's supper time my Lord, it's nine a clocke.

The dead of night passes with the procession of ghosts, then Ratcliffe rouses the King with news of cockcrow, then one of his lords tells Richmond it is four o'clock, the King announces it is an hour past sunrise. For the passing of time there is a more emotional parallel in *Antony and Cleopatra*, but for the mystery of place it has no parallel. The two armies pitch their tents on either side of the stage, logically the camps are a safe distance apart, and the procession of ghosts in alternate sentences dishearten Richard and comfort Richmond, the simultaneity, by goodwill of the audience, is more powerful even than in those effects of the cinema, where the fire-engine and he advancing flames are shown in swiftly alternating scenes, or where the reprieve rushes along to the rhythm of the condemned man's progress to the scaffold. Expressionistic and post-expressionistic drama in Europe, in turning to the cinema for its systems of flickering alternation, is merely exploring a simple and sometimes crude Elizabethan device.

It is not uninstructive to take advantage of the bifurcation of the drama in its extremist modern forms for a technical analysis of the Shakespearian theatre. We have (whether it results in art is a matter for discussion) the completely visual element separated out in the cinema, the completely auditory in the wireless play. Both aspects may teach us something. The purely visual cinema play is one without explanatory sub-titles. Perhaps the greatest film of this kind, *Warning Shadows,* with Fritz Kortner, the great Shakespearian actor, as its chief player, achieved some of its success by taking the Shakespearian Othello theme as its motive, the bodies of the actors and their groupings were the sole material of the play, and our actors visited it to get a rare opportunity of learning their craft. At the other end of the scale it has been found that of all plays tested on the wireless Shakespeare's have been most successful, since there is not only verbal scene-painting, but verbal time-indications and lighting effects. The progress of these two attempts at art show remarkable parallels with the development of Elizabethan drama. We have seen the development from crude 'slapstick' to the miming subtleties of Mr. Charles Chaplin, we have seen the progress from crude action to sensitive psychology, we have even seen, as the Elizabethans saw, the change from a robust joyous mood to something bordering on the morbid. If the cinema is to be an art, we are in the unique position of being able to watch if from its birth, a privilege the modern world has been accorded by no other artistic manifestation. In the wireless play we have already seen Mr. Richard Hughes, a University wit, placing his drama in a coal mine where the visual element is completely eliminated. From such crude beginnings as these, whether in *Cambises* or *Gammer Gurton's Needle,* grew *Hamlet, The Broken heart,* and *Twelfth Night.*

It is seldom that we are permitted to see a Shakespearian play as one that must win its way by its pure theatrical quality. How then did Shakespeare succeed in subduing the unruly audience of the open-air theatre and make it listen to his play? In *The Tempest* 'A tempestuous noise of thunder and lightning' is heard, foul and technical words draw the audience's attention and the play is on its way. If that be unavailing, 'Enter Mariners wet', and ever-powerful realism completes the conquest. I have seen an audience at a melodrama hushed by the explosion of a submarine at the bottom of the sea, and the immediate appearance of the crew in dripping oilskins. Such violent means are not Shakespeare's sole prerogative, or his complete bag of tricks. Remember that *The Tempest* was his ripest play; his greenest, *Love's Labour's Lost*, begins with a boyish rigmarole,

> Let *Fame*, that all hunt after in their lives,
> Live registred upon our brazen tombes.

Such lines cannot quell or attract the groundlings. Small point as it is, perhaps in such an approach we have assistance in separating court plays from public shows. The same lack of initial attack characterises a *Midsummer Night's Dream* and *Cymbeline. The Taming of the Shrew* makes a bold enough beginning, and *Twelfth Night* opening with song is safe enough. Of the tragedies, *Coriolanus, Titus Andronicus, Romeo and Juliet*, *Julius Caesar*, *Macbeth*, and *Hamlet* all begin with noise and excitement, nuts, apples, and pamphlets are forgotten, and the play-world begins. In *Antony and Cleopatra* and *King Lear* the first few lines seem to give an opportunity for the hubbub to subside before the action begins. In *Troilus and Cressida* we have a bold experiment. *Julius Caesar* is clearly a play in two parts whose *theatrical* interest lies in the first half, including the murder, whose *dramatic* interest is after the manner of a Greek tragedy on the theme of the consequences of Caesar's death. In *Troilus and Cressida* it would seem as if Shakespeare wished to begin the play without pandering. He therefore brings out a prologue to warn the audience

> that our Play
> Leapes ore the vaunt and firstlings of those broyles,
> Beginning in the middle: starting thence away,
> To what may be digested in a Play.

Attention is therefore needed from the very first line, and with this first line:

> Call here my Varlet, lie unarme againe,

this fierce play fiercely begins.

We must not forget the contribution made by the actors. The German audiences were impressed by the unprecedented naturalism of the acting and the actor's intensity within his part. Richard Flecknoe, at some distance it is true, gives this description of Richard Burbage who played Lear, Hamlet, and Falstaff among other chief parts:

> He was a delightful Proteus, so wholly transforming himself into his Part, and putting off himself which his cloathes, as he never (not so much as in the Tyring-house) assum'd himself again until the Play was done . . .
>
> He had all the parts of an excellent orator (animating his words with speaking, and speech with action) his Auditors being never more delighted than when he spoke, nor more sorry than when he held his peace; yet even then, he was an excellent Actor still, never falling in his Part when he had done speaking; but with his looks and gesture, maintaining it still unto the heighth.

Such a description explains much, and more might have been understood if Nash had kept his promise to write, so that

> Tarlton, Ned Alleyn, Knell, Bentley shall be made known to Fraunce, Spayne and Italie; and not a part that they surmounted in more than other but I will here note and set down, with the manner of their habites and attyre.

We cannot know the detail of their movements, but of their costumes we know something. Even as early as *Fulgens and*

Lucres at the beginning of the sixteenth century, actors' costume was noted for its richness.

> I thought verely by your apparell
> That ye had bene a player.
>
> . . . .
>
> There is so myche nyce aray
> Amonges thes galandis now aday
> That a man shall not lightly
> Know a player from another man.

The magnificence of English actors' costumes dazzled German eyes, in spite of Fynes Moryson's disparagement of it. Specimens of costumes actually worn by these English actors in Germany still exist, as well as a sword used by them on the stage. From Henslowe's Diary and from the Revels accounts we know that special costumes were assigned to specific parts, an important aid in clarifying the action on the stage. We have also a description of a special clown's get-up worn by Tarlton, Who came like a rogue in a foul shirt without a band, and in a blew coat with one sleeve, his stockings out at the heeles, and his head full of straw and feathers.

I am convinced that one element in the successful illusion of the Elizabethans lay in the costume, which even when it was intended to be contemporary was of such magnificence as to constitute a stage livery that carried with it a heightened atmosphere. Archaeological accuracy of costume was not understood in its modem strictness, but some attempt at verisimilitude was made. In the Court Revels this was certainly done, and we have an interesting record by Leone de Sommi, an Italian producer at Mantua in the mid-sixteenth century:

> Since every novelty is pleasing, it is a delightful sight to see on the stage foreign costumes, varying from our usage; hence it is that the most successful comedies are those costumed in the Greek fashion, for this reason more than any other I have arranged that the scene of the piece which, God willing, we shall present Tuesday, is laid in Constantinople, so that we can introduce for men and for women a style of dress unfamiliar to us here . . . And if this succeeds well in Comedy, as by experience we are sure that it will, all the more will it succeed in Tragedy, in

costuming which the greatest care must be taken, never dressing the actors in the modern manner, but in the way that is shown in antique sculptures or pictures, with those mantles and that attire in which the persons of former centuries appear so charmingly.

The Shakespearian stage did not go anything like so far. The drama of which De Sommi speaks is rightly named the *Commedia Erudita*, the learned or written drama opposed to the popular and improvised *Commedia dell'Arte*. I hope shortly to give a thorough account of the contacts of this improvised comedy with Elizabethan England, but for the purpose of this immediate inquiry it is sufficient to say that more interest was taken in it by actors than by authors. Shakespeare's advice to the players is not merely an attack on improvisation, but on this particular school of improvising. The players are described by Hamlet before he sees them and form a stock *Commedia dell'Arte* company. 'He that plays the king', 'the adventurous knight', the sighing lover, the humorous man, *i.e.*, the elderly pantaloon, the clown, and the lady. They can play both learned and improvised drama, 'law of writ and the liberty', they have a stock of speeches out of which they make their patchwork improvisations, they use miming or dumb-show, and spoken words. At the time Hamlet was being written, if we take 1600 as a possible date, the travelling actors were returning from the Continent and bringing their theatrical bad manners with them, their habit of improvising and 'inexplicable dumb shows and noise'. It may be, as Dr. Harrison suggests, that Shakespeare is mocking a rival company, but if this is so, they are merely scapegoats for a broader technical principle. Shakespeare's interest in the *Commedia dell'Arte* is shown again in one of the best remembered of his speeches, Jacques' 'All the world's a stage'. This speech contains description of four of the stock characters of this comedy of types, the lover, the soldier or capitano who is used by Shakespeare himself as Armodo in *Love's Labour's Lost*, the justice, and finally, mentioned by his Italian name, the Pantaloon as he appears in the old engravings, lean and slippered with spectacles on nose and pouch on side.

It is because he cannot neglect any manifestation of theatrical art that he includes this Italian kind in his allusions; it is because he seeks finer effects than mere bodies can give that he condemns it. Shakespeare's subtlest effects are musical, musical and vocal tones, and magical, compelling, hypnotic atmospheres. Otto Ludwig many years ago spoke of symphonic and concerted scenes. It is possible to find melodies and harmonies, arias, duets, trios, quartets, and further in such a play as *Midsummer Night's Dream.* In a mild form we have, at the beginning of his career in *Love's Labour's Lost*, an interesting attempt at comic mass music in the two successive vocal waves, first when Holofemes, in the masque at the end (Act V, Scene ii) is being 'ragged', and again in the wilder hullbaloo during the fight between Costard and Holofemes. This second tumult is a crude though successful device to render theatrically effective the announcement of the King's death. In this reputedly unplayable play we find laid bare for our inspection some of the mechanics of playwriting, and like good machinery, though simple, it is effective. In *Merchant of Venice,* Act V, Scene i, we have an interesting use of the vocal duet between Lorenzo and Jessica to point the scenery and atmosphere of 'such a night as this'.

It is a commonplace to speak of *King Lear* as a symphony, but I hope to show how the musical elements have their practical bearing in the theatre. I take the dramatical problem of *King Lear* to be the discord raised when Lear and Cordelia, who are one harmonious being, are by dramatic fiction torn roughly apart. The musical movement of the play emphasizes this discord and demands a reconciliation. I find this dramatic and musical reconciliation occurs during the exquisite duet in Act IV, Scene vii, when Lear comes to his senses, his mental discord is resolved, and his Cordelia is at last restored to him. All this part is Shakespeare's own invention. There is nothing in the old legends, nothing in the old play. The crescendo of the discord is rightly regarded as one of Shakespeare's summits of dramatic achievement, but it must not be neglected as a theatrical achievement. The theme is boldly stated at the beginning of the play:

Give me the map there. Know that we have divided into three our Kingdom.

The height of his disruption, his mental kingdom divided into the three of himself, Edgar, and the Fool, occurs amid an eruption of the elements. It is a mistake to suppose that there was no physical storm on the stage. 'Storme and Tempest' are clearly called for in the stage directions:

> Drummers make Thunder in the Tyring-house, and the twelve-penny Hirelings make artificial Lightning in their Heavens.

The storm is stilled to allow the actors ot speak, and there is no need of thunder and lightning when Lear has such words as these to speak:

> Blow windes, & crack your cheeks; Rage, blow
> You Cataracts, and Hyrricano's spout,
> Till you have drench's our Steeples, drown the Cockes.
> You Sulph'rous and Thought-executing Fires,
> Vaunt-currious of Oake-cleaving Thunder-bolts,
> Sindge me white head. And thou all-shaking Thunder,
> Strike flat the thicke Rotundity o'th' world,
> Cracke Natures moulds, all germaines spill at once
> That makes ingratefull Man.

That such crashing storm-music comes to so exquisite and end in the reconciliation duet is proof enough of Shakespeare's theatrical capacity.

It seems, however, that he was not satisfied; the duet was too soon over, and in a play not far from *King Lear* in time, in *Pericles*, he gives us one of the greatest of all his musical scenes, Act V, Scene i, in which the reconciliation of Marina and Pericles is so full of happiness for him that hallucinations of music come to close the scene with a dying fall and a vision. Farther than this scene his accomplishment did not go.

It has often been denied that the Elizabethans used descriptive or atmospheric music. In its crudest form martial music for battle purposes has been shown by Mr. W.J. Lawrence to have subtle differences. In atmospheric quality the song 'Come away, come away, death', in *Twelfth Night* is not lacking. As a clue to character, 'When that I was and a little tiny boy', brings a note of tragedy to end a very serious play. But outside Shakespeare there is more definite evidence. In Marston, *Wonder of Women*,

Act IV, 'Infernal musick plays softly whilst Erictho enters, and, when she speaks, ceaseth'. In *Fedele and Fortunio, Two Italian Gentlemen,* between the acts there is 'a pleasant Galliard' and 'a sollemne Dump'. In the *Duchess of Malfi*, madmen sing 'to a dismal kind of music', and in *The Chaste Maid in Cheapside,* 'While all the Company seeme all to weepe and moume, there is a sad Song in the musicke Roome'. These should be sufficient to indicate the possibilities of supporting the atmospheric value of the spoken words, in the way in which some modern producers of Greek plays support the choruses. Two instances are clear enough. In *Antony and Cleopatra* the masterly scene, Act IV, Scene iii, of the passing of the night with the watchmen on guard is intensified, 'Musicke of the Hoboyes is under the Stage'. Music is a flux to smooth the conjuring up of a vision; it happens so in *Pericles*, and again in *Julius Caesar*, Act IV, Scene iii, where Lucius falls asleep over his song. It is a structural scene, and, therefore, receives special emphasis as the final pivot of the play. Music is used as a solvent, as an atmospheric veneer, used to swing over moods, to prepare for tragedies and catastrophes, to harmonize discordances. Such is the music that labels itself, but the subtlest of all Shakespearian music eludes the statistician. The purely vocal music that gives colour to a character's speeches, that differentiates one man from another, one mood from another, is the most difficult of all to pin down and to analyse. Of the separate vocal melodies are built up scenic harmonies and concerted music. If ever we were able to record the tonal qualities of verse, its quivering over-tones and vocal mysteries, we should be on the thresh-old of Shakespeare's real workshop. Until we have this certainty it is not allowable to cut or to prune a speech, however trivial it may see. Certainly to cut out a whole scene or character without understanding its tonal function is criminal, to cut out the opening lines of a speech is foolish, for we do not know as yet the relation between speech and character in poetic drama. If there must be cutting, let it be in the middle of a speech, so that its impact and its final notes are unimpaired. Shakespeare the producer, in the days of his maturity, was conceivably unable to supervise his plays in person; to that end many of his later scenes are actor-proof, but it would need a bold person to consider them producer-proof.

These suggestions I have put forward are in many cases personal, and cannot have their justification except in the test of practice. It seems brutal to speak of a dramatic laboratory, but if we are to be more than amateurs in the study of Shakespeare, as I fear have been many eminent and erudite scholars, it would be well to devote at least a part of our attention to that side of his work which shows Shakespeare as a practical man of the theatre. If a national theatre is permitted by the temper of this country it does not seem too much to ask that some part of its activity may concern itself with the basic elements of dramatic and theatrical effect as exemplified in the work of the greatest wielder of the English language. It is this language, spoken under the conditions of the theatre, that is the chief clue to the effects that Shakespeare's poetical mind demanded from the theatre.

13

Shakespeare's Significances[1]

Edmund Blunden

Cryptography has long since taken up her abode at a spiritual Stratford or St. Albans, and, though the direction and temper of most of the consequent investigations have been ludicrous, there is a sense in which all critics of Shakespeare must be cryptographers. 'A sort of riddling terms' is found in Sophocles; the short and unadorned dialogue there vibrates with additional tragic purposes; no wonder then if Shakespeare, in a country full of proverb, metaphor, parable and pun, is supremely skilful in conducting his characters to their destiny by means of oracular and laconic utterances. For stage presentation, it is very probable that only the external and immediate references of these needs to be grasped. Upon my submitting some instances of what I take to be the Shakespearian sublimation of the pun, a friend of the highest judgement in poetical mysteries observed: 'Very well; but according to your theory Shakespeare's audiences would have to be all Shakespeares.' Ultimately, it might be so; but for the transitions and logic of the moment, not so. In the cinematography we have a scarcely surpassable case of sheer surface and rapid narrative supplying all that 'the public wants' on the spur of the moment. But even there, what King Lear calls a 'darker purpose' is the secret of continued liking and demand. It is on this account that Chaplin, the Elizabethan of the films, is the only creator of works that can be seen again and again with pleasure. In story and situation the films with which he has captured the world and held it for ten years are swift enough,

1. From the Shakespeare Association Lecture (1929): reprinted in *The Mind's Eye* (1934).

various enough to satisfy the least thoughtful. But he never fails to include some deeper theme or characteristic which repays more painful thinking. The fight for the tramp on the highway of human society has sustained his work first and last, and hardly a gesture escapes him without strong emotional reason. Consider, for instance, the ending of his recent play, *The Circus*. The wanderer, who entered a world in which romance and even money came his way, and who has left it again as lonely and possessionless as when he began, sits over the ashes; plays with a relic, with *the* relic of the whole episode; crumples it up and casts it from him, and then walks with his pathetic comic peculiarity out of view. But, as he goes, one swift glance right and left, one lively skipping step, tell us that he is master of himself. It is morning, it is freedom, and in that glance we have the spirit of 'fresh woods and pastures new'. Napoleon, or Charlie?

Of this quality, and of unique degree, are the significant gestures of Shakespeare, and without pretending of offer very much that is not already extant somewhere in the commentators, or perfectly well apprehended by every good reader of Shakespeare, I shall now attempt to produce a series of examples of his myriad-mindedness from a play in which he delineates one of his most perplexing subjects. That play is *King Lear.* I do not know that it can be called a study of insanity. It is rather a revelation of the sanity, or inevitable sequence, underlying and co-ordinating what superficially seems incoherence. And, since the play of character, incident and feeling is subtle, attention must be subtle also, even though the course of our curious considerings may make us run the risk of being styled cryptographers with a difference. I begin by noticing the way in which Shakespeare invites us to watch the similarities in initials of tragedy, or the contrasts in things which have the marks of similarity. We have heard Cordelia reply to her father, 'Nothing, my lord'. It is honesty's voice, and it sounds the call for Lear's disaster. Lear plays on the word. In the end of the scene, he grimly answers Burgundy's proposal to accept Cordelia with a dowry:

> Nothing: I have sworn: I am firm.

Already it is a danger-signal. We come presently to the menace of a secondary tragedy, when Edmund is plotting against Edgar. Again, this word: dishonesty's voice:

> *Glo.* What paper were you reading?
> *Edm.* Nothing, my lord.

And Gloucester, like Lear, plays on the word which sets his misery, if he knew it, in motion.

There is a development of pathos akin to this in the high words between Kent and Lear at the beginning, and their echoes in Gloucester's courtyard. 'See better, Lear', said Kent at the outset, but the answer is 'Now by Apollo', and the oath being answered again, Lear finally seals the banishment of Kent with 'By Jupiter'. When under very different conditions Lear finds Kent, disguised, in the stocks, another combat of opinion occurs, and concludes

> *Lear.* By Jupiter, I swear, no.
> *Kent.* By Juno, I swear, ay.

There is a pause here. Will the strong candour of this opposition, even to the shouting back of his oaths, remind Lear of that other occasion, and make him 'see better'?

But Lear's thought has receded to original sources, as he thinks them. It was his way from the beginning. His mind, seizing on a notion, is apt to work on that without a chance of being redirected in time. Cordelia's 'Nothing' is followed by a beautiful and complete declaration, ending with emphasis:

> Sure I shall never marry like my sisters
> To love my father *all*.

Lear responds, 'But goes thy heart with *this?*' He has not heard. He means still, with 'nothing'. He himself illustrates this fatal insistency in the figure of the dragon and his prey. It becomes a dominant method in his madness to catch up some idea, whether suggested to his memory by circumstances or to his mind by the conversation he hears, and to retain it and shape other matters to it with a kind of pride. This, of course, is readily seen when 'poor Tom', himself the centre of a tragic whirlwind, comes before Lear on the heath, and Lear cannot discover any explanation of this companion of rats and rain other than that he too had 'unkind daughters'. That way the summit of his madness lies, but there are other and less dreadful aspects of his iterating to himself one particular theme.

I may choose one prolonged example of these, which has not, so far as I can find, received close attention. Lear, from the first, is portrayed as being a little inclined to remember his school education. His reply to Cordelia's unhappy 'Nothing' is exactly a thesis of the old natural philosophers: 'An Aliquid producatur ex Nihilo?'

> Nothing will come of nothing.

Soon after, with a reference to 'the barbarous Scythian', he appears to have Horace in mind. He breaks into Latin — 'Hysterica passio' — when describing his physical trouble, a 'fit of the mother'; he compares himself to Prometheus with a vulture at his heart. And in the third act, he listens to the wild account that 'poor Tom', with his blanket only to protect him, gives of his tribulations, such as 'riding on a bay trotting-horse over four-inched bridges'. Lear listens to this recital of vivid wretchedness, and his mind fastens on the case of 'poor Tom'. Presently he refers to him as 'this philosopher', and propounds to him a question, not solely suitable to the war of elements all round, but familiar among the ancient philosophers. 'What is the cause of thunder?' Even in this is involved, not only the academic interest of Lear, his notion of 'poor Tom' and the weather, but some allusion to the clash of hot and cold, of his own ardent love confronted with the marble-hearted ingratitude of his daughters. We proceed. 'Riding over four-inched bridges' and other visions raised by poor Tom's autobiography have stirred Lear's recollection of a famous passage. '*Modo* is he called and Mahu' chances to chime with that. The next title he gives poor Tom is 'learned Theban', and after a little while that is changed for 'good Athenian'. In short, fascinated by Tom's amazements, Lear is all this time contemplating the position through the first Epistle of the second book of Horace, and particularly through these lines:

> Ille per extentum funem mihi posse videtur
> Ire poeta, meum qui pectus inaniter angit,
> Irritat, mulcet, falsis terroribus implet,
> Ut magus; et modo me Thebis, modo ponit Athenis.

'That is the poet for me, the man who can walk the whole tightrope of his art, the man who distresses me with imaginings, who angers, comforts, fills with unreal horror like a wizard, who makes me be at Thebes one minute and the next at Athens.' So, there is a unity between the scattered eccentricities of Lear.

When this Horatian by-play is still happening in Lear's mind, Edgar chances to originate another stubborn notion.

> *Lear*. What is your study?
> *Edg*. How to prevent the fiend, and to kill vermin.
> *Lear*. Let me ask you one word in private.

At this point Kent intervenes, but we can guess what the question would have been. How did he kill his daughters? Duly the word 'vermin' works; and in the scene in the farm-house later, when Lear prepares to 'arraign them straight', he addresses the *idola* of his daughters according to its significance, 'Now, you she- foxes!' Towards the close of that scene, he reverts to his caprice of quoting Horace, and orders poor Tom to find some better 'garments' — he had only a blanket: 'you will say they are Persian attire, but let them be changed'. This witty stroke is fully appreciated if we see that it plays on the last ode of Horace, Book First: 'Persicos odi, puer, apparatus' ('My boy, Persian attire and I don't agrec').

With poignant chances of recovery, no sooner discovered than destroyed, Lear passes into deeper insanity; his talk then leaps from one subject to another with wilder haste; and still there is a contexture in it. He has now the additional confusion of the rumoured war with France among his principal motives. And so, when he has made his escape at Dover, and comes with his crown of weeds to the side of Gloucester and Edgar, he begins: 'No, they cannot touch me for coining'; the metaphor echoes, and he changes it into actuality, 'There's your press-money'. He is 'the king himself, preparing his army for the quarrel with France, inspecting recruits. 'That fellow handles his bow like a crow-keeper'. Again we must see not only the fantasy of Lear, but the bird-boy passing over the farm. 'Look, look! a mouse'; apparently a reminiscence of the classical proverb, certainly a Falstaffian comment on a supposed recruit's usefulness, and clearly a remark brought on by his spying a field-mouse in the com. 'O! well flown, bird', by no great extension of this, is his enthusiasm for falconry bursting forth as he sees the hawk drop on that mouse. We have from him a picture both of the country circumstances and his life and times, 'Give the word', he finishes, like a sentry. 'Sweet marjoram', says Edgar. It sounds 'aloof from the entire point'; yet Lear says 'Pass'. And with good secret reason. Sweet maqoram was accounted, according to Culpeper, a blessed remedy for diseases of the brain. Edgar was clearly a friend. Some other oblique significances in this scene have been well displayed by the eighteenth-century commentators. Gloucester, eyeless, is speaking with Lear:

> Dost thou know me?
> *Lear*. I remember thine eyes well enough. Dost thou squiny at me? No, do thy worst, blind Cupid; I'll not love.

The final depths of distress indicated by this disinterested justing would be enough, but Shakespeare's mark is abundance. We are to feel, even here, that Lear is pondering the grossness of mortality; for 'blind Cupid' was the sign painted over the door of brothels. More bewildering still is the accurate inevitability which brings Lear back from his philosophy to his mad hope, as it is explained by Johnson:

> *Lear*. . . . I will preach to thee: mark.
> [He takes a hat in his hand, and turns it about.]
> When we are born, we cry that we are come
> To this great stage of fools.
> [He pauses, looks at the hat; admires the fashion of it.]
> This' a good block!

[*That is, the mould of a felt hat. It suggests something*:]

> It were a delicate stratagem to shoe
> A troop of horse with felt; I'll put it in proof,
> And when I have stolen upon these son-in-law,
> The kill . . .

In this manner every circumstance is made an agent as well as an accompaniment of the chief misery; it is not safe for Lear even to look at a hat or a straw.

The country symbolism of flowers, which at length resulted in those little pretty gift-books of the *Language of Flowers*, was known to Shakespeare, and contributed its colours to the full beauty of his plays. I imagine that wildflowers were not so remote from the Londoner's life in his day that his choosing some of them to suit a particular dramatic moment from more than one point of view would pass without appreciation. It is in *Hamlet* rather than *King Lear* that his garlanding of blooms and messages pleases his creative mind most notably; there we have the rosemary for remembrance, the pansies for thoughts, and the other bitterly sweet flowers; there, too, the 'fantastic garlands' that Ophelia has taken with her to the pool are more than the chance companions of her drowning. They are the omens and the ghosts of it. Yet in *King Lear*, also, we are to use our sense and our tradition, too, when flowers come into the tragedy. I have not at the moment the means to explore fully the association of 'all the idle weeds' that Cordelia names as making up Lear's 'crown' — already we see that they carry a meaning beyond that of mere picturesque detail of madness. They are his crown of thorns. But among them the *nettle* that throngs about graves, the *hemlock* with its fame for poison and narcotic, the sickly and usurping *darnel*, can quickly be perceived as speaking to the imagination of the spectator on the elements of Lear's affliction. The same touch, I believe, occurs in the study of Othello, where he calls Desdemona

> Thou weed
> Who art so lovely fair and smell'st so sweet
> That the sense aches at thee.

These rural instants, in colour lovely and in purpose and association sinister, may well be illustrated from the most exact botanist among our rural poets, John Clare. In his *Shepherd's Calender* for the month of May, he runs into a catalogue of the 'idle weeds' — there are Othello's

> Corn-poppies, that in crimson dwell,
> Called 'head-aches' from their sickly smell,

and there, red and purple

> fumitory too — a name
> That Superstition holds to fame.

'Rank fumiter' is the first of the items in Lear's mockery crown that Cordelia distinguishes.

It will be forgiven me if I transcribe several more lines from Clare's poem on 'May', although it is not one of his happiest songs of Flora, with the object of testing Shakespeare's significances in *King Lear.*

> With its eyes of gold
> And scarlet-starry points of flowers,
> Pimpernel, dreading nights and showers,
> Oft called 'the Shepherd's Weather-glass',
> That sleeps till suns have dried the grass,
> Then wakes, and spreads its creeping bloom
> Till clouds with threatening shadows come —
> Then close it shuts to sleep again:
> Which weeders see, and talk of rain;
> And boys, that mark them shut so soon
> Call 'John that goes to bed at noon'.

Now let me revert to the play, and to the moment when Lear in Gloucester's farmhouse is about to rest and save his mind. The storm seems past. The Fool, shivering in his drenched clothes, waits on his master.

Lear. Make no noise, make no noise, draw the curtains: so, so, so. We'll go to supper i' the morning: so, so, so.

Fool. And I'll go to bed at noon.

I do not wish to rhapsodize, over these last seven words, but they impress me with their seven meanings:

1. They are a sort of tried ironical joke on Lear's late hours.
2. They make a playful complaint that the Fool would like a little food before going to bed.
3. There is a pun on the people's name for the scarlet pimpernel. The weak-bodied Fool with his coxcomb looks like that flower.
4. But, if so, he shuts late. Surely there has been storm enough during the night.
5. There will be a worse storm still; and at once.
6. It is the last time that the Fool speaks during the play. He presages his untimely death, with a secondary meaning in the word 'bed' of 'grave'.
7. He takes off his coxcomb for the last time to please his old friends the audience.

It is the chief Arcanum of the Fool's difference from others that he should combine and encipher his meanings; he is the inspired child, the comical but uncheatable percipient of the true and the false. 'Not altogether fool' is a reserved way, Kent's way, of describing his telepathy. Duly then we find him crying out his paradoxes and snatches of songs, and, since most of them are to achieve the ordinary reward of clowning, the laugh of the majority, their connexion with the matter in chief is not profoundly masked. But, when we come to that part of the play in which the sexual ferocity and treachery of Regan and Goneril are revealed in broad day, we may look back and notice that there was one character who from the beginning knew all about the secret. This was the Fool. I will quote one of his hints on the subject:

Lear. Take heed, sirrah; the whip.

Fool. Truth's a dog must to kennel; he must be whipped out when Lady the brach may stand by the fire and stink.

I had for a long time passed this by, as being merely a figurative contrast between the fate of frankness and flattery, when a friend who knows his dogs as well as Shakespeare knew them chanced to read the passage with me, and informed me that there was a latent and unmistakable allusion in it. The persons under the discussion of the Fool and the King are Regan and Goneril. 'Brache' was a 'mannerly' Elizabethan term for she-hounds, both canine and human.

It is in their prodigious ability with cant terms that the Elizabethan dramatists eclipse all after-comers at the huge game of reporting human nature. It is in working knowledge of those cant terms, which even in their immorality have the genius of a strong and spirited race, and not the second-hand smirking pettiness of more recent impropriety, that the older exponents of Shakespeare, Beaumont and Fletcher, Massinger and the others have the advantage of the modems. Change of manners prevents us from applying the openness of a Francis Grose to all dark sayings even in *King Lear,* but, if we understand the aims of Shakespeare, we shall see the play better in its lights and shades. 'Anger hath a privilege', and when the deeps of these oceanic lives are troubled, then there must be a muddy violence on the surface. Thence comes the satire and the imprecation on women from Lear. Thence, too, such a detail as where Kent threatens to pound Oswald into mud, and calls him 'you wagtail'. The term describes the self-confident way of Oswald, yes; but more — the wagtail will be seen at such comers as the outflow of drains; more again — it was a term given to the character of a loose woman; and that finally achieves its full meaning in the play when at last Regan challenges Oswald on his relation with Goneril. 'I, madam!'

The character of Gloucester is built up with many touches which are not all conspicuous, and which have the difficult duty of making his tragedy 'his own fault', yet none the less pathetic, and always distinctly lower than that of Lear. The jovial coarseness in his introduction of his illegitimate son to Kent appears to indicate the worse side of his earlier life. He is included in Kent's equivocation:

> I have seen better faces in my time
> Than stands on any shoulder that I see
> Before me at this instant.

When he comes over the heath in the storm with his torch, the Fool's exclamation is ominous: 'Now a little fire in a wide field were like an old lecher's heart; a small spark, all the rest on's body cold. Look! here comes a walking fire'. And finally, we have to learn from Edgar that the farmhouse, which seemed so welcome a refuge for Lear, the 'dark tower', held another secret, and was grimly concerned with the making of the tragedy. The eminence of Gloucester is his conscience. He is almost grateful for his affliction:

> If I could bear it longer, and not fall
> To quarrel with your great opposeless wills,
> My snuff and loathed part of nature should
> Burn itself out.

Of Lear we have many incidental characteristics. As has been shown, he is a curious student, and even at his worst times can approach his torture with the calm of a Harvey: 'Then let them anatomize Regan, see what breeds about her heart. Is there any cause in nature that makes these hard hearts?' He is a lover of the English scene, and even as he points to the map he expresses it

With shadowy forests and with champains rich'd,
With plenteous rivers and wide-skirted meads.

He is a reader of the classics, and seems when he mentions 'the mystery of things' to have the title of Lucretius' poem in his system; his 'thunder-bearer' and 'high-judging Jove' are of the old poets. In hunting, hawking, archery, tournament, the art of war, and even football he has acquitted himself well, and through his decline lights up at the thought of them. The magnificence of the English sportsman is presented in most affectionate though smiling fashion when, even at the culmination of his tragedy, as he holds dead Cordelia in his arms, Lear catches at a compliment to his mastery.

Lear. I killed the slave that was a-hanging thee.
Officer. 'Tis true, my lords, he did.
Lear. Did I not, fellow?
I have seen the day, with my good biting falchion,
I would have made them skip.

'Every inch a king', he has fallen short of perfection; but he has never fallen short of the desire for it, and under the punishment of fate and age and the wilderness he continues to 'have one part in his heart' that receives whatever may make his rule more equal, his feelings more imaginatively open to the problems of the unprivileged man. In short, Lear is, without 'daubing it further', as gifted and as generous a sovereign as ever could have the title of the King of Britain; but we must know so much without any illuminated addresses from Shakespeare.

It may be that a closer acquaintance with Shakespearian criticism would have kept me from botching in my way the trains of thought already dignified by the scholarship of others. I will, however, run the risk of repeating the known or the obvious, while I touch with pleasure on a facet of this play singularly bright with the originality of Shakespeare, yet composed of gleams and glances finely unstrained. As *King Lear* proceeds, much occurs to lighten the movement of the passions and allure the audience along, yet so, that the ultimate darkness must be deepened. One great instrument of this is the season and scenery. At first, this topic is unimportant; we are indoors. There have been eclipses in the sun and moon, but those can have but a chimerical concern with us. It remains good hunting weather, but the plot turns, and the year turns. When Edgar is driven out, he must

> with presented nakedness outface
> The winds and persecutions of the sky;

Siberian days, with beggars' withered arms among withered trees and shaking 'sheepcotes and mills'. When Lear is driven out, the green before the bloom has yet to come; the hawthorn is merely the effigy of bony nakedness, and rain and hurricare seem to conspire to destroy even the seed of life in the mould. Shelter itself is a war on humanity: 'Fathom and half, fathom and half shrills poor Tom from his outhouse. But this is Nature's last paroxysm. Afterwards she softens, and speaks.

> In better phrase and matter than she did.

The human tempest, wintriness and hunger do not follow her example. They become intenser. Gloucester may be blinded, but he comes to the 'chalky bourn' of Dover through fields of corn and flowers; above him the 'shrill-gorged lark' makes music, and below the lazy sea is murmusing, and the samphire-gatherer and fisherman are out and about. Lear may be demented, but he too moves among the ripening fields, and pulls flowers for his head, once unbonneted, wherever he likes; his eye meets the mating wren and 'small gilded fly'. In his final love-song or hymn to Cordelia, we feel that the sunshine is playing, and the gilded butterflies' are coming even through prison bars.

> As it fell upon a day
> In the merry month of May —

the sun goes out, the butterflies vanish, 'all's cheerless, dark, and deadly'.

In making these notes upon the richness, and intuitive complexity, and choral harmony of Shakespeare's significances, I have limited myself to one play, and of that I have done little more than scratch the surface, with nothing like a plough. I fear, too that such a style of literal criticism as I have attempted may make me seem guilty of shallow presumptuousness, like the 'critic fly' in Thomson's *Seasons*, who settled on the dome of St. Paul's, and decided that the architecture of St. Paul's was interestingly rough. But the points in *King Lear* which attracted me are not roughnesses, but unions of perfection; the mind of the dramatist is such that wherever we are perplexed we are safe in agreeing with the rustic summing up 'the mystery of things': 'It all be done for a purpose' — several purposes.

14

The Othello Music[1]

G. Wilson Knight

In *Othello* we are faced with the vividly particular rather than the vague and universal. The play as a whole has a distinct formal beauty: within it we are ever confronted with beautiful and solid forms. The persons tend to appear as warmly human, concrete. They are neither vaguely universalized, as in *Lear* or *Macbeth*, nor deliberately mechanized and vitalized by the poet's philosophic plan as in *Measure for Measure* and *Timon* — where the significance of the dramatic person is dependent almost wholly on our understanding of the allegorical or symbolical meaning. It is true that Iago is here a mysterious, inhuman creature of unlimited cynicism: but the very presence of the concrete creations around, in differentiating him sharply from the rest, limits and defines him. *Othello* is a story of intrigue rather than a visionary statement. If, however, we tend to regard Othello, Desdemona, and Iago as suggestive symbols rather than human beings, we may, from a level view of their interaction, find a clear relation existing between *Othello* and other plays of the Hate-theme. Such an analysis will be here only in part satisfactory. It exposes certain underlying ideas, abstracts them from the original: it is less able to interpret the whole positive beauty of the play. With this important reservation, I shall push the interpretative method as far as possible.

Othello is dominated by its protagonist. Its supremely beautiful effects of style are ever expressions of Othello's personal passion. Thus, in first analysing Othello's poetry, we shall lay

1. *The Wheel of Fire* (1930).

the basis for an understanding of the play's symbolism: this matter of style is, indeed, crucial, and I shall now indicate those qualities which clearly distinguish it from other Shakespearian poetry. It holds a rich music all its own, and possesses a unique solidity and precision of picturesque phrase or image, a peculiar chastity and serenity of thought. It is, as a rule, barren of direct metaphysical content. Its thought does not mesh with the reader's: rather it is ever outside us, aloof. This aloofness is the resultant of an inward aloofness of image from image, word from word. The dominant quality is separation, not, as is more usual in Shakespeare, cohesion. Consider these exquisite poetic movements:

> O heavy hour!
> Methinks it should be now a huge eclipse
> Of sun and moon, and that the affrighted globe
> Should yawn at alteration.

(V. ii. 98)

Or,

> It is the very error of the moon;
> She comes more nearer earth than she was wont,
> And makes men mad.

(V. ii. 109)

These are solid gems of poetry which lose little by divorce from their context : wherein they differ from the finest passages of *Lear* or *Macbeth*, which are as wild flowers not to be up torn from their rooted soil if they are to live. In these two quotations we should note how the human drama is thrown into sudden contrast and vivid, unexpected relation with the tremendous concrete machinery of the universe, which is thought of in terms of individual heavenly bodies : 'sun' and 'moon'. The same effect is apparent in:

> Nay, had she been true,
> If heaven had made me such another world
> Of one entire and perfect chrysolite,
> I'd not have sold her for it.

(V. ii. 143)

Notice the single word 'chrysolite' with its outstanding and remote beauty: this is typical of *Othello*. Now the effect is such passages is primarily one of contrast. The vastness of the night sky, and its moving planets, or the earth itself — here conceived objectively as a solid, round, visualized object — these things, though thrown momentarily into sensible relation with the passions of man, yet remain vast, distant, separate, seen but not apprehended; something against which the dramatic movement may be silhouetted, but with which it cannot be merged. This poetic use of heavenly bodies serves to elevate the theme, to raise issues infinite and unknowable. Those bodies are not, however, implicit symbols of man's spirit, as in *Lear*: they remain distinct, isolated phenomena, sublimely decorative to the play. In *Macbeth* and *Lear* man commands the elements and the stars: they are part of him. Compare the above quotations from *Othello* with this from *Lear*:

> You nimble lightnings, dart your blinding flames
> Into her scornful eyes! Infect her beauty,
> You fen-suck'd fogs, drawn by the powerful sun,
> To fall and blast her pride.
>
> (II. iv. 167)

This is typical: natural images are given a human value. They are insignificant, visually: their value is only that which they bring to the human passion which cries out to them. Their aesthetic grandeur, in and for themselves, is not relevant to the Lear-universe. So, too, Macbeth cries

> Stars, hide your fires;
> Let not light see my black and deep desires.
>
> (I. iv. 50)

And Lady Macbeth:

> Come, thick night,
> And pall thee in the dunnest smoke of hell,
> That my keen knife see not the wound it makes,
> Nor heaven peep through the blanket of the dark,
> To cry 'Hold, hold!'
>
> (I. v. 51)

Here, and in the *Lear* extract, there is no clear visual effect as in *Othello*: tremendous images and suggestions are evoked only to the blurred as images by the more powerful passion which calls them into being. Images in *Macbeth* are thus continually vague, mastered by passion; apprehended, but not seen. In Othello's poetry they are concrete, detached; seen but not apprehended. We meet the same effect in:

> Like to the Pontic sea,
> Whose icy current and compulsive course
> Ne'er feels retiring ebb, but keeps due on
> To the Propontic and the Hellespont,
> Even so my bloody thoughts, with violent pace,
> Shall ne'er look back, ne'er ebb to humble love,
> Till that a capable and wide revenge
> Swallow them up. Now, by yond marble heaven,
> In the due reverence of a sacred vow
> I here engage my words.
>
> (III. iii. 453)

This is, indeed, a typical speech. The long comparison, explicitly made, where in *Lear* or *Macbeth* a series of swiftly evolving metaphors would be more characteristic, is another example of the separateness obtaining throughout *Othello*. There is no fusing of word with word, rather a careful juxtaposition of one word or image with another. And there are again the grand single words, 'Propontic', 'Hellespont', with their sharp, clear, consonant sounds, constituting defined aural solids typical of the Othello music: indeed, fine single words, especially proper names, are a characteristic of this play — Anthropophagi, Ottomites, Arabian trees, 'the base Indian', the Egyptian, Palestine, Mauretania, the Sagittary, Olympus, Mandragora, Othello, Desdemona. This is a rough assortment, not all used by Othello, but it points the Othello quality of rich, often expressly consonantal, outstanding words. Now Othello's prayer, with its 'marble heaven', is most typical and illustrative. One watches the figure of Othello silhouettend against at flat, solid, moveless sky: there is a plastic, static suggestion about the image. Compare it with a similar Lear-prayer:

> O heavens,
> If you do love old men, if your sweet sway
> Allow obedience, if yourselves are old,
> Make it your cause; send down and take my part!
>
> (II. iv. 192)

Here we do not watch Lear: 'We are Lear'. There is no visual effect, no rigid subject-object relation between Lear and 'the heavens', nor any contrast, but an absolute unspatial unity of spirit. The heavens blend with Lear's prayer, each is part of the other. There is an intimate interdependence, not a mere juxtaposition. Lear thus identifies himself in kind with the heavens to which he addresses himself directly: Othello speaks of 'you marble heaven', in the third person, and swears by it, does not pray to it. It is conceived as outside his interests.

Now this detached style, most excellent in point of clarity and stateliness, tends also to lose something in respect of power. At moments of great tension, the Othello style fails of a supreme effect. Capable of fine things quite unmatched in their particular quality in any other play, it nevertheless sinks sometimes to a studied artificiality, nerveless and without force. For example, Othello thinks of himself as:

> . . . one whose subdued eyes,
> Albeit unused to the melting mood,
> Drop tears as fast as the Arabian trees
> Their medicinal gum.
>
> (V. ii. 348)

Beside this we might place Macduff's

> O I could play the women with mine eyes
> And braggart with my tongue! But, gentle heavens,
> Cut short all intermission . . .
>
> (IV. iii. 230)

Now Othello's lines here have a certain restrained, melodic beauty, like the 'Pontic sea' passage; both speeches use the typical Othello picturesque image or word; both compare, by simile, the passion of man with some picture delightful in itself, which is developed for its own sake, slightly over-developed — so that the final result makes us forget the emotion in contemplation of the image. Beauty has been imposed on human sorrow, rather than shown to be intrinsic therein. But Macduff's passionate utterance has not time to paint word-pictures of 'yon marble heaven', or to search for abstruse geographical images of the Hellespont, or Arabia. There is more force in his first line than all Othello's slightly over-strained phraseology of 'subdued eyes' and melting mood'. Its strength derives from the compression of metaphor and the sudden heightened significance of a single, very commonplace word ('woman'), whereas the other style deliberately refuses power in the level prolixity of simile, and searches always for the picturesque. The Othello style is diffuse: leisurely, like a meandering river; the Macbeth style compressed, concentrated, and explosive; often jerky, leaping like a mountain torrent. But metaphor is not essential to intensest Shakespearian power. Another, still finer, passage from *Lear* on the same theme might be adduced:

> *Cordelia*. How does my royal lord? How fares your majesty?
> *Lear*. You do me wrong to take me out o' the grave:
> Thou art a soul in bliss; but I am bound
> Upon a wheel of fire, that mine own tears
> Do scaled like molten lead.
>
> (IV. vii. 44)

The extraordinary force of that ending is gained by simile: but there is no diffusion of content, no accent that does not carry the maximum of emotion. It is even more powerful than Macduff's speech, since it lacks excitability: it has the control and dignity of Othello's with the compressed, explosive quality of Macduff's. The Othello style does not compass the overpowering effects of *Macbeth or Lear*: nor does it, as a rule, aim at them. At the most agonizing moments of Othello's story, however, there is apparent weakness: we find an exaggerated, false rhetoric. There is a speech in *Othello* that begins in the typical restrained manner, but degenerates finally to what might almost be called bombast. It starts:

> Where should Othello go?
> Now, how dost thou look now? O ill-starr'd wench!
> Pale as they smock! When we shall meet at compt,
> This look of thine will hurl my soul from heaven,
> And fiends will snatch at it. Cold, cold, my girl!
> Even like thy chastity.
>
> (V. ii. 271)

Here we have the perfection of the Othello style. Concrete, visual, detached. Compare it with Lear's, 'Thou art a soul in bliss . . . ', where the effect, though perhaps more powerful and immediate, is yet vague, intangible, spiritualized. Now this speech, started in a style that can in its own way challenge that of *Lear*, rapidly degenerates as Othello's mind is represented as collapsing under the extreme of anguish:

> O cursed slave!
> Whip me, ye devils,
> From the possession of this heavenly sight!
> Blow me about in winds! Roast me in sulphur!
> Wash me in steep-down gulfs of liquid fire!
> O Desdemona! Desdemona! Dead!
> Oh! Oh! Oh!

There is a sudden reversal of poetic beauty: these lines lack cogency because they exaggerate rather than concentrate the emotion. Place beside these violent eschatological images the passage from *Lear*:

> And my poor fool is hang'd! No, no no life!
> Why should a dog, a horse, a rat have life,
> And thou no breath at all? Thou'lt come no more,
> Never, never, never, never, never!
> Pray you, undo this button: thank you, Sir.
> Do you see this? Look on her, look, her lips,
> Look there, look there!
>
> (V. iii. 305)

Notice by what rough, homely images the passion is transmitted — which are as truly an integral part of the naturalism of Lear as the mosaic and polished phrase, and the abstruse and picturesque allusion is, in its best passages, a characteristic of Othello's speech. Thus the extreme, slightly exaggerated beauty of Othello's language is not maintained. This is even more true elsewhere. Othello, who usually luxuriates in deliberate and magnificent rhetoric, raves, falls in a trance:

> Lie with her! lie on her! We say lie on her, when they belie her. Lie with her! that's fulsome — Handkerchief — confessions — handkerchief! To confess, and be hanged for his labour; first, to be hanged, and then to confess — I tremble at it. Nature would not invest herself in such shadowing passion without some instruction. It is not words that shake me thus. Pish! Noses, ears, and lips. — Is't possible? — Confess — handkerchief! — O devil!
>
> (IV. i. 34)

Now, whereas Lear's madness never lacks artistic meaning, whereas its most extravagant and grotesque effects are presented with imaginative cogency, Othello can voice words like these. This is the Iago-spirit, the Iago-medicine, at work, like an acid eating into bright metal. This is the primary fact of Othello and therefore of the play: something of solid beauty is undermined, wedged open so that it exposes an extreme ugliness. When Othello is represented as enduring loss of control he is, an Macbeth and Lear never are, ugly, idiotic; but when he has full control he attains an architectural stateliness of quarried speech, a silver rhetoric of a kind unique in Shakespeare:

> It is the cause, it is the cause, my soul, —
> Let me not name it to you, you chaste stars! —
> It is the cause. Yet I'll not shed her blood;
> Nor scar that whiter skin of hers than snow,
> And smooth as monumental alabaster.
> Yet she must die, else she'll betray more men.
> Put out the light, and then put out the light:
> If I quench thee, thou flaming minister,
> I can again thy former light restore,
> Should I repent me: but once put out they light,
> Thou cunning'st pattern of excelling nature,
> I know not where is that Promethean heat
> That can thy light relume. When I have pluck'd the rose
> I cannot give it vital growth again,
> It needs must wither: I'll smell it on the tree.
>
> (V. ii. 1)

This is the noble Othello music: highly-coloured, rich in sould and phrase, stately. Each word solidifies as it takes its place in the pattern. This speech well illustrates the Othello style: the visual or tactile suggestion — 'whiter skin of hers than snow', 'smooth as monumental alabaster'; the slightly over-decorative phrase, 'flaming minister'; the momentary juxtaposition of humanity and the vast spaces of the night, the 'chaste stars'; the concrete imagery of 'thou cunning'st pattern of excelling nature', and the lengthy comparison of life with light; the presence of simple forward-flowing clarity of dignified statement and of simile in place of the super logical welding of thought with molten thought as in the more compressed, agile, and concentrated poetry of *Macbeth* and *Lear*; and the fine, outstanding single word, 'Promethean'. In these respects Othello's speech is nearer the style of the aftermath of Elizabethan literature, the settled lava of that fiery eruption, which gave us the solid image of Marvell and the 'marmoreal phrase' of Browne: it is the most Miltonic thing in Shakespeare.

Now this peculiarity of style directs our interpretation in two ways. First, the tremendous reversal from extreme, almost over-decorative, beauty, to extreme ugliness — both of a kind unusual in Shakespeare — will be seen to reflect a primary truth about the play. That I will demonstrate later in my essay. Second, the concreteness and separation of image, word, or phrase, contrasting with the close-knit language elsewhere, suggests a proper approach to *Othello* which is not proper to *Macbeth* or *Lear*. Separation is the rule throughout *Othello*. Whereas in *Macbeth* and *Lear* we have one dominant atmosphere, built of a myriad subtleties of thought and phraseology entwining throughout, subduing our minds wholly to their respective visions, whereas each has a single quality, expresses as a whole a single statement, *Othello* is built rather of outstanding differences. In *Othello* all is silhouetted, defined, concrete. Now instead of reading a unique, pervading, atmospheric suggestion — generally our key to interpretation of what happens within that atmosphere — we must here read the meaning of separate persons. The persons here are truly separate. Lear, Cordelia, Edmund all grow out of the Lear-universe, all are levelled by its characteristic atmosphere, all blend with it and with each other, so that they are less closely and vividly defined. They lack solidity. Othello, Desdemona, Iago, however, are clearly and vividly separate. All here — but Iago — age solid, concrete. Contrast is raised to its highest pitch. Othello is statuesque, Desdemona most concretely human and individual, Iago, if not human or in any usual sense 'realistic', is quite unique. Within analysis of these three persons and their interaction lies the meaning of *Othello*. In *Macbeth* or *Lear* we interpret primarily a singleness of vision. Here, confronted with a significant diversity, we must have regard to the essential relation existing between the three main personal conceptions. Interpretation must be based not on unity but differentiation. Therefore I shall pursue an examination of this triple symbolism, which analysis will finally resolve the difficulty of Othello's speech, wavering as it does between with at first sight appear an almost artificial beauty and an equally inartistic ugliness.

Othello radiates a world of romantic, heroic, and picturesque adventure. All about him is highly coloured. He is a Moor; he is noble and generally respected; he is proud in the riches of his achievement. Now his prowess as a solider is emphasized. His arms have spent 'their dearest action in the tented field' (I. iii. 85). Again,

> The tyrant custom, most grave Senators,
> Hath made the flinty and steel couch of war
> My thrice-driven bed of down.
>
> (I. iii. 230)

His iron warriorship is suggested throughout. Iago says:

> Can he be angry? I have seen the cannon,
> When it hath blown his ranks into the air,
> And, like the devil, from his very arm
> Puff d his own brother: — and can he be angry?
> Something of moment then: I will go meet him:
> There's matter in't indeed, if he be angry.
>
> (III. iv. 134)

And Lodovico:

> Is this the nature
> Whom passion could not shake? Whose solid virtue
> The shot of accident, nor dart of chance,
> Could neither graze nor pierce?
>
> (IV. i. 276)

But we also meet a curious discrepancy. Othello tells us:

> Rude am I in my speech,
> And little bless'd with the soft phrase of peace.
>
> (I. iii. 18)

Yet the dominant quality in this play is the exquisitely moulded language, the noble cadence and chiselled phrase, of Othello's poetry. Othello's speech, therefore, reflects not a soldier's language, but the quality of soldiership in all its glamour of romantic adventure: it holds an imaginative realism. It has a certain exotic beauty, is a storied and romantic treasure-house of rich, colourful experiences. He recounts his adventures, telling of

> antres vast and deserts idle,
> Rough quarries, rocks, and hills whose heads touch heaven,
>
> (I. iii. 140)

of Connibals, and the Anthropophagi, and 'men whose heads do grow beneath their shoulders' (I. iii. 144). He tells Desdemona of the handkerchief given by 'an Egyptian' to his mother:

> 'Tis true: there's magic in the web of it:
> A sibyl, that had number'd in the world
> The sun to course two hundred compasses,
> In her prophetic fury sew'd the work;
> The worms were hallow'd that did breed the silk,
> And it was dyed in mummy which the skillful
> Conserved of maidens' hearts.
>
> (III. iv. 69)

Swords are vivid, spiritualized things to Othello. There is his famous line:

> Keep up your bright swords, for the drew will rust them.
>
> (I. ii. 59)

And in the last scene, he says:

> I have another weapon in this chamber;
> It is a sword of Spain, the ice-brook's temper.
>
> (V. ii. 252)

In his address at the end, he speaks of himself as

> one whose hand,
> Like the base Indian, threw a pearl away
> Richer than all his tribe.
>
> (V. ii. 346)

His tears flow as the gum form 'Arabian trees' (V. ii. 350); he recounts how in Aleppo he smote 'a malignant and a turban'd Turk' (V. ii. 352) for insulting Venice. Finally there is his noble apostrophe to his lost 'occupation'.

> Farewell the plumed troop and the big wars,
> That make ambition virute! O, farewell!
> Farewell the neighing steed and the shrill trump,
> The spirity-stirring drum, the ear-piercing fife,
> The royal banner and all quality,
> Pride, pomp, and circumstance of glorious war!
> And, O you mortal engines, whose rude throats
> The immortal Jove's dread clamours counterfeit,
> Farewell Othello's occupation's gone.
>
> (III. iii. 349)

Again, we have the addition of phrase to separate phrase, rather than the interdependence, the evolution of thought from thought, the clinging mesh of close-bound suggestions of other plays. Now this noble eulogy of war is intrinsic to the Othello conception. War is in his blood. When Desdemona accepts him, she knows she must not be 'a moth of peace' (I. iii. 257). Othello is a compound of highly-coloured, romantic adventure — he is himself 'coloured' — and War; together with a great pride and a great faith in those realities. His very life is dependent on a fundamental belief in the validity and nobility of human action — with, pherhaps, a strong tendency towards his own acheivement in particular. Now war, in Shakespeare, is usually a positive spiritual value, like Love. There is reference to the soldiership of the protagonist in all the plays analysed in my present treatment. Soldiership is almost the condition of nobility, and so the Shakespearian hero is usually a soldier. Therefore Othello, with reference to the Shakespearian universe, becomes automatically a symbol of faith in human values of Love, War, of Romance in a wide and sweeping sense. He is, as it were, conscious of all he stands for : from the first to the last he loves his own romantic history. He is, like Troilus, dedicate to these values, has faith and pride in both. Like Troilus he is conceived as extraordinarily direct, simple, 'credulous' (IV. i. 46). Othello, as he appears in the action of the play, may be considered the high-priest of human endeavour, robed in the vestments of Romance, whom we watch serving in the Temple of War at the Altar of Love's Divinity.

Desdemona is his divinity. She is, at the same time, warmly human. There is a certain domestic feminity about her. She is 'a maiden never bold' (I. iii. 94). We hear that 'the house affairs' (had Cordelia any?) drew her often from Othello's narrative (I. iii. 147). But she asks to her the whole history:

> I did consent,
> And often did beguile her of her tears,
> When I did speak of some distressful stroke
> That my youth suffered. My story being done,
> She gave me for my pains a world of sighs :
> She swore, in faith, 'twas strange, 'twas passing strange,
> 'Twas pitiful, 'twas wondrous pitiful:
> She wish'd she had not heard it, yet she wish'd
> That heaven had made her such a man.
>
> (I. iiii. 155)

The same domesticity and gentleness is apparent throughout. She talks of 'to-night at supper' (III. iii. 57) or 'to-morrow dinner' (III. iii. 58); she is typically feminine in her attempt to help Cassio, and her pity for him. This is how she describes her suit to Othello:

> Why, this is not a boon;
> 'Tis as I should entreat you wear your gloves,
> Or feed on nourishing dishes, or keep you warm,
> Or sue to you to do a peculiar profit
> To your own person . . .
>
> (III. iii. 76)

— a speech reflecting a world of sex-contrast. She would bind Othello's head with her handkerchief — that handkerchief which is to become a terrific symbol of Othello's jealousy. The Othello world is eminently domestic, and Desdemona expressly feminine. We hear of her needlework (IV. i. 198), her fan, gloves, mask (IV. ii. 9). In the exquisite 'willow'-song scene, we see her with her maid, Emilia. Emilia given her 'her nightly wearing' (IV. iii. 16). Emilia says she has laid on her bed the 'wedding-sheets' (IV. ii. 105) Desdemona asked for. Then there is the Willow-Song, brokenly sung whilst Emilia 'unpins' (IV. iii. 34) Desdemona's dress:

> My mother had a maid called Barbara:
> She was in love, and he she loved proved mad
> And did forsake her . . .
>
> (IV. iii. 26)

The extreme beauty and pathos of this scene is largely dependent on the domesticity of it. *Othello* is eminently a domestic tragedy. But this element in the play is yet to be related to another more universal element. Othello is concerely human, so is Desdemona. Othello is very much the typical middle-aged bachelor entering matrimony late in life, but he is also, to transpose a phrase of Iago's a symbol of human — especially masculine — 'purpose, courage, and valour' (IV. iii. 217), and, in a final judgement, is seen to represent the idea of human faith and value in a very wide sense. Now Desdemona, also very human, with an individual domestic feminine charm and simplicity, is yet also a symbol of woman in general daring the unknown seas of marriage with the mystery of man. Beyond this, in the far flight of a transcendental interpretation, it is clear that she becomes a symbol of man's ideal, the supreme value of Love. At the limit of the series of wider and wider suggestions which appear from imaginative contemplation of a poetic symbol she is to be equated with the Divine Principle. Now in one scene of *Othello,* and one only, direct poetic symbolism breaks across the vividly human, domestic world of this play. As everything in *Othello* is separated, defined, so the plot itself is in two distinct geographical divisions: Venice and Cyprus. Desdemona leaves the safety and clam of her home for the stormy voyage to Cyprus and the tempest of the following tragedy. Iago's plot begins to work in the second part. The storm-scene, between the two parts, is important.

Storms are continually symbols of tragedy in Shakespeare. Now this scene contains some most vivid imaginative effects, among them passages of fine storm-poerty of the usual kind:

> For do but stand upon the foaming shore,
> The chidden billow seems to pelt the clouds;
> The wind-shaked surge, with high and monstrous mane,
> Seems to cast water on the burning bear,
> And quench the guards of the ever-fixed pole:
> I never did like molestation view,
> On the enchafed flood.

(II. i. II)

This storm-poetry is here closely associated with the human element. And in this scene, where direct storm-symbolism occurs, it is noteworthy that the figures of Desdemona and Othello are both strongly idealized:

Cassio. Tempests themselves, high seas and howling winds,
The gutter'd rocks and congregated sands, —
Traitors ensteep'd to clog the guiltless keel, —
As having sense of beauty, do omit
Their mortal natures, letting go safely by
The divine Desdemona.
Montano. What is she?
Cassio. She that I spake of, our great captain's captain,
Left in the conduct of the bold Iago,
Whose footing here anticipates our thoughts
A se'nnight's speed. Great Jove, Othello guard,
And swell his sail with thine own powerful breath,
That he may bless this bay with his tall ship,
Make love's quick pants in Desdemona's arms,
Give renewed fire to our extincted spirits,
And bring all Cyprus comfort!
Enter Desdemona, & *c*.
O, behold,
The riches of the ship is come on shore!
Ye men of Cyprus, let her have your knees.
Hail to thee, lady! and the grace of heaven,
Before, behind thee, and on every hand,
Enwheel thee round!

(II. i. 68)

Desdemona is thus endued with a certain transcendent quality of beauty and grace. She 'paragons description and wild fame' says Cassio: she is

One that excels the quirks of blazoning pens,
And in the essential vesture of creation
Does tire the ingener.

(II. i. 63)

And Othello enters the port of Cyprus as a hero coming to 'bring comfort', to 'give renewed fire' to men. The entry of Desdemona and that of Othello are both heralded by discharge of guns: which both merges finely with the tempest-symbolism and the violent strees and excitement of the scene as a whole, and heightens our sense of the warrior nobility of the protagonist and his wife, subdued as she is 'to the very quality' of her lord (I. iii. 252). Meeting Desdemona, he speaks:

> *Othello*. O my fair warrior!
>
> *Desdemona*. My dear Othello!
>
> *Othello*. If gives me wonder great as my content
> To see you here before me. O my soul's joy!
> If after every tempest come such calms,
> May the winds blow till they have waken'd death!
> And let the labouring bark climb hills of seas
> Olympus-high and duck again as low
> As hell's from heaven! If it were now to die,
> 'Twere now to be most happy; for, I fear,
> My soul hath her content so absolute
> That not another comfort like to this
> Succeeds in unknown fate.
>
> (II. i. 184)

This is the harmonious marriage of true and noble minds. Othello, Desdemona, and their love are here apparent, in this scene of storm and reverberating discharge of cannon, as things of noble and conquering strength: they radiate romantic valour. Othello is essential man in all his prowess and protective strength; Desdemona essential woman, gentle, loving brave in trust of her warrior husband. The war is over. The storm of sea or bruit of cannonade are powerless to hurt them: yet there is another storm brewing in the venomed mind of Iago. Instead of merging with and accompanying tragedy the storm here is thus contrasted with the following tragic events: as usual in *Othello*, contrast and separation take the place of fusion and unity. This scene is thus a microcosm of the play, reflecting its action. Colours which are elsewhere softly toned are here splashed vividly on the play's canvas. Here especially Othello appears a prince of heroes, Desdemona is lit by a divine feminine radiance: both are transfigured. They are shown as coming safe to land, by Heaven's 'grace', triumphant, braving war and tempestuous seas, guns thundering their welcome. The reference of all this, on the plane of high poetic symbolism, to the play as a whole is evident.

Now against these two Iago pits his intellect. In this scene too Iago declares himself with especial clarity:

> O gentle lady, do not put me to't;
> For I am nothing, if not critical.
>
> (II. i. 119)

His conversation with Desdemona reveals his philosophy. Presented under the cloak of fun, it exposes nevertheless his attitude to life: that of the cynic. Roderigo is his natural companion: the fool is a convenient implement, and at the same time continual food for his philosophy. Now Othello and Desdemona are radiant, beautiful: Iago opposes them, critical, intellectual. Like cold steel his cynic skill will run through the warm body of their love. Asked to praise Desdemona, he draws, a picture of womanly goodness in a vein of mockery. And concludes:

> *Iago*. She was a wight if ever such wight were —
>
> *Desdemona*. To do what?
>
> *Iago*. To suckle fools and chronicle small beer.
>
> (II. i. 159)

Here is his reason for hating Othello's and Desdemona's love: he hates their beauty, to him a meaningless, stupid thing. That is Iago. Cynicism is his philosophy, his very life, his 'motive' in working Othello's ruin. The play turns on this theme: the cynical intellect pitted against a lovable humanity transfigured by qualities of heroism and grace. As Desdemona and Othello embrace he says:

> O you are well turned now!
> But I'll set down the pegs that make this music,
> As honest as I am.
>
> (II. i. 201)

'Music' is apt: we remember Othello's rich harmony of words. Against the Othello music Iago concentrates all the forces of cynic villainy.

Iago's cynicism is recurrent:

> Virtue! a fig! 'tis in ourselves that we are thus or thus . . .
>
> (I. iii. 322)

Love to him is

> . . . merely a lust of the blood and a permission
> of the will.
>
> (I. iii. 339)

He believes Othello's and Desdemona's happiness will be short-lived, since he puts no faith in the validity of love. Early in the play he tells Roderigo:

> It cannot be that Desdemona should long continue her love to the Moor . . . nor he his to her . . . These Moors are changeable in their wills . . . the food that to him now is as luscious as lacusts, shall be to him shortly as bitter as coloquintida. She must change to youth: when she is sated with his body, she will find the error of her choice: she must have change, she must.

This is probably Iago's sincere belief, his usual attitude to love: he is not necessarily deceiving Roderigo. After this, when he is alone, we hear that he suspects Othello with his own wife: nor are we surprised. And, finally, his own cynical beliefs suggest to him a way of spiting Othello. He thinks of Cassio:

> After some time, to abuse Othello's ear
> That he is too familiar with his wife.
>
> (I. iii. 401)

The order is important: Iago first states his disbelief in Othello's and Desdemona's continued love, and next thinks of a way of precipitating its end. That is, he puts his cynicism into action. The same rhythmic sequence occurs later. Iago witnesses Cassio's meeting with Desdemona at Cyprus, and comments as follows:

> He takes her by the palm: ay, well said, whisper: with as little a web as this will I ensnare as great a fly as Cassio. Ay, smile upon her, do; I will gyve thee in thine own courtship . . .
>
> (II. i. 170)

Iago believes Cassio loves Desdemona. He has another cynical conversation with Roderigo as to Desdemona's chances of finding satisfaction with Othello, and the probability of her love for Cassio (II. I. 223-79). A kiss, to Iago, cannot be 'courtesy': it is

> Lechery, by this hand; and index and obscure prologue to the history of lust and foul thoughts.
>
> (II. i. 265)

Iago is sincere enough and means what he says. Cynicism is the key to his mind and actions. After Roderigo's departure, he again refers to his suspicions of Othello — and Cassio too — with his own wife. He asserts definitely — and here there is no Roderigo to impress — his belief in Cassio's guilt:

> That Cassio loves her, I do well believe it;
>
> That she loves him, 'tis apt and of great credit.
>
> (II. i, 295)

In this soliloquy he gets his plans clearer: again, they are suggested by what he believes to be truth. I do not suggest that Iago lacks conscious villainy: for from it. Besides, in another passage he shows that he is aware of Desdemona's innocence (IV. i. 48). But it is important that we observe how his attitude to life casts the form and figure of his meditated revenge. His plan arises out of the cynical depths of his nature. When, at the end, he says, 'I told him what I thought' (V. ii. 176), he is speaking at least a hald-truth. He hates the romance of Othello and the loveliness of Desdemona because he is by nature the enemy of these things. Cassio, he says,

> hath a daily beauty in his life
>
> That makes mine ugly.
>
> (V. i. 19)

This is his 'motive' throughout: other suggestions are surface deep only. He is cynicism loathing beauty, refusing to allow its existence. Hence the venom of his plot: the plot is lago — both are ultimate, causeless, self-begotten. Iago is cynicism incarnate and projected into action.

Iago is thus utterly devilish: there is no weakness in his casing armour of unrepentant villainy. He is a kind of Mephistopheles, closely equivalent to Goethe's devil, the two possessing the same qualities of mockery and easy cynicism. Thus he is called a 'hellish villain' by Lo.dovico (V. ii. 368), a 'demi-devil' by Othello (V. ii. 301). Othello says:

> I look down towards his feet; but that's a fable.
>
> If that thou be'est a devil, I cannot kill thee.
>
> (V. ii. 286)

Iago himself recognizes a kinship:

> Hell and night
> Must bring this monstrous birth to the world's sight.
>
> (I. iii. 409)

And,

> Divinity of hell!
> When devils will the blackest sins put on,
> They do suggest at first with heavenly shows
> As I do now.
>
> (II. iii. 356)

He knows that his 'poison' (III. iii. 325) will 'burn like the mines of sulphur' (III. iii. 329) in Othello. Thus Iago is, to Othello, the antithesis of Desdemona: the relation is that of the spirit of denial to the divine principle. Desdemona 'plays the god' (II. iii. 353) with Othello: if she is false, 'heaven mocks itself (III. iii. 278). During the action, as Iago's plot succeeds, her essential divinity changes, for Othello, to a thing hideous and devilish — that is to its antithesis:

> Her name that was as fresh
> As Dian's visage, is now begrimed and black
> As mine own face.
>
> (III. iii. 386)

She is now 'devil' (IV. i. 251, 256) or 'the fair devil' (III. iii. 478); her hand, a 'sweating devil' (III. iv. 42); the 'devils themselves' will fear to seize her for her heavenly looks (IV. ii. 35). Thus Iago, himself a kind of devil, insidiously eats his way into this world of romance, chivalry, nobility. The word 'devil' occurs frequently in the latter acts: devils are alive here, ugly little demons of black disgrace. They swarm over the mental horizon of the play, occurring frequently. Iago is directly or indirectly their author and originator. 'Devil', 'hell', 'damnation' — these words are recurrent, and continually juxtaposed to thoughts of 'heaven', prayer, angels. We are clearly set amid 'heaven and men and devils' (V. ii. 221). Such terms are related here primarily to sexual impurity. In *Othello,* pure love is the supreme good; impurity, damnation. This pervading religious tonal significance relating to infidelity explains lines such as:

> Turn thy complexion there,
> Patience, thou young and rose-lipped cherubin, —
> Ay, there, look grim as hell!
>
> (IV. ii. 62)

Othello addresses Emilia:

> You, mistress,
> That have the office opposite to Saint Peter
> And keep the gate of hell!
>
> (IV. ii. 90)

Here faithful love is to be identified with 'the divine', the 'heavenly'; unfaithful love, or the mistrust which imagines it, or the cynic that gives birth to that imagination — all these are to be identified with 'the devil'. The hero is set between the forces of divinity and hell. The forces of hell win and pure love lies slain. Therefore Othello cries to 'devils' to whip him from that 'heavenly' sight (V. ii. 277). He knows himself to have been entrapped by hell-forces. The Iago-Devil association is of importance.

Now it will be remembered that *Othello* is a play of concrete forms. This world is a world of visual images, colour, and romance. It will also be clear that the mesh of devil-references I have just suggested show a mental horizon black, formless, colourless. They contrast with the solid, chiselled, enamelled Othello-style elsewhere. This devil-world is insubstantial, vague, negative. Now on the plane of personification we see that Othello and Desdemona are concrete, moulded of flesh and blood, warm. Iago contrasts with them metaphysically as well as morally: he is unlimited, formless villainy. He is the spirit of denial, wholly negative. He never has visual reality. He is further blurred by the fact of his being something quite different from what he appears to the others. Is he to look like a bluff soldier, or Mephistopheles? He is a different kind of being from Othello and Desdemona: he belongs to a different world. They, by their very existence, assert the positive beauty of created forms — hence Othello's perfected style of speech, his strong human appeal, his faith in creation's values of Love and War. This world of created forms, this sculptural and yet pulsing beauty, the Iago-spirit undermines, poisons, disintegrates. Iago is a demon of cynicism, colourless, formless, in a world of colours, shapes, and poetry's music. Of all these he would create chaos. Othello's words are apt:

> Excellent wretch! Perdition catch my soul
> But I do love thee! And when I love thee not?
> Chaos is come again.
>
> (III. iii. go)

Chaos indeed. Iago works at the foundations of human values. Cassio is a soldier: he ruins him as a soldier, makes him drunk. So he ruins both Othello's love and warrior-heart. He makes him absurd, ugly. Toward the end of the play there is hideous suggestion. We hear of 'cords, knives, poison' (III. iii. 388), of lovers 'as prime as goats, as hot as monkeys' (III. iii. 403); we meet Bianca, the whore, told by Cassio to 'throw her vile guesses in the devil's teeth' (III. iv. 184); there are Othello's incoherent mutterings, 'Pish! Noses, ears and lips!' (IV. i. 42), he will 'chop' Desdemona 'into messes' (IV. i. 211); she reminds him of 'foul toads' (IV. ii. 61). Watching Cassio, he descends to this:

> O! I see that nose of yours, but not that dog I shall throw it to.
>
> (IV. i. 146)

Othello strikes Desdemona, behaves like a raging beast. 'Fire and brimstone!' (IV. i. 245) he cries, and again, 'Goats and monkeys!' (IV. i. 274). 'Heaven stops the nose' at Desdemona's impurity (IV. ii. 77). Othello in truth behaves like 'a beggar in his drink' (IV. ii. 120). In all these phrases I would emphasize not the sense and dramatic relevance alone, but the suggestion — the accumulative effect of ugliness, hellishness, idiocy, negation. It is a formless, colourless essence, insidiously undermining a world of concrete, visual, richly-toned forms. That is the Iago-spirit embattled against the domesticity, the romance, the idealized humanity of the Othello-world. Here, too, we find the reason for the extreme contrast of Othello's two styles: one exotically beautiful, the other blatantly absurd, ugly. There is often no dignity in Othello's rage. There is not meant to be. Iago would make discord of the Othello music. Thus at his first conquest he filches something of Othello's style and uses it himself:

Not poppy, nor mandragora,
Nor all the drowsy syrups of the world,
Shall ever medicine thee to that sweet sleep
Which thou owed'st yesterday.

(III. iii. 330)

To him Othello's pride in his life-story and Desdemona's admiration were ever stupid:

Mark me with what violence she first loved the Moor, but for bragging and telling her fantastical lies: and will she love him still for prating?

Iago, 'nothing if not critical', speaks some truth of Othello's style — it is 'fantastical'. As I have shown, it is somewhat over-decorative, highly-coloured. The dramatic value of this style now appears. In fact, a proper understanding of Othello's style reveals Iago's 'motive' so often questioned. There is something sentimental in Othello's language, in Othello. Iago is pure cynicism. That Iago should scheme — in this dramatic symbolism forged in terms of interacting persons — to undermine Othello's faith in himself, his wife, and his 'occupation', is inevitable. Logically, the cynic must oppose the sentimentalist: dramatically, he works his ruin by deceit and deception. That Othello often just misses tragic dignity is the price of his slightly strained emotionalism. Othello loves emotion for its own sake, luxuriates in it, like Richard II. As ugly and idiot ravings, disjointed and with no passionate dignity even, succeed Othello's swell and flood of poetry, Iago's triumph seems complete. The honoured warrior, rich in strength and experience, noble in act and repute, lies in a trance, nerveless, paralysed by the Iago-conception:

Work on, my medicine, work.

(IV. i. 45)

But Iago's victory is not absolute. During the last scene Othello is a nobly tragic figure. His ravings are not final: he rises beyond them. He slays Desdemona finally, not so much in rage as for 'the cause' (V. ii. I). He slays her in love. Though Desdemona fails him, his love, homeless, 'perplexed in the extreme' (V. ii. 346), endures. He will kill her and 'love her after' (V. ii. 19). In that last scene, too, he voices the grandest of his poetry. The Iago-spirit never finally envelops him, masters him, disintegrates his soul. Those gem-like miniatures of poetic movement quoted at the start of my essay are among Othello's last words. His vast love has, it is true, failed in a domestic world. But now symbols of the wide beauty of the universe enrich his thoughts : the 'chaste stars', the 'sun and moon', the 'affrighted globe', the world 'of one entire and perfect chrysolite' that may not buy a Desdemona's love. At the end we know that Othello's fault is simplicity alone. He is, indeed, 'a gull, a dolt' (V. ii. 163); he loves 'not wisely but too well' (V. ii. 344). His simple faith in himself endures: and at the end he takes just pride in recalling his honourable service.

In this essay I have attempted to expose the underlying thought of the play. Interpretation here is not easy, nor wholly satisfactory. As all within *Othello* — save the lago-theme — is separated, differentiated, solidified, so the play itself seems at first to be divorced from wider issues, a lone thing of meaningless beauty in the Shakespearian universe, solitary, separate, unyielding, and chaste as the moon. It is unapproachable, yields itself to no easy mating with our minds. Its thought does not readily mesh with our thought. We can visualize it, admire its concrete felicities of phrase and image, the mosaic of its language, the sculptural outline of its effects, the precision and chastity of its form. But one cannot be lost in it, subdued to it, enveloped by it, as one is drenched and refreshed by the elemental cataracts of *Lear,* one cannot be intoxicated by it as by the rich wine of *Antony and Cleopatra*. *Othello* is essentially outside us, beautiful with a lustrous, planetary beauty. Yet the Iago-conception is of a different kind from the rest of the play. This conception alone, if no other reason existed, would force the necessity of an intellectual interpretation. Thus we see the Iago-spirit gnawing at the root of all the Othello-values, the Othello-beauties; he eats into the core and heart of this romantic world, worms his way into its solidity, rotting it, poisoning it. Once this is clear, the whole play begins to have meaning. On the plane of dramatic humanity we see a story of the cynic intriguing to ruin the soldier and his love. On the plane of poetic conception, in matters of technique, style, personification — there we see a spirit of negation, colourless, and undefined, attempting to make chaos of a world of stately, architectural, and exquisitely coloured forms. The two styles of Othello's speech illustrate this. Thus the different technique of the Othello and Iago conceptions is intrinsic with the plot of the play: in them we have the spirit of negation set against the spirit of creation. That is why Iago is undefined, devisualized, inhuman, in a play of consummate skill in concrete imagery and vivid human delineation. He is a colourless and ugly thing in a world of colour and harmony. His failure lies in this: in the final scene, at the moment of his complete triumph, Emilia dies for her mistress to the words of Desdemona's willow-song, and the Othello music itself sounds with a nobler cadence, a richer flood of harmonies, a more selfless and universalized flight of the imagination than before. The beauties of the Othello-world are not finally disintegrated: they make 'a swan-like end, fading in music'.

15

The Early Shakespearian Manner and Development to the Mature Style[1]

George Rylands

Morton Luce finds the *Lucrece* far inferior to the *Venus and Adonis*. 'We have less nature, less melody, less beauty, less poetry than in the earlier poem.' The answer is that we have more Shakespeare, more of the dramatic poet. He himself promises in his dedication of the first poem that the second is to be 'some graver labour'.

Ornament in the *Venus and Adonis* is supplied by similes. The bird tangled in the net, the dive-dapper peering through a wave, the shooting star, the night-wanderer, the snail with trader horn, the nurse's song, seem to belong to a more natural world. The shrill-tongued tapsters, the breeding jennet (taken from Du Bartas),

> What recketh he his rider's angry stir,
> His flattering 'Holla' or his 'Stand, I say'?

and poor Wat, the hunted hare, even if academic imitations, are free and simple in spirit and style. Delightful and individual is the little cry with which Shakespeare introduces his decoration:

> Lo, here the gentle lark, weary of rest.
> Look, when a painter would surpass the life.
> Look, how a bright star shooteth from the sky.
> But lo, from forth a copse that neighbours by.

1. Two chapters form *Words and Poetry* (1928).

Lucrece is dramatic. Shakespeare is striving to realize the sensations of the two protagonists. There is a conflict in Tarquin before the rape, similar to that in the heart of Macbeth:

> But as he is my kinsman, my dear friend,
> The shame and fault finds no excuse or end.
> He's here in double trust;
> First, as I am his kinsman and his subject;

and to Brutus's 'insurrection in the state of man':

> Between the acting of a dreadful thing
> And the first motion.

Again when Tarquin prays that the heavens may countenance his sin, he starts reflecting:

> The powers to whom I pray abhor this fact,
> How can they then assist me in the act?

and he is in the same position as Claudius:

> O what form of prayer
> Can serve my turn?

Dramatically imaginative is the meeting between Lucrece and her maid; even more so her misinterpretation of the 'homely villein's' bashful blushes as consciousness of her shame.

In this piece poetry gives place to rhetoric, simile to metaphor, description to soliloquy, Spenserian imagery to euphuistic, antithetical conceits. The metaphors are pursued laboriously and at length in a way which is very characteristic of Shakespeare's early manner; for although *Lucrece* is more dramatic, the plays, especially (and naturally so) the chronicle plays, suffer stylistically from their narrative qualities.

Here the metaphorical idea of an army setting siege to a city, which is found elsewhere in Shakespeare and the Elizabethans, for example:

> She will not stay the siege of loving terms
> Nor bide the encounter of assailing eyes
>
> (*Romeo and Juliet*)

is elaborated over eight stanzas (427-83). Here also the familiar conceits upon 'windy sighs', 'the ocean of tears beating on the rocky heart', which are to be found even in the final plays. *Lucrece*, weighty, prest, obstructive, contains most of the material, the superstitions, saws, fables, and unnatural history, out of which *Henry VI, Richard III* and *II* and *Romeo and Juliet* are composed.

> Nor read the subtle-shining secrecies
> Writ in the glassy margents of such books.
>
> (*Lucrece*)

> And what obscured in this fair volume lies
> Find written in the margent of his eyes.
>
> (*Romeo and Juliet*)

> Mud not the fountain that gave drink to thee.
>
> (*Lucrece,* three uses)

> The purest spring is not so free from mud
> As I am dear from treason to my sovereign.
>
> (*2 Henry VI*)

> Roses have thorns and silver fountains mud.
>
> (*Sonnets*)

> Thou sheer, immaculate and silver fountain,
> From whence the stream through muddy passages
> Hath held his current and defiled himself.
>
> (*Richard II*)

The proverbial instance is elaborated, as often.

> And now this pale swan in her watery nest
> Begins the sad dirge of her certain ending.
>
> (*Lucrece*)

> I am the cygnet to this pale faint swan,
> Who chants a doleful hymn to his own death.
>
> (*King John*)

> The face, that map which deep impression bears
> Of hard misfortune.
>
> (*Lucrece*)

> I see as in a map the end of all.
>
> (*Richard III*)

> In thy face I see
> The map of honour, truth and loyalty.
>
> (*2 Henry VI*)

> Thus is his cheek the map of days outworn.
>
> (*Sonnets*)

> Poor broken glass, I often did behold
> In thy sweet semblance my old age new born.
>
> (*Lucrece*)

> Thou art thy mother's glass and she in thee
> Calls back the lovely April of her prime.
>
> (*Sonnets*)

Lucrece has the seeds of the history plays — the few examples above could be multiplied. The style is dense and cumbersome, a cloak worn without grace, whereas the style of the tragedies, no less compact and closely woven, falls gracefully from the shoulder and does not cramp the movement.

Movement: there lies the weakness of the early plays: there are no *gestures,* as it were, and little variety of speed. Paradoxes, proverbs, and euphuisms litter one's path.

> Smooth runs the water where the brook is deep.
>
> *(2 Henry VI)*
>
> The smallest worm will turn being trodden on.
>
> *(3* Henry VI)
>
> Seems he a dove? His feathers are but borrowed,
> For he's disposed as is the hateful raven.
> Is he a lamb? His skin is surely lent him,
> For he's inclined as is the ravenous wolf.
>
> *(2 Henry VI)*
>
> Or as the snake rolled in the flowering bank.
>
> *(2 Henry VI)*

Even in *Romeo and Juliet* the diction sometimes impedes the pace:

> O serpent heart hid with a flowering face,
> Did ever dragon keep so fair a cave?
> Dove-feathered raven! Wolfish-ravening lamb!

All the animals in and out of Aesop and Pliny are herded together with the heroes of Greece and Rome. The similes are careful and lengthy. Here are two from *Henry VI*, Pt. 3:

> Look, as I blow this feather from my face,
> And as the air blows it to me again,
> Obeying with my wind when I do blow,
> And yielding to another when it blows,
> Commanded always by the greater gust:
> Such is the lightness of you common men.
> Why then I do but dream on sovereignty;
> Like one that stands upon a promontory,
> And spies a far-off shore where he would tread,
> Wishing his feet were equal with his eye,
> And chides the sea that sunders him from hence,
> Saying, he'll lade it dry to have his way.

These are straightforward, excellent in their way; but it is the narrative, not the dramatic way, the way of *Sohrab and Rustum.*

There is a natural pause at the end of each line and the lines are piled one upon the other. This form of versification which is so common in all his work previous to 1600 is the versification of poetry which is to be read, not spoken. It is the versification of Spenser, of *Venus and Adonis* and *Lucrece*, and it was some time before Shakespeare grew out of it. For one thing, it jingles prettily, for another, it helps to increase the speed. The actor can take the lines at a run. We will take an example from each play.

The time was once when thou unurged wouldst vow
That never words were music to thine ear,
That never object pleasing in thine eye,
That never touch well welcome to thine hand,
That never meat sweet-savoured in thy taste,
Unless I spake or look'd or touch'd or carved to thee.

(*Comedy of Errors*)

His words are bonds, his oaths are oracles,
His love sincere, his thoughts immaculate,
His tears pure messengers sent from his heart,
His heart as far from fraud as heaven from earth.

(*Two Gentlemen*)

So many hours must I tend my flock;
So many hours must I take my rest;
So many hours must I contemplate;
So many hours must I sport myself;
So many days my ewes have been with young;
So many weeks ere the poor fools will ean;
So many years ere I shall shear the fleece.

(*3 Henry VI*)

O, who can hold a fire in his hand
By thinking on the frosty Caucasus?
Or cloy the hungry edge of appetite
By bare imagination of a feast?
Or wallow naked in December snow
By thinking on fantastic summer's heat?

(*Richard II*)

Our instruments to melancholy bells,
Our wedding cheer to a sad burial feast,
Our solemn hymns to sullen dirges change,
Our bridal flowers serve for a buried corse
And all things change them to the contrary.

(*Romeo and Juliet*)

You, Lord Archbishop,
Whose see is by a civil peace maintained,

Whose beard the silver hand of peace hath touched,
Whose learning and good letters peace hath tutored,
Whose white investments figure innocence. . .

(2 *Henry IV*)

If ever you have look'd on better days,
If ever been where bells have knoll'd to church,
If ever sat at any good man's feast,
If ever from your eyelids wip'd a tear
And know what 'tis to pity and be pitied,
Let gentleness my strong enforcement be.

(*As You Like It*)

This might best be called *stanza movement*. The Shakespearian sonnet (*e.g.* LXVI) is similar, but on a rather larger scale. Out of numerous examples in *Lucrece*, I quote one:

Let him have time to tear his curled hair,
Let him have time against himself to rave,
Let him have time of Time's help to despair,
Let him have time to live a loathed slave,
Let him have time a beggar's orts to crave; (981)

ant one from Spenser:

I hate to speak, my voice is spent with crying,
I hate to hear, loud plaints have dulled my ears,
I hate to taste, for food withholds my dying,
I hate to see, mine eyes are dimmed with tears,
I hate to smell, no sweet on earth is left,
I hate to feel, my flesh is numb'd with fears;
So all my senses from me are bereft. (*Daphnaida*)

The movement is not uncommon in other plays of the time, in Greene and Kyd. A subtle usage occurs in *Arden of Feversham*.

Wilt thou not look? Is all thy love o'erwhelmed?
Wilt thou not hear? What malice stops thine ears?
Why speak'st thou not? What silence ties thy tongue?
Thou hast been sighted as the eagle is,
And heard as quickly as the fearful hare,
And spoke as smoothly as an orator,
When I have bid thee hear or see or speak;
And art thou sensible in none of these?

The accumulation and the management of the pauses are skilful. The speed rises and then comes to rest. Marlowe's verse climbs the same staircase, but he never jingles, not even in the Zenocrate refrain: there is less repetition. One foot is always planted firmly upon the next stair — they succeed each other. Shakespeare in the quotations above seems to draw himself up one foot at a time.

In close combination with this method of laying line upon line, we may take the Shakespearian habit of accumulating words, a rhetorical device which also increases the speed. It survives in a modified form even in his final style. In *Venus and Adonis*:

> Were I hard-featured, foul, or wrinkled-old,
> Ill-nurtured, crooked, churlish, harsh in voice,
> O'erwom, despised, rheumatic and cold,
> Thick-sighted, barren, lean, and lacking juice,
> Then might'st thou pause . . .

In *Love's Labour's Lost*:

> This wimpled, whining, purblind, wayward boy,
> This senior-junior, giant-dwarf, Dan Cupid;
> Regent of love-rhymes, lord of folded arms,
> Thc anointed sovereign of sighs and groans,
> Liege of all loiterers and malcontents,
> Dread prince of plackets, king of codpieces,
> Sole imperator and great general
> Of trotting 'paritors.

Regent, lord, sovereign, liege, prince, king, imperator, general: this is the 'dictionary method' of Burton. John of Gaunt's England speech, Othello's 'Farewell, the plumed troop', Macbeth's 'Innocent sleep . . .' provide other examples among many. The device is worth noticing, as one reads, for two reasons: first, because it tended to break down end-stopping; secondly, because, like scales and five-finger exercises, as it were, it makes the vocabulary richer and more flexible.

This practice is characteristic of Shakespeare's style; it contributed to his development. But it is not the cause of the complete although gradual change between his two styles. The child is father of the man, the first brought forth the second; but there comes a year when the gulf between the two seems a wide one. That year was roughly 1600. It marks a change in Shakespeare and in Elizabethan poetic diction. How did the change in his style come about? What was the reason of it? I have never found that critics answered these questions.

There are, on my own reading, two reasons:

1. A reaction against the diction and versification of the day, *which led to the study of prose.*
2. Character and dramatic realism breaking through fashions and conventions.

The two go hand in hand, for the study of character occasioned, if it did not cause, the reaction.

Language is the subject of *Love's Labour's Lost.* Shakespeare is still half-enchanted by the golden net in which he is entangled. Armado, with his fire-new words and congruent epithetons; Boyet, honey-tongued, wit's pedlar; Berowne, conceit's expositor, represent three degrees of the courtly and the fantastical. The play jangles with puns and parodies, showing a nimble, critical, satirical spirit. (I can add little to Pater's *Appreciation.)* A remark of Holofemes deserves attention:

Ovidius Naso was rhe man; and why indeed, Naso but for smelling out the odoriferous flowers of fancy, the jerks of invention? *Imitari* is nothing; so doth the hound his master, the ape his keeper, the 'tired horse his rider.

The odoriferous flowers soon withered. Shakespeare was never as seduced by Ovid as were the university wits.

The play also gives the reaction against verbal fashions and imitations to 'russet yeas and kersey noes'.

Berowne. My love to thee is sound sans crack or flaw.
Rosalind. Sans 'sans', I pray you.
Berowne. Yet I have a trick
Of the old rage; bear with me, I am sick;
I'll leave it by degrees.

And Shakespeare did. The dramatic reality of Berowne and the tragic situation tumble over the card house. 'Honest plain words best suit the ear of grief.'

There are plenty of other instances of Shakespeare tilting at the diction of the day. Take Demetrius:

O, Helen, goddess, nymph, perfect, divine;
To what, my love, shall I compare thine eyne?

Crystal is muddy. O, how ripe in show
Thy lips, those kissing cherries, tempting grow;
This pure congealed white, high Taurus' snow,
Fann'd with the eastern wind turns to a crow;
When thou holdst up thine hand.

It is written with the tongue in the cheek, an amusing parody.

Twelfth Night has many little touches; the clown's — 'Oh! this age. A sentence is but a cheveril glove to a good wit; how quickly the wrong side may be turned outward', and 'words are grown so false, I am loath to prove reason with them', and 'I might say "element", but the word is overworn', and 'Vent my folly! He has heard that word of some great man, and now applies it to a fool. I prithee now ungird thy strangeness and tell me what I shall vent to my lady'; or Sir Andrew's admiration for Viola's 'Jerks of invention'. 'Odours, pregnant, and vouchsafed. I'll get 'em all three ready.' Or take the musicians in *Romeo and Juliet* scratching their heads over 'music with her silver sound', or Speed, 'your old vice still; mistake the word'.

Everywhere one remarks this awareness and sensibility to words and with it an increasing feeling of reaction from the artificial and the pretty. Crystal, cherries, the lily and rose, tears of pearl, the buds of youth, and other similar conceits cease, with a few exceptions to be considered elsewhere, in the later plays.

The reaction against rhetoric and bombast is too obvious to be dwelt on. The parody put in the mouth of ancient Pistol takes a more passionate note in Hamlet's denunciation of the players. Every tongue had caught the trick of Marlowe and Kyd. Their blank verse had taken the town by storm, just as *Poems and Ballads* took the undergraduates and set them marching and chanting up and down King's Parade. Shakespeare turned to prose:

Orlando. Good day, and happiness, dear Rosalind.

Jaques. Nay, then, God be wi' you, an you talk in blank verse. *(Exit)*

Character, or rather a particular character, is interfering. Beside Berowne place Richard III, Hotspur, the Bastard. They all speak with the same accent; they are all realistic, commonsensical, prosaic, energetic figures. They take the verse into their own hands and break down the barriers of diction. Gloucester gives the point of view of them all.

> Because I cannot flatter and speak fair,
> Smile in men's faces, smooth, deceive, and cog,
> Duck with French nods and apish courtesy,
> I must be held a rancorous enemy.
> Cannot a plain man live and think no harm,
> But thus his simple truth must be abused
> By silken, sly, insinuating Jacks?

Or take Faulconbridge's ridicule of the citizen of Angiers:

> Here's a large mouth indeed,
> That spits forth death and mountains, rocks and seas,
> Talks as familiarly of roaring lions
> As maids of thirteen do of puppy-dogs . . . .
> 'Zounds, I was never so bethumped with words
> Since I first called my brother's father dad;

and of the Dauphin's Petrarchan conceits:

> Drawn in the flattering tablet of her eye!
> Hang's in the frowning wrinkle of her brow!
> And quarter'd in her heart, he doth espy
> Himself love's traitor: this is pity now,
> That hang'd and drawn and quarter'd, there should be
> In such a love so vile a lout as he.

One regrets that he was not present instead of Hubert to counter Arthur's frigid fancies over the burning coal.

Take Hotspur's account of the lord 'perfumed like a milliner':

> he made me mad
> To see him shine so brisk and smell so sweet
> And talk so like a waiting-gentlewoman
> Of guns and drums and wounds;

or his trouncing of Glendower:

> I had rather be a kitten and cry mew
> Than one of these same metre ballad-mongers;
> I had rather hear a brazen canstick turned,
> Or a dry wheel grate on the axle tree;
> And what would set my teeth nothing on edge,
> Nothing so much as mincing poetry:
> 'Tis like the forc'd gait of a shuffling nag;

or last with Lady Percy:

Not yours, in good sooth. Heart, you swear like a comfitmaker's wife. Not you, 'in good sooth', and 'as true as I live', and 'as God shall mend me', and 'as sure as day'.

And giv'st such sarcenet surety for thy oaths,
As if thou never walk'dst further than Finsbury.
Swear me, Kate, like a lady as thou art,
A good mouth-filling oath; and leave 'in sooth',
And such protest of pepper-gingerbread,
To velvet-guards and Sunday-citizens.

All these passages have critical significance. I do not fall into the snare of identifying Shakespeare with his *dramatis personae* and making his views theirs; but these voices demanded a new medium, verse which will allow colloquial emphases and prose order, or else prose itself, the prose which Hamlet and Edmund and Iago were to speak. Dramatic effect must war with poetic decoration. In the early plays it is the characters who are really alive that mould and modify the verse. Thus the nurse in *Romeo and Juliet* in the famous speech (Act I, Sc. iii) with its repetitions, parentheses and oratio recta, breaks up the rhythms:

I never should forget it; 'Wilt thou not, Jule', quoth he; and her

And a good lady, and a wise, and virtuous, and Capulet's rebukes of Tybalt. In the *Midsummer Night's Dream* the vitality of the dialogue begins to get the better not only of metre but even of rhyme. Repetition again is a useful instrument of realism.

She, sweet lady, dotes,
Devoutly dotes, dotes to idolatry,
Upon this spotted and inconstant man.
Am I not Hermia? Are not you Lysanter?
Is't not enough, is't not enough, young man,
That I did never, no, nor never can,
Deserve a sweet look from Demetrius' eye,
But you must flout my insufficiency?
Good troth you do me wrong, good sooth you do,
In such disdainful manner me to woo.

The transitional period begins with *The Merchant of Venice* (1596). The clowns, old Gobbo and Launcelot, speak prose; that is nothing new. Portia and Nerissa have a light prose scene, where Julia and Lucetta had been hampered by verse. It is, however, antithetical, euphuistic prose: 'The brain may devise laws for the blood' but a hot temper leaps o'er a cold decree; such a hare is madness the youth, to skip o'er the meshes of good counsel the cripple.' This is of the same order as Hotspur's 'I tell you, my lord fool, out of this nettle, danger, we pluck the flower, safety'. Sebastian in *Twelfth Night* is another who 'speaks holiday' — 'My determinate voyage is mere extravagancy'. The style is excellently parodied by Falstaff. But the significant fact is that Shylock speaks prose, and he is of tragic dimensions. He speaks prose, not all the way through, certainly, but at his best moment (Act III, Sc. i). It is mannered prose, as Shakespearian prose always is, antithetical, cumulative in effect, like the verse passages already noted: but it is passionate. Above all, for the moment character has banished verse, drama has banished poetry.

What follows? *Henry IV, Henry V, Much Ado, As You Like It.* Everyone is speaking prose, court prose or comic prose, and Shakespeare is mocking blank verse or transposing the chronicles. The characters are taking the words into their own hands. Falstaff, Quickly, Shallow, Caius, Mine Host, Beatrice and Benedict, Fluellen, Rosalind, all are alive and speaking prose, both light and serious, while Hotspur rattles his metrical fetters.

In *The Merchant of Venice* also Shakespeare rides his verse with ease over flat country. That is to say he runs on in a natural colloquial way; for instance, Portia's speech, 'It is enacted in the laws of Venice' (Act IV, Sc. i). Inversion is comparatively rare, ornament has been pruned away, and for a short period Shakespeare's verse is less mannered than his prose. Jaques is colloquial in verse.

The new style was beginning, packed with matter, a style that could gallop at a touch, with freer rhythms and higher emotional pressure. We shall find the first hint of it in the second part of *Henry IV.*

> O God, that one might read the book of fate,
> And see the revolution of the times
> Make mountains level, and the continent—
> Weary of solid firmness — melt itself
> Into the sea! And, other times, to see
> The beachy girdle of the ocean

Too wide for Neptune's hips; how chances mock,
And changes fill the cup of alteration
With divers liquors! O, if this were seen,
The happiest youth, viewing his progress through,
What perils past, what crosses to ensue,
Would shut the book and sit him down and die.
'Tis not ten years gone
Since Richard and Northumberland, great friends . . .

That is the accent of Hamlet. We have the pauses and parentheses and exclamations, the changes of construction, the broken and shortened lines of the tragedies. *The study of dramatic prose made Shakespeare master of dramatic verse.*

After King Henry's speech above, comes Warwick's:

There is a history in all men's lives
Figuring the nature of the times deceased . . .

which is a pair to Brutus's:

There is a tide in the affairs of men
Which taken at the flood leads on to fortune.

This one might call the Greek Chorus manner. The many examples of it in the chronicle plays gave place to the soliloquies of the tragedies. It is weighty and controlled, something between the poetic and the dramatic, tending very often towards the rhetorical. Pater, speaking of the opening lines of *Love's Labour's Lost*, notes the 'monumental' manner of the *Sonnets*, and it is in passages in this manner that the earlier Shakespeare excels. Time is not rarely the subject, and the model, Ovid,

Jamque opus exegi, quod nec Jovis ira, nec ignis,
Nec poterit ferrum, nec edax abolere vetustas.

and the 'Exegi monumentum' of Horace. *Lucrece* has fine stanzas and there are similar lines in the *Sonnets*.

Time's thievish progress to eternity.

(*Sonnets*)

Thou ceaseless lackey to eternity.

(*Lucrece*)

Let fame that all hunt after in their lives
Live registered upon our brazen tombs,
And then grace us in the disgrace of death;
When spite of cormorant devouring Time.
The endeavour of this present breath may buy
The honour which shall bate his scythe's keen edge,

